RILEY LIBRARY
NORTHWEST NAZARENE COLLEGE
NAMPA. IDAHO 83686

DATE DUE

FEB 1 9 2013			
GAYLORD			PRINTED IN U.S.A.

HOW TO STAND UP FOR YOUR RIGHTS— AND WIN!

ROY M. COHN

A FIRESIDE BOOK

Published by Simon and Schuster
NEW YORK

130197

First Fireside Edition, 1982

Published by Simon and Schuster
A Division of Gulf & Western Corporation
Simon & Schuster Building
Rockefeller Center
1230 Avenue of the Americas
New York, New York 10020

FIRESIDE and colophon are trademarks
of Simon & Schuster

Designed by Irving Perkins

Manufactured in the United States of America

1 3 5 7 9 10 8 6 4 2
1 3 5 7 9 10 8 6 4 2 Pbk.

Library of Congress Cataloging in Publication Data

Cohn, Roy M.
How to stand up for your rights—and win!

1. Law—United States—Popular works. I. Title.
KF387.C53   349.73   81-5612
                 347.3   AACR2

ISBN 0-671-25341-7
ISBN 0-671-25342-5 Pbk.

AUTHOR'S
NOTE

I would like to acknowledge the substantial contribution made by Professor Robert Blecker, my close friend, sometime adversary, and colleague at New York Law School. Robert's legal editorship and philosophical bent blended well with my experience. Without him this book would have been very different. On the other hand, his naive idealism is his own, and the clarion call to legal arms in these pages is mine. I assume complete responsibility.

ACKNOWLEDGMENTS

I AM ALWAYS indebted to Joan and Joe Foley, my literary agents, who goad me from one project to the next, with worry and care well beyond the call of duty.

This particular book, in its overall concept, bears the unmistakable imprint of the master himself, Michael Korda, editor-in-chief of Simon and Schuster. His able associate John Cox improved the product and eliminated over my vigorous objection about two hundred pages of potential libel.

Research on cases was done primarily by Robert Salvia, a top honors student at the New York Law School, and by young associates of mine at Saxe, Bacon & Bolan.

Instead of making the ritualistic disclaimer that all names and events are fictitious and bear no resemblance to reality, I assure the reader that all names used refer to actual persons. I have often deliberately omitted names of past and present clients, and details of their legal situations, even when they are matters of public record, so as to accord with my belief in the attorney-client confidence, even when law and ethics make it inapplicable.

Many lawyers and judges of renown have contributed to my legal education—and the actual courtroom experiences which form the basis for it. But one above all taught me, often the hard way, the art of cross-examination, the elements of drama in a trial that so often overshadow the issues. Most of all this person taught me that you can fight hard and retain a sense of integrity. It is to his memory that I fondly dedicate this book—to my archrival in the Army-McCarthy hearings—JOSEPH N. WELCH.

CONTENTS

PREFACE

JUST ABOUT every day, we encounter situations in which someone is trying to take unfair advantage of us. It happens to rich and poor and middle-income alike. Often what we need is not so much a lawyer as the confident knowledge that the law can be on our side, and the ability to exercise our legal rights on the spot. This book deals with the common types of everyday person-to-person confrontations in which so many of us ordinarily feel abused. Its goal is to make your world fairer to you and easier to handle: It will show you how to stand up and fight back for rights that are legally yours.

For a good part of my life, I have had to fight back. When I was twenty-three years old, and the prosecutor in the Julius and Ethel Rosenberg atom-spy trial, I had to fight back to overcome the distorted criticism of the case, and to establish their guilt—and I'm still fighting back against the ignorance and emotion being used to obscure the facts.

I've had to fight back against my own upbringing and heritage. The son of a highly regarded Jewish liberal Democratic judge, I sacrificed a surefire career when I chose to take my legal legacy and use it not to advance in elective New York politics but to help fight back against what was and remains a real threat to the free world—Communism.

When I went to Washington at age twenty-five—still a bit wet behind the ears—I had to fight back against the Army, the State Department, the Democratic leadership in the Senate, Vice President Nixon, and the White House.

Whenever I've made political enemies, they've turned into deadly ones. Thus when I returned to New York, my former assistant, Bobby Kennedy, who was by then his brother's and the country's Attorney General, placed me right at or near the top of his hit list. As a result I had to fight back against three separate criminal indictments over a nine-year period—charging me with just about everything. The government forced eleven of my good friends to testify against me. By these experiences I learned the value of lawyers, friends, and fighting back.

I had to fight back against poisonous articles in *Life* magazine which mysteriously appeared as my jury was about to be selected. I had to fight back against a federal judge who in my opinion stopped at nothing to try to bring about my conviction. I won each fight. Three separate juries, 12–0, voted me not guilty. After my own personal fights, my life changed. I began to practice law and fight back for my clients. I have fought back against adversaries in one challenging lawsuit after another, in virtually all fields. I have fought to make deals and successfully conclude negotiations that were good for both sides. I have fought back against the ''legal establishment'' which thinks I should calm down and play by the Marquess of Queensberry rules. I've had to fight back against the ''club'' which wants to strip law of its adversary nature, and substitute a ''contest'' where only one group succeeds—the lawyers. I have had to fight back against those who think problems surrounding the law should be low-keyed and handled gently, instead of with toughness and by going for the jugular.

Some people, like Morley Safer on a *60 Minutes* profile, find me not at all an enigma—he said I'm the kid on the block the others picked on; I determined to get rich and get even, and I have. We are all the kids on the block. We all want to get rich and get even.

The mind of man has devised an infinite variety of get-rich-quick schemes; many have found their way into print. This book is not another one. The purpose here instead is to help you get even when you've been unfairly disadvantaged; and more important, to help you prepare so that you will not be unfairly disadvantaged in the first place. So many times in everyday life we feel at the mercy of others to whom we must trust our lives, our possessions— money, or the greatest possession we have, our time. Too often, having hastily agreed, we suffer the consequences of others' foul-ups. This book is designed to help you help yourself in advance to stay ahead so you will not later need to get even. You travel, you buy a house, you sign a contract, you get married or divorced, you write a will, you're served bad food at a restaurant. How should you avoid problems by anticipating them? If they occur nonetheless, how can you fight back? That's what this book is about primarily. It is for those who want to fight back, on the spot, and for those who want to make more of their own lives.

I don't expect anyone to agree with everything in this book. I do want to give encouragement and support to those who are willing to stop being the Casper Milquetoasts of the world. The Bible says that the meek shall inherit the earth. But in my experience the only earth the meek inherit is that in which they are eventually buried. I write for those who would take charge of their own lives, those who are willing to stand up for their rights!

EMBARRASSMENT:
A FOREWORD ON
BEING FORWARD

IF YOU think about it, you can probably recall hundreds of incidents in your experience when you ended up poorer because you failed to speak up, because you were afraid to ask for more information—"How much does it actually cost?"—or because you were afraid to suggest a possible solution for fear of seeming pushy. "OK, we agree you paint the outside of the house for $1,800, but you also throw in the inside touchups for nothing." Or you were afraid to make a demand, hold firm, and risk the relationship by walking out or sending the other person packing. "Let's forget the whole thing. If you won't give me a two-year written guarantee on the system, I'll find a company that will. Goodbye."

The freedom to attack and retreat, to come actively into situations and to flee from them, to change the shape of things, to make moves, is most seriously hampered for many people by a discomfort at getting what's theirs. Perhaps you failed to speak up lest you appear untrusting—to a contractor, waiter, barber, builder, baby-sitter. Maybe you really were not trusting, and for good reason. By speaking up firmly and admitting your skepticism, you may, rather than ruin things, save yourself a lot of money. By openly displaying your distrust in advance, thereby forcing the other person to demonstrate his reliability, you may save your own or your child's life. Yet all the time, people who are playing life's

RILEY LIBRARY
NORTHWEST NAZARENE COLLEGE
NAMPA, IDAHO 83686

big-stakes games are embarrassed out of taking necessary precautions—it all seems so forward.

For example, you are about to agree on future work to be done and payments to be made. The other person has impressed you with his presentation and references; an air of optimism and hope pervades the scene. Everything is just fine, and you don't want to spoil this spirit by injecting grubby unpleasant details, like written guarantees in advance, or responsibility for failures in the project. It seems impolite, uncouth, to destroy the fine feeling. So you hold back your unpleasant observations, you stifle in your breast all nagging doubts. You say nothing and do nothing; you allow the deal to slide along its so far obviously slotted course. All to your own disadvantage.

You failed to act on your own behalf because you were embarrassed to play the game of your own life aggressively, to make an offensive move, lest you give offense. But all successful passive receivers need perfect passes from fortune—it's true in cards, football and life. It's probably also true with radios, but I don't know enough about them to be sure. No matter how magnificent your chosen route, you can't catch it and run with it if the ball's not there.

Let's start with the ultra-ultra-fearful. Passive, we'll call him, walks into an antique shop, say for the first time, or even worse, time after time. He sees an interesting and charming item—an old country kitchen pine table whose wood wears its age with rich deep red-brown scars. Passive asks the storekeeper, "How much?" "$800." Or perhaps it's a shipmaker's tool for $80, or a knickknack for $8. Passive and many others like him think that a price tag indicates the price you must pay if you are legally to acquire the item offered for sale. To the Passives, the idea of bargaining, of haggling, is unpleasant, to be avoided at all costs. (Perhaps Passive would try it in a bazaar in Afghanistan, but in the United States today, never.) Such people excel in large department stores; their cunning is restricted to buying items on sale and clipping coupons at supermarkets.

But anyone who deals directly, person-to-person, with the

owner of a thing for sale knows that there is almost always give in the price!

It's simple. You each have a threat. You can refuse the sale, *refuse to buy* a thing or service. You can decline to spend your money. The seller, on the other hand, can refuse to sell to you for less than the marked price. Who has the advantage? At this point, almost always you, the buyer. With a few exceptions, like tankerfuls of oil, there are more things for sale in the West than there is money to pay for them. Money talks. Don't muzzle it. The usual prevailing currency in personal day-to-day negotiation for sale and purchase of goods and services is the buyer's money. If the buyer is the employer, he controls the paycheck; if he is the purchaser, he controls the sale. The promise to pay and the complementary threat not to pay unless satisfied can be used time and again to make your life better. But you are embarrassed.

Some businesses deal with consumers only *as a class*. While prostrating themselves to satisfy consumers' tastes and preferences in order to get their dollars, they will treat consumers rigidly as a group in setting the price. It's "take it or leave it" from the start. Individual treatment is reserved for "returns" and other problems which arise after the sale. These are the department stores, the supermarkets, the gas stations—unless you happen to do a lot of business with them.

Thus the first general rule: The greater the amount at stake, usually the more you can gain in dollars and cents by making the correct moves. As a percentage of the total purchase price, however, the amount that's involved in personal give and take tends to shrink as the volume grows. That's because, among regulars, there arises a common expertise. Both buyer and seller develop the same way of looking at the world, and there is less room to bluff. By and large, both parties know and agree on how much a thing's worth.

Second rule: *Do not fall prey to the psychology of scale.* Do not forget that a dollar is a dollar in every possible situation. Otherwise the pennies you save clipping coupons at the supermarket for a year you will squander as a "mere" $50 in the purchase of a car. A dollar saved is a dollar earned. Benjamin Franklin was right.

Keep in mind that at the time of agreement, there is usually room to better your position. Find it, and move in! "Easy to say, hard to do," you complain. Maybe, but the first giant rule for all but those who are already masters or generally obnoxious is to fight. Overcome shyness, and help yourself make it in your world! Ask the dealer, "How much is your realistic bottom price on that painting?" After you hear it, you already will have saved yourself a good bit if you end up buying it. But even if you've appeared to touch bottom there are almost always further concessions to gain. Offer to pay in cash. Almost never is there anything illegal about paying money for what you buy. Almost no one will ever force you to pay by credit card or check. The storekeeper may or may not report the sale for income tax purposes, but that is his business. Perfectly legitimately, he may well want your cash now for a quick purchase of wholesale goods, or to pay bills. Whatever the case, it is perfectly appropriate to ask him if there is a cash discount. Do it! If the storekeeper says yes, which he very often will —as he, in turn, doesn't have to pay the credit-card company 5 percent or more—you will have reduced the purchase price further, often substantially. Of course, if you want to keep on haggling and playing the personalities of the situation by trying to be charming, acting poor or important, or any other such shenanigans, you are most likely a person who isn't "ultra-fearful" to begin with.

Speaking up and asking the price can save you money in situations in which there is no bargaining to be done. How many times have you agreed to a service and been disgruntled when you found out how much it cost *after* it was done? You were embarrassed to ask how much it was before deciding to do it; it would have made you look cheap or poor to admit that price might be a factor in your decision. Thus, you don't ask the beautician the cost of the feather s/he is putting in your hair as s/he does you up for the gala ball. You don't ask the dentist how much the crown is going to cost before s/he constructs it. You don't ask the waiter how much the day's special costs, nor the innkeeper how much the rooms are. Presumably, the price of many of these things will not change by your inquiry, but your decision whether to take up the inflexible offer may well. People often accept with resignation the price tag for things they wouldn't have chosen at all had they known how much in the first place. They feel embarrassed to ask. Somehow, the seller never feels embarrassed to present the bill.

If you care *about* yourself, care *for* yourself. *Demand information* when you know it will help you make informed choices; it doesn't cost anything extra except merely finding out. The action is out there in the world; your voice must be heard, your influence felt, unless you don't care how you fare in any particular situation. A few of my wealthier clients feel this way. They can afford to for a few generations, and fortunately they have lawyers who don't. By and large, however, the world of those blown by the currents is composed of desperate hangers-on.

A related rule: When you do pay for something, *ask for a receipt.* I have known fools to guard every penny at the supermarket, only to fall in love with a painting of their dreams, pay for it with a year's savings, feel relieved that the storekeeper accepted their perfectly valid check, and exit, confident it will be shipped to their out-of-state home, as promised, the next week. They walk out gaily not having a receipt. Assume the gallery owner is perfectly honest. What happens if the check is cashed and an electrical fire sweeps the gallery before the painting is shipped? Ask for receipts. Designate a barrel in your house that you like as an ornament and store receipts in it.

And know what you are being charged. I know people who are embarrassed to check the addition on the restaurant tab and would be mortified to "squabble over a mere $5 or $10." First of all, errors come in all columns. But that issue aside, it is not a sign of ill-breeding but of an aware and active nature to make certain you are not being ripped off. It is a sign that a person, from whatever class, should be and probably will be in control. I asked one of the owners of the expensive "21" Club in New York whether in his opinion it is unseemly to carefully check the amounts and addition on the check. His answer: Anyone who doesn't is stupid. Mistakes can and do happen.

From now on, I will consider it established that price tags are generally negotiable. They constitute an offer. There are two possible responses to an offer. One is called "sucker's gambit." It consists in immediately resigning oneself to the price and either paying it or walking away. There is a twin sin here. You will not only pay too much when you do pay, but often you will fail to make deals when you could have gained from them. You will fail because you were scared off too early by the high asking price. The second response, of course, is negotiation.

So if you're paying too much, heed. It very often pays to fight back by speaking up, even to supermarkets and utilities. Speak up! Don't be embarrassed. The worst that can happen is that someone will say no, and in that case, nothing's changed, except that you asked—you were going to reconcile yourself to the settlement anyway. It was rejected? You weren't, your offer was. And if you were, so what? You've paid no other price for speaking up except saying it; and you will sometimes get big benefits. Say it and reap.

Suppose you're not frightened, just sensitive to other people's feelings. You don't want them to get the message that you don't trust them when you do. Beware. It is a common and costly mistake to assume falsely that "honest" means "caring." The two are quite different. Many people who are basically honest, who will not cheat you, will delight in letting you cheat yourself.

Closely related to denying indications of distrust is caring inordinately for others' feelings. You call in a carpenter to ask for an estimate on some built-in units in your living room. The carpenter, very bright and cultured and, judging from his portfolio, accomplished and widely displayed, looks at your problem and suggests a couple of arrangements that have possibilities. You are basically satisfied with this person. He asks a high price, which you would rather not pay, but you are ultimately willing to if necessary. The next move is yours. If you wish to move forward, you must commit a few hundred dollars for an extended discussion as to your precise needs and life-style, and follow-up sketches. Then, subject to your approval, a completed unit will be constructed for a few thousand dollars.

Things are moving along fine at this first meeting. Finally the carpenter says, "Would you like to give me a deposit now? That way I can schedule our next meeting to plan the units." You feel embarrassed to say: "No. I like you very much at this first meeting. You sound right for my problem. But I want to think it over, and perhaps get another estimate, and then I'll get back to you." That ten-second speech might save you $1,000: The carpenter, fearing to lose the sale, might ask you if price is the problem, and be willing on the spot to come down. At the very least, he will be alerted to the fact that you are careful and demanding in your dealings.

Why does the carpenter ask for the deposit? Does he need it? Not likely. I know a master carpenter whose skill with wood was exceeded only by his salesmanship. He said to me once at a museum exhibition which included his work: "The most important thing is to make them stake you." He used to demand a nominal, fully refundable deposit. His philosophy was simple. Get them committed. Get them to give something as an expression of their favorable expectation. Make them keep in touch with the present pleasant moment in which they now trust and like you and your work.

A classic case in which the embarrassment problem arises is the contract between friends. A handshake is fine as long as things work out. But when things fall apart, the word, the promise, goes just before the friendship itself. The way around this genuine problem of appearing not to trust a friend is to use an attorney as the bad guy who insists on a contract in writing.

We all tend to feel embarrassed at asking for it in writing; it seems as if we don't trust the other person. It seems as if we're making a situation of friendly exchange into a hostile and distrustful adversary process. This embarrassment evaporates on analysis: Either the other person at the time of the promise is intending to fulfill it or not. If his intentions are good, that person will be more than willing to back them up by putting them on paper. It impresses you that he's serious about them. If, however, the other person is not seriously intending to go through with it, he will be hesitant and there will be an embarrassing pause. The shame you feel in that case is projection—how you would feel if you were a phony. The silence on the other side is caution: The con game becomes more difficult when a future swearing contest is avoided by black and white.

So don't feel embarrassed. No reputable business person will ever refuse to make a promise in writing. There should be a reason not to, rather than a reason to put it in writing. Make sure it's signed and dated. Get into the habit; it becomes easy. You'll be respected. If you need an excuse, blame it on your brother or spouse, or friend who is a lawyer and fights with you unless everything is in writing, or blame it on past instances where you've been burned.

The response to the old "What's the matter, don't you trust me?" should be a puzzled "If I didn't trust you, I wouldn't do business with you. What I don't trust is memories, yours or mine." When things end up in dispute, often the best of intentions become the worst of memories and the best of friends the worst of enemies. Stop the argument before it starts; get it in writing. Another good reason for getting it down in writing can be put this way: "I'd never think of asking if it were just you and I. But we both run the risk of an accident or worse, and thus have to provide for the possibility that one of us won't be around."

A friend of mine wanted to buy someone a birthday present and paid a small deposit on an old gold coin. The next week, he went to pick up the coin and pay the remainder. But the store owner informed him that the price of gold had risen so substantially that she "could not afford" to sell the coin to him at the original orally agreed price. He was furious, but she steadfastly refused. He was so agitated that he stormed out forgetting to get back his deposit. He happened to mention the story to me in passing, asking me what he should have done, and whether he had a legal right to the coin. I told him there was plenty he could do.

Basically a person is entitled to receive what he has contracted for once there has been an agreement and he has given a deposit or something of value—the law calls it "consideration." As we'll see, there are exceptions to this rule, but in this case I felt sure the sudden price rise of gold was not such an exception. My friend had made a good investment, and the merchant, whose business it was to assess gold values, had simply miscalculated the state of the world. I told my friend that he had every legal right to the coin at the agreed-upon price.

But having a right to something and actually getting it are two different things. I hope that if this book does nothing else, it will at least convince you of this—that having a legal right and effectively exercising it to your own advantage are not the same thing. Many rights may be too expensive to enforce. This principle is well understood by merchants. Generally it is not worthwhile to spend $200 to get back $100. (People who play slot machines seem to miss this point.)

The basic problem in these situations becomes how to convince the other person that you are not thinking strictly economically. If the other person realizes that it is not in your best financial interests to sue him, he may laugh off your threats. So how do you use your legal right to your monetary advantage?

This is a very important question, and it crops up frequently. The follow-up confrontation with the storekeeper must be done right or you will get nothing. There are some general rules that apply here.

1. Think of the problem from other people's perspective. The situation must be presented so that they understand it to be in their best interests to give you what you want.
2. Where the monetary costs to you of vindicating a right—such as court costs and time expenditure—exceed the value of the right, and the other party knows this, you must convince him that you are operating by a different calculus than cost-benefit. "The principle of the thing" is bandied about but is rarely pursued for its own sake. On the other hand, the other person must not be allowed to operate by that same nonmonetary calculus. Do not allow him to put his ego on the line against you. Encourage the opposite: Allow him to feel good in mak-

ing you whole, and let him understand it is to his advantage to deliver as promised.

3. Give the other person a way by which s/he wins. For example if the gold coin that you're being refused is one that s/he had in stock, point out that s/he's still making a profit over cost on that original coin. Yes, gold is more expensive, but that's gold s/he'll be buying and selling in a new market.

   If the coin isn't in stock, then the best carrot I can think of is that the shopkeeper's courtesy and integrity in dealing with this matter will be rewarded with future business, your own and your friends'.

4. Do not emphasize your profit from the purchase of the coin, but your noneconomic loss in the failure to deliver: e.g., a birthday party to which you will have to go empty-handed; you will be humiliated. The excuse of having made promises to other people is often effective; e.g., you have put a deposit on a gold chain and have designed a case with a jeweler.

5. Communicate your determination to have the contract enforced at any cost, but do not get belligerent. It may not be economically rational to proceed to court, and both of you may know this, but the other person must be convinced that you are governed by other than an economic calculus.

The strategy is, therefore, to set up tripwires—that is, to commit yourself automatically in advance to respond and disable yourself from reassessing afterward. To commit yourself in advance to a response which may not be cost-effective at a later time—i.e., to commit yourself to the "irrational"—may itself be rational and effective.

The power of the "irrational"—in this case, the advantage that may be gained when one side convinces the other that it is committed to act in a fashion that is not strictly in its own immediate best interests—is enormous. When the Iranians took the Americans hostage, one of the reasons the United States was unable to respond by threatening was that Khomeini was perceived as "irrational," as committed and willing to suffer greater costs to achieve aims not otherwise worthwhile.

It is essentially no different in situations of lesser importance. "To get your gold coin," I explained to my friend, "you must convince the shopkeeper that you will suffer great embarrassment if you do not have it and will be forced to institute legal proceedings in order to prove to others that you had purchased it on time, even if you must pay more than you win."

It worked. My friend, flushed with confidence, returned and calmly informed the store owner that he had shopped around, could not find any comparable coin and absolutely insisted on the sale, because of the humiliation, etc. . . . He got the coin at the original price. By the way, between the time he was first refused and the time he eventually got it, gold had gone up another 10 percent again!

The advice here is much more dependable than the price of gold. Timid? Uncomfortable? Don't be. The real embarrassment is being taken. Avoid that shame!

I
PERSONAL
CONTRACTS

MANY PEOPLE think of a contract as a carefully constructed written agreement, duly notarized, and drafted by lawyers in archaic abstruse language nobody, including the lawyers who fashioned it, fully understands. Somehow these massive documents govern the complex arrangements of vast commercial enterprises and are stored in vaults, to be taken out and utilized as proof only in the direst of emergencies. Many business contracts are not so unlike that. Bevies of lawyers have agonized over every imaginable specification and nuance and contingency to produce several hundred pages of such dreary prose that no one person ever reads it in its entirety. I'll leave all discussion of these complex agreements to the corporations and their law firms, including my own.

Somewhat closer to the everyday lives of most of us are the agreements that we enter into with companies or firms. Often they are nothing more than a form we are forced to sign in order to obtain goods and services. These written forms are forced on us on a take-it-or-leave-it basis; there is no room for negotiation, they are not bargained for, and we often don't bother to read them. As a result, as we shall see in later sections, courts sometimes void them—when the red, white and blue of fair play controls the black and white of legalese.

Closer to home, and the primary focus in this section, are personal contracts. Often there are no lawyers involved. Sometimes that's an advantage to both parties; often it's a means by which the sophisticated schemer takes advantage of the naively trusting. Such contracts may be informal. Indeed, they need not be written; they may be oral. At the very extreme, they need not have been spoken or expressed at all, but may be *implicit* in an ongoing relationship. A contract may arise from a long course of dealing, or from a long-standing intimacy. We'll explore some of the boundaries where things get sticky. But first, a few simple rules.

A contract, any contract, is basically a promise, an agreement between two or more people that creates, modifies or terminates a legal relation. The promise must be mutual. The minds of both parties must meet: They must agree to the same thing and know

31

they are agreeing to the same thing. Otherwise there is no deal. Mutuality also implies that both parties were free and able to bargain and shape the agreement—i.e., the agreement must be one which a sensible person "not under delusion, duress, or in distress" would make. The justice of this is obvious, the law prohibits any person from selling himself into slavery and would void any such agreement. While no one I know has actually sold himself into slavery, too many friends and clients have come close by giving themselves away.

Furthermore, in addition to a mutual and uncoerced meeting of the minds, a valid contract must involve "consideration"—an inducement to agree, something of value moving from each party to the other which seals it. The consideration need not be a material thing. Instead, one party can *do* something, or even forgo something to which he had every legal right. For example, if you and I agree that if you stop smoking for a year I will give you $5,000, and you stop smoking for a day, at which point I want to back out of the deal, I may be forced to go through with it once you've forgone smoking for even a brief period. That is adequate consideration in itself. But the consideration must be legal and not against public policy. Traditionally, as we'll see, I can't claim benefits under a contract with you on the grounds that the consideration is that I was your lover. Adultery, fornication and the like, being illegal, are not adequate consideration. In short, a contract against public policy will be voided—although, as we'll see, the times are a-changin'.

Contract is the legal institution more than any other which expresses and puts into practice our faith in the importance of free-willing adults, free to choose and promise and bind themselves and others. The irony of contract is that we achieve our freedom by mutual bondage. Nowhere is this truer than in marriage, which is the most basic personal contract, affecting more of us than any single other.

1.
ANTICIPATING DISAGREEMENTS

THE SECRET to winning battles is avoiding the necessity of fighting them. It's true in war, sport and life. The greatest generals are those who plan and move so that the enemy will not attack, but will surrender because of the overwhelming power deployed against him. Threats work when they prevent adverse reaction: The best weapons are those never fired in action. The successful defensive back in football covers a zone to which no opposing quarterback would pass. Life's demolition derby is like that; the winner is often the person who has engaged in the fewest mutually destructive combats. Successful people have known this for centuries: "A stitch in time saves nine," "An ounce of prevention is worth a pound of cure." These maxims have become almost trite, but their message is still very sound.

ELECTRONIC RECORDING

How many times has another person denied s/he ever said what you heard with your own two ears? How often has another person publicly proclaimed just the opposite of what s/he has privately said to you? It happens in business, in politics, and between husband and wife, parent and child, friend and friend. So many fruitless and bitter arguments take the form "You did too say that," "I never said that." How easily and quickly these arguments could be settled if only the original conversation had been recorded by a device which has no interest in distorting past statements in light of present circumstances. It takes a camera to produce the photo-finish winner of a neck-and-neck horserace. We do not trust the human eye. And instant playbacks at football and baseball games from time to time contradict a referee's or umpire's ruling. So the human eye and ear are far from infallible. How much less reliable is the human mind.

With all its formal trappings, a written contract's major purpose is to record both parties' expressed intentions and promises to which each can later refer. Daily life is mostly quick and informal. Discussions and promises rarely ripen into contracts. And besides, a contract has to be signed by both parties, whereas a secret recording can operate with the knowledge of only one, or none. How high are the stakes which often rest on what was actually said, how great the emotional and monetary consequences of failing to establish another's past promises and representations in noncontract situations! How many times we wish somehow there had been a recording!

The technology is available to make a record of your interactions with the world around you. Some of it is very inexpensive. A simple suction-cup device which plugs into any standard tape recorder and is widely available at audio shops for under $2 enables you easily to record your own telephone conversations. Less readily available, and more expensive but certainly not prohibitive for most people, are concealed body recorders, which are regularly used by undercover agents working for law-enforcement agencies and which enable you to record live conversations without notifying the other person. Don't you wish you'd had one working the last time you dealt with the auto-repair shop, the used-car salesman, or perhaps even your own lawyer or doctor? When you think about it, recording yourself can help you greatly to stand up and fight back.

On the other hand, of course, the resignation of Richard Nixon as President of the United States is the most dramatic recent proof that there are times when secretly taping your own conversations can come back to haunt you. Is it legal secretly to tap, tape and bug your own and others' conversations? Should you? Neither question can be answered with a simple yes or no.

Governmental law enforcement relies heavily on bugs and taps and concealed audio and now videotape to uncover and prove various types of crimes—witness recent successful investigations of major drug dealers, and major cases of official corruption, most recently the ABSCAM FBI sting operations against members of Congress and other public officials. It was also revealed in *The New York Times* that the British government had bugged the hotel and private conference rooms of the opposing parties in the Rhodesian negotiations, enabling the mediators to know when to stand firm and when to yield.

Yet all this monitoring is not without its serious dangers. In 1927, Supreme Court Justice Brandeis observed:

> The evil incident to invasion of privacy of the telephone is far greater than that involved in tampering with the mails. Whenever a telephone line is tapped, the privacy of the persons at both ends of the line is invaded, and all conversations between them upon any subject, and although proper, confidential, and privileged, may be overheard. Moreover, the tapping of one man's telephone line involves the tapping of the telephone of every other person whom he may call, or who may call him. As a means of espionage, writs of assistance and general warrants are but puny instruments of tyranny and oppression when compared to wiretapping.

Although generally a law-and-order conservative, I have always been deeply troubled by the invasion of privacy involved in such things as wiretapping, searches and seizures, and mail interceptions by government. It might be a shock to those who think I go for the jugular in every lawsuit—I don't deny it in principle—but during my years as a prosecutor, never once to my recollection did I authorize a wiretap, a mail interception, or a search and seizure. With a few possible exceptions—e.g., national security and kidnapping cases—I believe that law enforcement can get along quite well without these inherently distasteful invasions of privacy.

Shifting our attention from law-enforcement agencies to private citizens, let's look first at the legality and then move on to the morality and wisdom of taping your own conversations, tapping your own phone, or bugging your home, office, car, etc. Obviously where all parties agree to the taping of a conversation, there is no legal or ethical problem, although it is not always wise to make such a record. Legal problems begin when at least one party to a conversation does not know that it is being recorded.

The theory behind prohibiting secret taping, tapping or bugging of conversations is that such "eavesdropping" violates a right of privacy. In most states "the wrongful intrusion into one's private activities" gives the victim the right to collect money damages from the intruder. Such acts may also be serious crimes.

In 1968, Congress basically preempted the field when it passed Title III of the Omnibus Crime Control and Safe Streets Act. The act was motivated by a feeling on the one hand that widespread governmental surveillance was necessary to combat organized crime and on the other by a fear that the widespread use of surveillance in the private sector had already gotten completely out of hand. Commercial espionage and marital espionage were rampant. Private detectives, with the full support of the lawyers who hired them, were tapping phones. Senator Edward V. Long, chairman of a Senate subcommittee conducting hearings on invasions of privacy, said: "The three large areas of snooping in this [nongovernmental] field are (1) industrial, (2) divorce cases and (3) politics. So far, we have heard no real justification for continuance of snooping in these three areas."

As enacted, federal law made it a crime punishable by five years in prison and a $10,000 fine as well as a civil cause of action whenever a person "willfully intercepts or procures any other person to intercept any wire or oral communication." In the original bill this far-reaching prohibition had one major exception: "It shall not be unlawful where one of the parties to the communication has given prior consent to such interception.'' In other words, whenever one party to a conversation consented, the other person was vulnerable. The motives of the person secretly recording were irrelevant. How the tapes were used also would have been irrelevant.

But, objecting that this exception destroyed essential protections, Senator Hart of Michigan observed that although the proposed act contained ''blanket prohibitions'' on all ''third-party'' (unconsented-to) interception by private persons, and although it placed strict controls on the use of such interceptions by law-enforcement officers, it was ''totally permissive with respect to surreptitious monitoring of a conversation by a party to the conversation, even though the monitoring may be for insidious purposes such as blackmail, stealing business secrets, or other criminal or tortious acts in violation of federal or state laws. The use of such outrageous practices is widespread today, and constitutes a serious invasion of privacy.''

His observations had their effect. Today federal law against secret interceptions continues to prohibit strangers to a conversation from surreptitiously recording the conversation without the consent of some party involved. And it prohibits secret interception even where one of the parties to the conversation has consented when ''such communication is intercepted for the purpose of committing any criminal or tortious act in violation of the Constitution or laws of the United States or of any state *or for the purpose of committing any other injurious act.*''

Thus, the situation today is far from clear. Certainly, a person may not secretly record a conversation in which he takes part and then use the tape to blackmail another person. For the statute prohibits making secret recordings for the purpose of ''injuring'' another person. But does that include business loss? If I wish to protect myself and later hold you to promises by secretly recording our conversation, and I use that recording to your disadvantage in a financial confrontation, have I ''injured'' you? Suppose I use it to prove your infidelity or cruelty, and thereby force you into a divorce on less favorable terms; have I injured you? It is not surprising that the courts were soon called on to answer this very question.

FEDERAL RESTRAINTS

Floyd Meredith, whose job involved lifting and loading, began to suffer from a very painful hip injury. He filed for workmen's compensation, claiming that the injury resulted from an accident suffered on the job. After an investigation and unsuccessful offer to compromise the claim, the insurance company refused to pay, alleging that Meredith had admitted to one of its investigators that the injury was caused by the ordinary strain of lifting heavy objects and not by an on-the-job accident. One day, it seems, Meredith had called the claims manager to ask again why his claim wasn't being paid. Without informing Meredith, the manager switched on his dictaphone recording machine. During their conversation, the manager read to Meredith an unsigned prior statement he'd made to an investigator and got Meredith to admit that he had in fact once made that statement.

When Meredith's workmen's compensation claim finally went to a formal hearing, Meredith testified that he had suffered his injury when his foot slipped on some debris on the floor. He denied ever having made the statement to the investigator and denied ever having acknowledged to the manager over the phone that he had made it to the investigator. Whereupon the lawyer for the insurance company revealed the secret recording and offered to play it. In the end, the workmen's compensation referee entered an award in favor of Meredith for a 15 percent disability. Meredith then sued the insurance company and its manager, alleging that the secret recording of his telephone conversation and its use at the workmen's compensation hearing had violated the federal law.

Both sides conceded that the purpose of making the recording was not to commit a crime or tort. The specific question before the court, then, was whether the conversation had been intercepted "for the purpose of committing any other injurious act."

The trial court decided that *the statute did not prohibit this recording*. Reviewing the legislative history of the act, a federal appeals court affirmed, holding that by using the term "injurious act" in conjunction with "criminal and tortious acts" Congress had intended to prohibit certain kinds of harmful conduct which might not be strictly criminal or tortious. What was aimed at was the "intent to use that interception against a nonconsenting party in some *harmful way and in a manner in which the offending party had no right to proceed.*" Here, said the court, the purpose of the recording was "to protect the insurance company's position, not to positively harm the plaintiff."

Of course, that's a very difficult distinction to put into practice —I can surreptitiously record our conversation and use it only in order to protect myself, not to injure you. Sometimes the best defense is a devastating offense. The court was apparently aware that it was laying down an elusive standard by which private citizens should decide whether and when to secretly record: "The term [injury] is very vague. The scope of such harmful conduct must be determined on a case-by-case basis." And the court obviously was uncomfortable with its own distinction between affirmative injury and defense: "A judgment at law can be injurious to the losing party. A bankruptcy case can injure creditors with scant resources." And, naturally, the insurance company's successful resistance to Meredith's unsupported claim would be injurious to him. "But all parties have a right to proceed under the law and to protect their own rights."

One of the morals of the story is that Meredith ought never to have spoken to the investigator, period. Or if he had to for some reason, he should have first consulted the workmen's compensation regulations or someone in the know who would have informed him that he could collect only if his injury was due to an on-the-job accident. He had told the investigator that he wasn't sure whether or not he had slipped. Had he understood his own best interests *before* saying anything, his memory might have been a bit sharper. Shutting up at the right times and getting help at the right times are subjects covered elsewhere.

So, can we protect ourselves from the lies of other people, and also from their suits at our secretly recording their past statements? It's not clear. In support of his own amendment, Senator Hart had said: "One party consent is . . . prohibited when the party acts in any way with an intent to injure the other party to the conversation in any other way. For example, for the purpose of blackmailing the other party, threatening him, or publicly embarrassing him. . . . [But the act does not] *prohibit such recording in other situations when the party acts out of a legitimate desire to protect himself and his own conversations from later distortion or other unlawful or injurious uses by the other party.*"

It seems to me therefore that if your motives are self-protection, if you want to stand up and fight back for your rights, then under federal law, as a precaution, you may secretly tape any conversation in which you are a party, as long as state law doesn't prohibit it.

STATE RESTRAINTS

All states make it a crime for outside parties surreptitiously to bug, tape and record. Some states have written into their constitution "the right of the people to be secure against unreasonable interception of telephone and telegraph communications," immediately following the traditional "right of the people to be secure in their persons, houses, papers, and effects, against unreasonable searches and seizures." These states, like New York, implement that guarantee by making eavesdropping a felony. But most states provide for the basic exception that "consent by one participant in a conversation to a recording precludes any violation."

Illinois, however, has made it a criminal offense for a person to "use an eavesdropping device to hear or record all or any part of any conversation unless he does so with the consent of *all* of the parties to such conversation." But for the vast majority of the country, the consent of one party permits the secret recording of all.

It seems but a small step from the surreptitious legal recording by the insurance claims manager in order to protect the company against Meredith's "phony" claim to the acts of an Atlanta soft-drink bottling company. Ms. McDaniel claimed she'd been injured by a foreign object in a soda bottle. The company placed a bug in her hospital room, recording and monitoring her conversations from a room directly above. They overheard many intimate conversations between her and her husband, nurses and friends. Ms. McDaniel sued the company. The great mental pain and distress, embarrassment and humiliation caused by the surreptitious recording were held to constitute an invasion of her right to privacy, even though the company in good faith believed that she had faked her injury and claim, and the company had not communicated to anyone else the facts and conversations it recorded.

What's the difference between these two cases? Easy. In the first, one of the parties to the conversation gave permission for the recording, whereas here, no party gave permission. But even this apparently clear-cut distinction takes on additional complications when we move away from the business world to the world of fighting spouses.

INTERSPOUSAL IMMUNITY A client of mine owned a four-story townhouse and came home earlier than usual one afternoon, repairing to the upper bedroom. The phone rang. As he picked it up upstairs, his wife, who did not know he was home, picked it up downstairs. My client was treated to a conversation which clearly suggested her unfaithfulness. He hired detectives and caught his wife *in flagrante delicto* with her lover, who just happened to be one of the leaders in the ultra-liberal movement.

He didn't record this conversation. Yet by listening in he was surreptitiously eavesdropping on a conversation to which he was not a party. Had he committed any violation of law? For example, could he successfully be sued by his wife's lover? I think it can be said that he was well within his rights. The United States Supreme Court has itself written: "Common experience tells us that a call to a particular telephone number may cause the bell to ring in more than one ordinarily used instrument. Each party to a telephone conversation takes the risk that the other party may have an extension telephone and may allow another to overhear the conversation. When such takes place there has been no violation of any privacy of which the parties may complain."* This to me is legalese for saying that since it was his—or at least "their"—telephone, he had a right to pick up an extension; and it was his wife's risk when she had the incriminating conversation over the home phone. Picking up an extension to hear a chance conversation is one thing. Tapping your own phone is another.

Can one spouse sue another for such surreptitious eavesdropping?

The chief prosecutor for the Justice Department in illegal-surveillance cases once estimated that 30 percent of all such actions concerned domestic relations. With the advent of the sexual revolution in the 1960s there came to be a sudden shift in the gender of the eavesdropping party. One private investigator commented that whereas at the beginning of the 1960s, 80 percent of the domestic eavesdrops were women checking their husbands, by its midpoint, 80 percent were husbands checking their wives. Presumably as society reaches sexual symmetry, it will achieve a 50–50 split.

Marital identity has long been a tradition in the law. For the purposes of civil suits, husbands and wives are one person—the husband. Therefore, one spouse could not sue the other for, for example, invasion of privacy or anything else. Increasingly, it has been recognized that spouses' upper limbs are employed not only to embrace each other, but also to keep each other at arm's length. Increasingly, this so-called "interspousal immunity" has been abolished in various states.

An obvious question is whether such spousal exception was implicit in the federal act. Or did the flat prohibition against nonconsensual eavesdropping apply to a husband and wife, thereby allowing either to sue the other?

The first major case to consider the question of an "interspousal electronic surveillance immunity"—whether one spouse could eavesdrop on another spouse's conversation with third parties—involved one Mr. Simpson, who, suspecting his wife's faith-

---

* *Rathbun* v. *U.S.* 355 US 107 1957.

lessness, had tapped his home phone, recording "mildly compromising" conversations between his wife and another man. The other man was making advances and his wife was resisting in something less than a "firm and final fashion." Convinced that he had "caught her," the husband played portions of the tapes to family members and neighbors. He also played them for a lawyer, on whose advice Mrs. Simpson agreed to an uncontested divorce.

The former Mrs. Simpson now sued her former husband under the federal statute. A federal appeals court concluded that although the statute on its face was all-inclusive and made no distinction between nonconsensual marital taps and other kinds, nevertheless Congress had not intended to intrude into domestic conflicts normally left to state law. The court, however, distinguished the immediate situation before them—one in which at the behest of the husband an outside person actually conducted the electronic surveillance—from other situations. The court held that involving any outside party in the surveillance was "an offensive act against a spouse's privacy of a much greater magnitude than is personal surveillance by the other spouse." The court even expressed some doubt about its own opinion, limiting it to the facts of the particular case, pointing out that the surveillance did not here physically extend beyond the marital home.

Soon after, a lower federal court allowed a civil cause of action to Clifford Remington against his wife, Kamila Remington, for hiring a detective agency to tap his home phone. Intimate conversations were recorded and played for other people, including the wife's lawyers. Mrs. Remington moved to dismiss the action on the grounds of interspousal immunity, which Pennsylvania recognized, and on the basis of the Simpson case. But the court distinguished *Simpson,* on the grounds that here there had been third-party participation in the eavesdropping.

The lesson seemed to be that you could invade your spouse's privacy, within your own home, as long as you did it yourself. These two cases were criticized. It was asked, for example, why it made a difference whether the spouse had help in installing the eavesdrop. So what that Simpson had done it alone? He had played it for various people. The invasion of privacy is no less if the installation is accomplished without aid, but the conversations are made public. How a tap is used, not how it is installed, should make the difference.

The next year, 1976, the question arose whether for the purpose of criminal prosecution under the federal statute it made any difference if the eavesdropping had been accomplished by a spouse unaided or by a detective agency on the spouse's orders. William Jones had lived with his wife in a house which his grandmother owned. The telephone in the house was listed in his name. He and his wife were separated in July 1974 and ceased to live together after that date. William filed for divorce in September, and the following month his wife was granted a restraining order prohibiting him from "coming about" her. Their divorce was granted in January 1975. He claimed that he had continued a sexual relationship with his wife even after he had moved out of the house, and that he returned on occasion to baby-sit. He testified that while baby-sitting in October 1974 he became suspicious that his wife was involved in an extramarital affair, and so he had tapped into the phone from outside the house and recorded the conversations. He used these recordings to obtain a divorce. The district judge dismissed the criminal indictments. But the circuit court of appeals reinstated them. There were many ways to distinguish Jones' situation from Simpson's and Remington's. *Jones* involved a criminal prosecution under the statute, whereas the other two cases involved civil suits. *Jones* involved monitoring from outside the home, whereas the other two cases were inside. Mr. Jones was at the time legally separated, whereas the other two were married. And the court noted these distinctions as being sufficient, but not necessary for the decision.

The court could have endorsed the Simpson-Remington distinction between unaided and third-party spousal surveillance for the purposes of civil suits while holding that distinction inapplicable in criminal actions. But instead it considered solo versus joint taps as unimportant—"a classic distinction without a difference." For purposes of federal wiretap law, "it makes no difference whether a wiretap is placed on a telephone by a spouse or by a private detective in the spouse's employ. The end result is the same—the privacy of the unconsenting parties to the intercepted conversation has been invaded.''

Although this court allowed a criminal indictment to stand for the unaided wiretap of a spouse by another spouse, it left unanswered the original situation of my client: picking up the extension and listening in. In a footnote the court said: "We express no opinion [as to whether Title III] reach[es] a family member's interception of a telephone conversation by use of an extension telephone in the family home, other than to note that there is a vast difference between overhearing someone on an extension and installing an electronic listening device to monitor all incoming and outgoing telephone calls.''

A decision of one federal court of appeals is not binding on any others. And, technically, no two decisions in this series directly conflict. But the law on this is far from settled. As of now, it might be that criminal liability would attach where civil liability would not. How odd. Sooner or later the Supreme Court of the United States will probably give us some clear guidelines about what a spouse may do concerning taping, tapping, and bugging his own home, his phone, his car. Under the circumstances outlined, where the husband innocently picked up the phone when it rang in his own room, I can hardly imagine a court's requiring him to hang up the minute he hears his wife arranging a rendezvous with another man. To require him to gently put the phone down in its cradle comes under the heading of impossibility of performance.*

---

* A friend of mine delights in telling how he made two of his biggest cases as a prosecutor. One involved an organized-crime figure who correctly guessed that the government was tapping his phone. Over dinner he pointed to the offending instrument and warned his wife not to say anything damning over it. She promised not to forget. Nor did she. Dutifully, five minutes later she called her best friend. As recorded by the government, the excited conversation began: "Maria, I'm calling you from the upstairs phone because John tells me not to say anything over the kitchen phone, you know his importing drugs and the government tapping . . ." In an unrelated case there was a savvy crooked businessman who also correctly guessed the government was tapping his phone and warned his wife not to talk over it. Terrified she might forget, she took the bedroom phone off the hook, thus converting the telephone tap into a bedroom bug which picked up the most revealing conversations imaginable.

The tide may be turning slowly against allowing a spouse the right to eavesdrop on a conversation between the other spouse and a third party. In December 1979 a federal district court in western New York refused to dismiss a civil suit filed by a man whose phone calls to the defendant's wife were recorded by a device the defendant had attached to his home phone.

SELF-TAPING

Although a few states as a matter of state law now prohibit taping phone calls even with one party consenting, generally it remains perfectly legal to record any conversation to which you are yourself a party. In January 1980, for example, the Ethics Committee of the New York State Bar Association modified its traditional ban on attorneys' recording telephone conversations without the consent of both parties to the conversation.

In 1974 the committee had concluded that "except in special situations it is improper for a lawyer engaged in private practice to record electronically a conversation with another attorney or any other person without first advising the other party." The committee had said that "even if secret electronic recording of a conversation with one party's consent is not illegal, it offends the traditional standards of fairness and candor that should characterize the practice of law." And the Bar Association had expressed the view that the use of extension phones to permit associates or secretaries to make records of, or simply listen to, telephone conversations without the knowledge or consent of the other parties involved would be unethical.

But now, six years later, the Ethics Committee has held squarely that even if lawyers may not themselves record conversations, they may advise their clients that it is legal for them to do it, and may advise them of the advantages of doing it. Presumably the tide will continue to turn.

Almost everywhere in this country, then, it is legal to secretly tape your own conversations, unless you are a lawyer engaged in private practice.*

---

* One other exception should be noted. The Federal Communications Commission has expressed a policy which most states have adopted that it is improper to record *interstate*

It is legal, but is it wise? This is a complicated question.

The example of Watergate leaps to mind. Recall that the Watergate break-in itself was for the purpose of planting a bug in Larry O'Brien's office. But tapes dominated the entire scene. Richard Nixon, for some reason unknown to anyone but himself, installed a secret taping system in the Oval Office, which was perfectly legal because he was a party to each taped conversation. That he could then have proceeded indiscriminately to tape his own seriously incriminating conversations is incredible. The most saintly among us, of which I surely am not one, say things in private that we wouldn't announce on television or to Bill Safire. To have indiscriminately taped these statements in the first place was itself remarkable, but to have preserved them, as Nixon did, when they were not yet under subpoena from any court or Congressional committee, and legally could have been destroyed, displays either an arrogance or an ineptitude that is thoroughly baffling and somewhat inconsistent with other actions of this unique man. There was and is no federal statute that explicitly makes destruction of possible evidence a crime. Of course once a document or other evidence has been subpoenaed, intentional destruction may be either criminal contempt or obstruction of justice. Not until well along into the Watergate investigation did Nixon have the legal obligation to preserve those tapes. On the subject of destruction of evidence: While it is true that "under federal law it is not illegal to destroy a document, no matter how relevant to future litigation provided no subpoena has been issued, and no grand jury or criminal investigation has yet begun," some states and professional codes have adopted a more stringent standard that makes it a crime to destroy documents or other real evidence "believing that an official proceeding or investigation is pending or about to be instituted" in order to "impair its verity or availability in such proceeding or investigation." A few states go even further and prohibit destruction of evidence if done for the purpose of

---

or *international* phone calls without the use of an automatic tone warning device. But as long as the calls are intrastate, or the conversations take place live, you may legally record the conversations.

making it unavailable in any future criminal or civil proceeding—that is, at any time regardless of the belief as to the likelihood of future proceedings.

The Senate version of the proposed reform of the criminal laws would have adopted such a new standard. The House version would have retained the old. The issue has not yet been resolved.

WIRETAPPING AND PRIVACY

Finally, there is a question of morality in all this. Was it fair and ethical to ask for and receive the candid advice of subordinates and confidences imparted by heads of state which they believed were thoroughly off the record, all the time preserving their comments for posterity? To have done so routinely, as Nixon did, raises serious questions. There may have arisen on occasion an exceptional need or warrant for taping. But these are two instances in which secretly taping one's own conversations backfired.

One more case from personal experience. Galveston, Texas, has produced many leaders in the business world. A modern example is John S. Samuels III, chairman of Carbomin Coal, who, as chairman of the New York City Opera and a director of Lincoln Center, is one of New York's cultural leaders. Decades before the rise of Samuels, Galveston's leading family was that of W. L. Moody. A fortune in insurance—American National Insurance Company (ANICO)—and shipping enabled Mr. Moody to create the $400 million Moody Foundation. Moody stipulated that there be only three trustees. Years later, in 1959, Will Wilson, the Texas attorney general, who was later to resign as head of the Criminal Division of the Justice Department in the wake of a scandal back home, forced a deal whereby three "outside" trustees were added to the foundation's board. After winning over one of the Moody family trustees under questionable circumstances, the outside trustees took control.

As a group and individually these outside trustees were pillars of the business community. One was chairman of a top Houston bank, another was the head of a large shipping and steel company listed on the New York Stock Exchange, and the third was a leading Texas oilman. While they were trustees of the Moody Foundation, which owned controlling interest in ANICO, some blatantly crooked deals were entered into by ANICO's then chairman and president. For example, multimillion-dollar loans were made to Las Vegas gambling casinos and other enterprises which resulted in huge personal kickbacks in the form of "points"; millions were lent to a broadcasting company which was controlled by the son of ANICO's president; and questionable loans were made in connection with the then highly controversial Teamsters Pension Fund.

In conjunction with Galveston's leading lawyer and one of the finest advocates I have ever known, V. W. "Boo" McLeod, we launched a lawsuit declaring that Mr. Moody's limitation of the number of trustees to three was controlling. At the deposition stage, we conducted an examination of the "outside" trustee who was "chairman" of the Moody Foundation, Paul R. Haas, an oilman from Corpus Christi. This was not to be a routine deposition. For however bleak our prospects of success might have looked to others before the examination, I knew we had a surprise for the distinguished chairman. He had hired a private detective to "get the goods" on the Moody family and me. Somehow or other we came into possession of a tape of a phone conversation between Haas and his detective in which the sanctimonious chairman made all sorts of gutter suggestions as to how to trap us.

Haas sat in the witness chair under oath refusing to acknowledge his tactics. I elicited some more of his standard sanctimony, putting him in concrete, then I produced a machine and played the tape. As Haas heard his own words echo across the room, he turned even paler than the bevy of ANICO and Moody Foundation lawyers sitting around the table. The Moodys and I enjoyed every minute of it. We won the lawsuit, and the Texas supreme court restored control of the Moody Foundation to the Moodys—Aunt Mary (Mrs. Mary Moody Northen), Robert Lee Moody, and Shearn Moody, Jr. Once again the tapes had hurt.

So what emerges from all this? Am I suggesting that it is always both wrong and stupid to tape yourself? No. You should have an inexpensive phone suction-cup tape recorder and you should on occasion use it. When? When you are talking to someone you don't trust, and who you believe will later turn on you or will conveniently forget.

Another time to tape conversations is when you agree to something with someone. If you don't want to put it in writing, you can save the formality and accomplish much the same thing: Hand him an inexpensive pocket dictating machine and ask *him* to dictate the terms of your agreement into the machine. This way he knows that you have a record as agreed to by him. Of course, this can cut both ways and serve as a check on your memory as well.

In my experience, taping oneself is somewhat analogous to keeping a gun in the house. It can accidentally go off at the wrong time, but, given the conditions out there, it ultimately makes sense, and I support the right of others to do it, legally.

Maybe I'm old-fashioned and ill-suited for the future. Maybe surveillance technology is an unalterable fact of life. Maybe the conditions that Congress understood in 1963 which led to Title III are here to stay:

> Commercial and employer-labor espionage is becoming widespread. It is becoming increasingly difficult to conduct business meetings in private. Trade secrets are betrayed. Labor and management plans are revealed. No longer is it possible, in short, for each man to retreat into his home and be left alone. Every spoken word, relative to each man's personal, marital, religious, political, or commercial concerns can be intercepted by an unseen auditor and turned against the speaker to the auditor's advantage.

But I hope not. If I were going to invest in a piece of today's newest technology in the surveillance field, it would be in a device which tells me whether others are tapping my phone, or wearing concealed tape recorders. It would be a device which enables both of us to rely on our minds and not machines; to be ourselves in private moments.

We are willing to die for freedom and fight any who would

deprive us of our liberty and autonomy. Let's be vigilant against voluntarily slipping into Big Brotherism—eternal posturing—because we embraced technology to our stainless-steel bosoms. Let's not become the devices of our devices. Let us ensure, in Joshua Lederberg's haunting phrase, that man doesn't become just another man-made thing.

2.
MARRIAGE

WHAT'S THE great American sport? Traditionalists say baseball. They're wrong. Others claim football or basketball. They're wrong, too. The right answer's easy: The matrimonial game—marriage, separation, divorce, remarriage and living together—occupies the serious attention of more Americans than any other. People who aren't married are living as if they were; people who are married are living as if they weren't. Some go through the formalities when they first join or split; others play the game later on. Family life is disintegrating as women's lib persuades married women to become just as selfish and unconcerned with the family unit as many of their husbands traditionally have been. With 40 percent of marriages ending in divorce, our children are suffering as their families shred at an alarming rate.

Once upon a time divorce was the private preserve of the rich. The grounds for divorce were few, the problems of proving adultery, for example, were great, and the costs of litigation were high. Today, with "no-fault" or multiple grounds for divorce in most states, it's much easier to get one. Lawyers now advertise and compete for the business at cheaper rates.

But although the divorce game is cheaper and easier to play and more people are playing it, the stakes are no less high. Many lives are ruined by bad moves on the part of the players and their lawyers. Because the overwhelming majority of adult Americans are involved directly or indirectly in the matrimonial game in one form or another, I've written this section to help you fight back and win. The purpose is not to enable you to avoid using a lawyer altogether, but to help you make the right use of your own lawyer when you need one, and, more important, to suggest some winning moves long before and long after any lawyer is involved.

I've played the matrimonial game a lot as the lawyer for some very rich and famous people. They may play for more money, but good moves are essentially the same for all economic classes. Your stakes are just as high. Your emotional well-being is no less valuable than theirs, and it might well be easier to achieve.

ANTE-NUPTIAL AGREEMENTS

It is easy to be cynical and declare that the best way to prevent a split is never to join in the first place. But for most people this is no solution; for the vast majority, a good marriage is much to be preferred to remaining single. However, there are strains in any alliance when the best interests of the parties diverge, and many pacts crumble as allies become enemies. Still, many marriages do work, and an important factor, I think, is that both parties come to terms with their relationship and want the same thing from it. In my experience that's very important.

Just as successful alliances run the gamut from loose and *ad hoc* confederations of interests to a single unified nation, so marriages range from a loose association of social and economic convenience to a couple living almost as one. The legal institution of marriage accommodates the entire range. While there are things that each of us wouldn't do for love or money, marriage is an act often undertaken for either motive, or both. Sometimes, moreover, they are difficult to separate. Accordingly, the odds of success in marriage are likely to be increased if both agree mutually, before marrying, what it is that each expects to put into the relationship and what each expects to get out. It's difficult to imagine and admit that the flush of the moment may become the flush of the toilet as the relationship goes down the tubes. But admitting it and providing for it up front will often prevent a breakdown later on. That's what this section is about.

ANTICIPATION OF DEATH

An ante-nuptial (that is, prenuptial) agreement is a contract entered into by prospective husband and wife which fixes just what either party will get on the other's death. In other words, it limits the rights of the survivor to what the agreement provides, rather than to what s/he would otherwise inherit under law. One of the lessons which emerges time and again from my experience is the wisdom of such an ante-nuptial agreement when a wealthy man marries a much-divorced, considerably younger lady. Let's talk some traditional black-letter law first. Parties to an ante-nuptial agreement are assumed not to deal at arm's length as in a business contract, but rather they must exercise the highest degree of good faith, candor and sincerity in all matters bearing on the agreement's terms. Fairness is the ultimate measure. The basic requirements for a valid ante-nuptial contract are *that it be freely entered into with an understanding of its terms without fraud and that it not be unjust or inequitable.* Otherwise, the courts will throw it out and allow the spouse to elect against the will.

The basis of an ante-nuptial agreement is contractual. The intended bride must understand her intended groom's financial status. She must also understand that when she becomes his wife, she would otherwise have an absolute right to a minimum portion of the estate (in New York, for example, her minimum is one-third if there are children of the decedent, one-half if there are not). Understanding these points, both parties are free to enter into a contract by which the intended bride waives or limits her rights to her husband-to-be's estate and vice versa. This becomes a legal contract. But like any other contract, it must be based on disclosure of relevant facts. The richer party must disclose the full extent of his assets so that the other party understands at the time s/he surrenders dower rights exactly what s/he is giving up. If not, once again, the court will dishonor the agreement.

For example, if the intended husband represents he is worth

$100,000 and agrees to leave the wife only $15,000 instead—fine. But suppose he misstated his worth and it was really $5 million—then the wife can later challenge the agreement on the ground of fraudulent concealment of assets.

From these general requirements, there emerges a typical almost inevitable pattern of litigation: Wealthier spouse, before remarrying, enters into an ante-nuptial agreement with his new bride-to-be, pursuant to which she gives up her rights in his estate in return for a fixed amount, or an annual income of a fixed amount; wealthier spouse dies, leaving all or most assets to children, friends or charities. Disinherited spouse challenges the validity of the ante-nuptial agreement, claiming it was fraudulently procured, and demands instead to elect against the will. That a spouse has surrendered something much greater than s/he's received in return is some evidence that the waiver of dower rights was not a fully informed one.

But this factor is not always determinative. For example, before marrying Allen Abbott, Yvonne signed a prenuptial agreement by which the parties stipulated that neither should acquire by their marriage any interest in certain enumerated items of property. Allen named Yvonne as the beneficiary of specified insurance policies, and she in turn agreed among other things that she would "make no claims against the estate" of Allen "by virtue of any statute of distribution, widow's allowance or otherwise." Referring to his ante-nuptial agreement in his will, Allen left his entire estate to his eight children. When the assets were added up, it turned out that the insurance policies which Yvonne had gotten were worth about $35,000, whereas the rest of his estate was worth about $600,000.

Although the ante-nuptial agreement had itemized the assets to which Yvonne was surrendering all rights without listing their value, and although she claimed that at the time of the agreement she'd been under the mistaken impression that the attorney who drew it up was representing both of them, nevertheless the court held that "the fact that the amount received by a widow under the ante-nuptial agreement is disproportionate to the value of the decedent's assets did not shift the burden of proof onto those who would take under the will to show that the ante-nuptial agreement was not fraudulent." In other words, doing poorly under the agreement wasn't enough; *she* had to prove she hadn't understood what she gave up at the time, or had been coerced. Yvonne lost.

In deciding whether to uphold an ante-nuptial agreement the courts will often consider the savvy of the parties. For example, where it was the second marriage for the husband and the third for his wife, who had previously been his bookkeeper and knew his assets, and where at first she'd rejected the ante-nuptial agreement but seventeen days before the wedding she'd signed it in his attorney's office after declining his lawyer's advice to retain her own attorney, the court upheld the wife's prenuptial forfeiture of dower.

It is not always necessary, therefore, that there be a *full* disclosure of assets, although to be safe there should be. Charlotte, a fifty-eight-year-old widow, met Perry, a sixty-nine-year-old widower, when each was gainfully employed. After an eighteen-month courtship, Perry proposed marriage but told Charlotte he wanted her to sign an ante-nuptial agreement by which she would accept $5,000 in lieu of dower or any other rights she might have were she to survive him. She took the agreement to her brother, a practicing attorney. Her brother asked if she knew how much her prospective spouse was worth. She said no, and he told her he thought the agreement was unfair and called for some further explanation. Notwithstanding his advice, she expressed a desire to sign it, and, not desiring to turn an ante-nuptial agreement into an anti-nuptial agreement, he simply drafted a second agreement by which Perry also relinquished any claim on her assets should he survive her. They were married in 1959. He died July 4, 1976. His estate was worth over $100,000.

The old rule in Massachusetts had been, as it is in many other states, that nothing short of proof of fraudulent concealment would invalidate an ante-nuptial agreement, irrespective of the unfairness of the agreement's provisions. The rule further provided: "The failure on his part to inform her of what he owned falls far short of fraudulent concealment. . . . Notwithstanding the confidential relations between the parties, the simple failure voluntarily to disclose the amount of his property does not constitute actionable fraud.''

The Massachusetts supreme judicial court was unhappy about this longstanding rule. But it seemed unfair to all who had entered into prenuptial agreements and were relying upon them to change the rule without prior warning. So the court used the occasion of Charlotte's suit to declare that in all Massachusetts ante-nuptial agreements entered into after March 1979, the burden is no longer on either party to *inquire* of the other, but on each to *inform* the other, "for it is only by requiring full disclosure of the amount, character, and value of the parties' respective assets that courts can ensure intelligent waiver of the statutory rights involved." Henceforth a court is to consider whether (1) the agreement contains a fair and reasonable provision for the party contesting the agreement as measured at the time of its execution; (2) the contesting party was fully informed of the other party's worth prior to the agreement's execution or had, or should have had, independent knowledge of the other party's worth; and (3) a waiver by the contesting party is set forth.

And the Massachusetts high court emphasized that the reasonableness of an agreement could not be judged in isolation but only in reference to such factors as the parties' respective worth, ages, intelligence, literacy, and prior family ties.

ANTICIPATION OF DIVORCE
Another traditional rule about ante-nuptial agreements was that they could deal only with one area—the rights of the parties in the event of death. Traditionally there could be no legally binding agreement as to alimony, support, or property division in the event of a separation or divorce. What was the purpose of restricting the agreement only to the split after death? Courts have construed "public policy" to favor the preservation and continuation of marriages, and therefore would not allow persons contemplating matrimony to predict and provide for the details of who gets what

after its collapse. The feeling was that such agreements, by making the breakup less painful, made it more likely. I often advise clients to include alimony provisions in prenuptial agreements anyway. Although not everywhere legally binding, they are likely to have some effect on a judge fixing alimony, if only a subconscious one. The judge would hardly avoid the impact of what the parties had worked out themselves and considered to be reasonable at the time.

There are still many places where the old rule generally holds. For example in 1978 the South Dakota supreme court set aside William and Thelma Connolly's ante-nuptial agreement by which he had relieved himself of any obligation to support his wife in the event of their divorce. The court held that post-divorce obligations of a husband to support an ex-wife are "affected with such public interest" that parties in a divorce action may not "conclusively agree" upon the terms of future support payments. After all, reasoned the court, the ante-nuptial agreement "may bear no reasonable relationship to the subsequent situation of the parties," in which case such agreements are against public policy, are void and unenforceable.

But while the court set this agreement aside, it denied any *per se* prohibition against all such nonsupport agreements. "At one time," the court said, "it was the rule that any attempt to diminish or waive by way of an ante-nuptial agreement a husband's duty to support his wife through alimony was unenforceable as being contrary to public policy. Some of the more recent decisions, however, seem to have receded from this flat prohibition against enforcing agreements of this nature in favor of a more flexible *ad hoc* approach that determines the validity of such an agreement on the basis of the facts in each case." Other states' high courts have followed this approach of frowning upon such agreements without flatly prohibiting them.

The courts are sometimes torn in these cases between a desire on the one hand to avoid an obvious harsh result to the wife, and on the other hand to recognize "the freedom of parties to contract, which is essential to both our society and system of government."

The flat prohibition against ante-nuptial alimony agreements, then, is a rule with widespreading exceptions and is in midair across the nation. Some states have recently changed their law. New York, for example, as of July 1980, now permits binding written agreements made before (or during) the marriage concerning alimony as long as the amount agreed upon is fair and reasonable at the time of agreement and isn't unconscionable at the time of divorce. The new law allows the ante-nuptial agreement to bind not only as to alimony but also as to property division, child support and even child custody as long as the court concludes the arrangements are in the child's best interests.

OTHER ANTE-NUPTIAL AGREEMENTS
So far I've been talking as if the issue is always money, money, money. But it's not. There are ante-nuptial contracts concerning other matters. One common one is about religion. These are less enforceable than property agreements because they generally involve children, and the courts' rule of thumb again is that whatever the wishes of the parents, it is the child's best interests that govern.

So for example in 1954 a court refused to conform with an ante-nuptial agreement that the child be brought up a Catholic and attend parochial school when neither the twelve-year-old nor his mother, who had custody, wanted him to be Catholic. (A dissent in this case pointed out that a child's desires and his best interests are not necessarily synonymous.)

The pattern is clear. In another case two Catholics married. They divorced and the wife got custody of the children. She converted to Judaism when she remarried and proceeded to bring the children up as Jews. The father sued to have them brought up Christian. But the court disallowed it, holding that the policy of the law with respect to religious upbringing of children is noninterference. "If the custodian is fit, s/he has exclusive control over the religious upbringing of the children."

This is the general rule, with few exceptions. Whoever has custody determines the upbringing regardless of ante-nuptial agreements to the contrary. And so in reverse of the last case another Catholic wife agreed before marrying the Jewish husband to convert and bring up the children as Jewish. She did. They were divorced. She remarried a Catholic and resumed Catholicism. The children's father moved to enjoin his former wife from attempting to change the religion of his four children. The court rejected his pleas, holding that the agreement didn't intend to encompass the situation of a future divorce, and even if it had, "ante-nuptial agreements regarding religious rearing of children are enforceable to the extent they provide for the best interest and welfare of the child. However, courts may modify their terms and provisions when confronted with appropriate evidence that the welfare of the child is not best served by a premarital agreement of the parents." Again the court emphasized its policy of not intruding into internal family affairs. "Only when moral, mental and physical conditions are so bad as seriously to affect the health or morals of children should the court be called upon to act." This father was distraught at what were to him his children's foreign beliefs. He used his visitation time to tell his children that they were Jews, that their mother was doing a sinful thing by taking them to her church and that they would suffer agonies of regret if they fell for their mother's religious indoctrination. But the court, without sympathy, chastised: "The father cannot expect to direct their lives by remote control. . . . the tragedy of these children being torn apart by a vindictive and insensitive father is the consequence of his own acts." The court added, "By inflicting his religious views, however sincerely held, on these hapless infants, he cannot redeem himself on earth or in heaven."

DIVORCE

We have seen that ante-nuptial agreements are often well advised. Ironically, it is not uncommon for them to prevent or forestall the very marital breakup they anticipate. Having modestly settled on shares after death or divorce, the poorer spouse often has more to gain by the continued good health not only of the wealthier partner, but also of the partnership itself.

However, with or without an ante-nuptial agreement, a large number of marriages are unstable, and I would guess that more than once, if only for a moment, most married people seriously consider a divorce. There are many more marital problems than there are marriages. And while I'm a lawyer and not a psychiatrist, reviewing thousands of marital breakups over the years does lead me to some general conclusions.

BEFORE SEPARATING

I once accompanied a woman client to the office of perhaps the nation's leading matrimonial law firm, which was representing her husband. Oddly, the clients and lawyers on both sides were personal friends as well. When the eminent counselor immediately launched into establishing trust funds and millions as a divorce settlement, my client, who was also his friend, cut him off abruptly. Indignant, she rose from her chair and said: "A marriage vow meant and means something to me. I only took it once, for better or worse. I intend to stand by it, and no matter how many millions you offer, I am not going to consent to a divorce." Subsequently, they had many happy moments together and were still married years later when he died, and she inherited the bulk of his estate. Would that more marrieds and more lawyers shared this sentiment.

An age-old question is whether a marriage should be kept intact just for the children. My answer is simple, if unfashionable: Yes, definitely. I know that many who consider themselves sophisticated and enlightened like to say that a bad marriage does the children no good, and that they are better off with a divorce. But in my experience that's generally not true. There are some cases where the parents are impossible around each other, doing little else but swearing at each other or hurling bottles along with the abuse. Here obviously the child is better off anywhere but in this environment. But in the average case I think it means a great deal to a child to have the security of knowing that both parents, each of whom loves the child, are living together with him. This may be more important than the other message which also filters through, that the parents don't get along with each other terribly well. I think the modern jargon about the health of the child being served by splitting is a rationalization to help the parents avoid the guilt and shame which they rightly ought to feel.

A little less psychiatry and a little more common sense would result in fewer marital breakups and happier children. In the olden days many marriages stayed together for the children, until the children went off to school, and then they stayed together for the long term comforts, and hobbies which the partners shared. That's not so bad really, not when compared to today's liberated, isolated egotistical solo acts.

At the risk of sounding like a preacher or marriage counselor, I offer a first piece of advice: Think twice before splitting up. It's much easier to destroy than it is to create. Don't measure your marriage against an impossible ideal; measure it against your alternatives. And if you do see a lawyer, it should be for the purpose of *exploring* the possibility of a divorce; don't feel forced to go through with it. I've actually known people who were too embarrassed to change their minds and save their marriage.

ACQUIRING INFORMATION. Sometimes, however, reconciliation is impossible, in which case there are many important steps to take *before* initiating formal divorce proceedings. Here it depends upon the factual situation, but a first basic rule is to gather information. If another lover is involved and your spouse is unaware that you know, it is often wise to hire a private investigator to document the liaison, so you can later prove it. This may also be a good time for a wife to accumulate as much information about her husband's finances as possible. Once he knows trouble is in the air, he is likely to dry up sources of information, such as bank and brokerage statements.

A wife is legally entitled to know more about her husband's income and assets that she often does in fact know. If the couple files joint income tax returns, she is entitled to copies of them. If the husband won't provide them, they may be obtained directly from the Internal Revenue Service. What a spouse is legally entitled to know about the other's assets varies from state to state, but in many states when a matrimonial action starts, both parties must fill out a form detailing income and assets. So ultimately there are not many secrets, unless the parties are sufficiently devious to conceal assets from each other, and from the court.

There can be an advantage in having this information early. I know a couple who file a "joint" return; the husband has his wife sign it when it's blank, and the accountant fills in the information later. If you know you're going to split up, you might make tax time a good time to find out about your husband's assets. Refuse to sign the return without looking at it. Ask your spouse whether in business s/he signs documents before reading them.

The point is that once you've concluded divorce is inevitable, acquire as much information as you can about your spouse's extra-curricular activities, income, and also about your life-style.

This leads me to a second point: How you live before you split will be an important factor in determining how you'll live after you split. Once a wife knows she's heading for a divorce, and while gathering information, she should raise her standard of living, without being too obvious about it. When seeking alimony and support payments, the wife should cast herself in the role not of gold digger, but of somebody who is asking for what is reasonable under the circumstances. Don't go on a spending spree. But remember that alimony is related to the spouse's life-style. A judge will look at the way the couple lived before the marriage broke up. If the couple lived frugally and the wife did her own housework and took the bus to the train, that's one thing. If, on the other hand, they had three expensive cars, the judge is going to look at it another way.

It's a funny thing. Women frequently misunderstand this. They react almost reflexively in the wrong way. They think that if they're going into a divorce, they'll appear in better light if they show what a cheapskate their husband is and has been. So they instinctively begin to cut back on frills in order to make a demonstration of how much they sacrificed. They feel it's worth it, that present sacrifice will yield future gains in the form of increased court-awarded support. What happens instead is that present sacrifice becomes permanent sacrifice as the court attempts to perpetuate the life-style which is presented it.

The fact is, the more a wife can show that her husband treated her lavishly, the more likely the husband is to get stuck with contributing more to keep up the standard of living to which the wife became accustomed.

The advice, again, to the wife contemplating divorce if she has some time within which to work is *gradually* to get things to a point where the standard of living is in decent shape. This increase in the standard of living should be accomplished subtly and delicately, not as done by one of my current clients who was mortally offended that her husband had run off with another woman. (She'd apparently forgotten that he'd previously run off with her.) This woman went right out to Tiffany and began buying diamond earrings. A judge seeing this is turned off, and is likely to reduce alimony substantially. Contemplating divorce, then, and with one eye toward the court, the dependent spouse should act decently and honorably so as to evoke sympathy, but at the same time should gather information and improve her standard of living.

From the last piece of advice, it's not too difficult to deduce what the other player should do when contemplating divorce in order to minimize future support payments: Cut back on life-style and make it seem as if the wife has gone on a spending spree. The husband should keep his wife in check and should bring to her attention in writing all departures from their accustomed pattern. He should write her a note and show it to a friend: "What's the matter with you? All of a sudden you've starting charging all sorts of clothes, and buying things way beyond our budget. We've always lived modestly, yet suddenly you go to the hairdresser twice a week." In short, the husband should cut back their life-style, and make a record of the modest way in which they live.

Sometimes the breakup comes suddenly. There is a serious fight and the husband walks out of the house. If the husband actually abandons the wife, and has in the past displayed violent temper fits, then there's nothing wrong with the wife's changing the locks. But beware: Locking a husband out from anger or spite and without fear of physical danger is a bad move and may later be costly.

It's a matter of judgment. If the wife is sure that the marriage is dead and the husband tries to come back in, she should tell him, "John, I wish you wouldn't. You walked out; you made your choice. After what you've done, I'd prefer we live apart." If he forces the issue and demands to return, especially when children are involved, it becomes sticky. If the wife, even at a cost, is determined to exclude a husband who wishes to come home, then she should make an application to the court for "exclusive possession" by her of the children, subject to such visitation rights as the court will award, or the parties can agree to. This application can be heard very quickly, and it's often the best route to go, as it puts a legal imprimatur on the exclusion. Otherwise, a husband determined to get back will renege on the agreement without fear.

Often the opposite problem occurs. Rather than wanting to get back in, the husband wants to walk out, but he fears that a court will later find he abandoned his wife. If the wife is glad to be rid of him, then the problem can easily be solved with a letter—usually between attorneys—from the wife to the husband giving permission for him to move out of the home, leaving her in possession. The letter should state further that the wife will not later claim the leaving as an act of abandonment.

If after a stormy fight a spouse has reason to believe that the other is about to clean out a bank account and flee the jurisdiction to escape from future judgments, s/he can make an application to the court for a restraining order. Where the account is a *joint* account, the fearful spouse should call up the bank immediately and seek to freeze the account. Most banks will cooperate gladly, if for no other reason than that an account which is "frozen"—which cannot be touched without the consent of both parties—tends to stay frozen for a while, thus guaranteeing the bank locked-in funds at a low interest rate.

UNCONTESTED DIVORCE

A truly uncontested divorce is about as common as a totally candid politician. No matter how amicably the breakup is begun, inevitably it degenerates into a squabble over something. Both spouses may agree that they'd prefer to be unhooked, but as long as there is property to be divided, and especially when there are children involved, there is bound to be disagreement over details. Psychologists tell us, and I've found it to be true in my experience, that the finality of a divorce can be so disturbing that the parties will subconsciously seize upon the most trivial disagreements to put a snag in it. This factor alone is reason enough to have lawyers work out a settlement even in a so-called "amicable" divorce.

In the rare instance in which there is little or no property, no children, a brief marriage, and a great desire to split, then both spouses can work things out between themselves without using lawyers. Libraries and stationery stores contain printed forms of agreements with instructions, and court clerks will be glad to help with the formalities, including the one court appearance that is usually necessary. But as I'll discuss, significant tax consequences often hinge on how an agreement is worded; a lawyer is likely to be more sensitive to these than a layman. An uncontested do-it-yourself divorce is possible, but rarely profitable. And the really "amicable" divorce is so rare that from here on in, I'll assume there is a contest—if not over whether to divorce, then at least over the terms.

CONTESTED DIVORCE

Divorces almost always have their ugly moments. Blackmail, however disguised, is present in almost all of them. What often starts off with sweet talk—"All I want is what's coming to me; I expect we'll remain good friends"—sooner or later degenerates into bitterness. Except in the rare case, anger, hurt and deep-seated resentments boil up and emotional considerations transcend financial ones.

Blackmail takes several forms. One of the most common is for the wife to threaten to expose improprieties in the husband's financial affairs. For example, if he has routinely given her substantial sums to pay household expenses, there arises the possibility that it came from unreported income. A detailed awareness of her husband's financial affairs gives the wife great additional leverage in negotiations. The threat to expose is always there, however implicit and unexpressed.

Having seen this operate countless times, I routinely give all my middle-class or wealthy married friends and clients a single piece of advice: *Do not share the financial details of your life with your spouse.* I know this sounds cynical and secretive, but I've seen many cases in which openness with the poorer spouse comes back to haunt you. Almost as routinely as I give the advice I get a response: "My wife and I are so close; we trust each other fully, and she knows everything I do." That is just marvelous. But three years from now, five years from now, maybe ten years from now, when one of you has found somebody else to love, or things are on the rocks, or you're fighting incessantly, I don't care who it is, when things get down to the nitty-gritty, the wife is going to say to her lawyer, "I didn't tell you this before, because I didn't want to bring it up, but . . ." Once upon a time a spouse was protected by a "marital privilege" and could prevent the other spouse from revealing in court anything said in confidence between them. But the privilege is being rapidly cut back across the country.

Of course, legally, you should report all of your income to the IRS. Nevertheless, the fact is that people in all walks of life do not. A husband, for example, who has not reported his income and has stored valuables in a safe-deposit box is liable to have his wife clean him out before he is aware that their marriage is doomed. He can't very well later claim to the judge: "Your honor, it is not necessary for me to pay this woman any alimony as she has removed two gold bars and $50,000 worth of bearer bonds which represent twenty years of unreported assets." If he should be so brazen as to try such a move and succeed by it in reducing alimony, his victory would be Pyrrhic. It can be more pleasant to share with a spouse than with the government. The point is that if the other spouse knows what you have and where you have it, you are vulnerable, later, to theft or blackmail. So I repeat the advice to you: Keep your financial secrets to yourself. If you're making the money, share the wealth with your spouse, not the information as to how it's made.

Blackmail takes many forms and often concerns subjects other than money. I don't care who it is, it takes a living saint not to bring up things. And once the process starts, it's difficult to brake it until all the poison is out and has injured both sides. I've seen wives accuse their husbands of having affairs with eight named females, and without pausing for breath, assert their impotence and homosexuality.

DIVORCE LAWYERS

I've mentioned that in most cases you should have a lawyer, and I've devoted an entire section of this book to help you make full use of your lawyer. But a few comments specifically as regards matrimonial lawyers are in order here.

It's easiest to begin with some negatives—that is, the kind of lawyer not to employ. Unless everything is really all agreed upon and merely has to be written up, *don't use your family lawyer,* who doesn't know much about divorce. If you live in New York, don't go near a "Wall Street" law firm; the same rule applies to big-name corporate firms in any city. With few exceptions, they have neither the knowledge nor the inclination to "dirty their hands" with divorce cases or criminal matters. Go to someone who knows the divorce field and won't be intimidated. Divorces get messy, and lawyers who can't roll up their sleeves often fail their clients.

If you're looking to save money and your divorce is uncontested, you might use a lawyer who advertises in mass-market publications. Remember, the quoted price is for uncontested divorces, and if yours involves property of any substance, you'd probably do better to avoid these inexpensive lawyers, who make their money on quick turnover with little attention paid to any individual client. The more costly mistake, however, is to use lawyers who advertise at the other end of the spectrum, in *Martindale*

Hubbell, the social register of law firms. In my opinion, it plays blatant politics and puffs up establishment firms which charge you loads of money regardless of the inattention their ivy-league associates grudgingly bestow on your grubby divorce. The best way to search is by personal recommendation: Talk to friends who have been through the process, and have been satisfied with their lawyers.

A lawyer has a primary responsibility to satisfy himself that reconciliation of the parties is out of the question before formally proceeding with a divorce. Reconciliation should be explored more than once, and its benefits should be emphasized. Many marital disputes could go either way, could ultimately be settled. But lawyers on both sides frequently adopt a working attitude that a divorce is a foregone conclusion. Countless times I've seen lawyers turn spats and threats into permanent splits which neither spouse really wanted. Of course, reconciliation goes against a lawyer's immediate self-interest in rolling up fees, but it is his initial and sometimes continuing duty to try to settle the dispute and save the marriage. If the lawyer is successful at keeping a marriage and family together, s/he may have lost a fee but will probably have gained a friend—something of much greater value.

Your next consideration is fee. Usually the size of the fee depends on the amount of money involved and the complexity of the case. Many lawyers charge for the initial consultation; I do not. It seems to me that a lawyer owes a potential client a free consultation during which each evaluates the other. I can afford this; not all lawyers can, and just because your lawyer charges you for the initial consultation does not make him a bad lawyer. Beware of "hourly" charges. Hourly charges are *prima facie* suspect; lawyers charging by the hour will spend more time keeping entries on every phone call they make, etc., than on applying themselves to the essentials of your case. Generally a flat fee should be agreed on—with a retainer down, and the amount of the remainder dependent on whether there is a settlement or the case goes through to trial. It is essential that you know how much it's going to cost you before hiring your lawyer. Lawyers and doctors, as well as other professionals, like to cloak themselves in an aura of "professionalism"—as if money is a subject too secondary to discuss—though in practice they're most accomplished in spending it. If the lawyer doesn't raise the issue, you raise it. Don't be embarrassed; the lawyer isn't doing you a favor by taking your case—you're doing him a favor by giving him the business.

This fee advice, incidentally, applies only to husbands. That is because husbands are responsible not only for their own attorney's fees but also for their wives', even though the latter have been incurred to promote divorces which the husbands oppose. This may seem unfair, but the rationale is that a husband is financially responsible for his wife's "necessaries," which include not only food and medicine but necessary legal fees. A lawyer hired by an impecunious wife should be willing to take her case without a down-payment retainer; his remedy is to ask the court to award enough money to cover her counsel fees. This application is generally made when temporary alimony is sought.

There is, however, no hard and fast rule that the husband pay the wife's lawyers' fees. The wife might have means of her own, and choose to pay her own lawyers' fees. And some law firms have a policy of requiring an initial retainer from the wife—among them a large firm on 57th Street in New York that has an extensive matrimonial practice.

A husband can deduct for tax purposes the money he pays *his* lawyer, and the wife can deduct the fee she pays her lawyer, but neither can deduct any fee paid to the other's attorney. Many lawyers circumvent this assymmetry by having the husband characterize the wife's lawyer's fees as "extra alimony," which is tax-deductible on the husband's return. The wife then pays her own lawyer from this, and she can deduct it. This double dip usually stands up.

Because a husband pays the wife's attorney and can influence the size of the fee, there is an inherent conflict of interest.

I've warned you against the lawyer who from the start is intent to split you apart, who treats your first approach as a reasoned, irreversible determination to get divorced, and influences you against even an attempt at reconciliation. In my experience the lawyer who eagerly splits a family for a fee will later sell out his client. When I sense this, if I represent the husband, ultimately responsible for the wife's lawyer's fee, I lay a trap. The following conversation has occurred many times with minor variations. I am speaking to the wife's attorney:

S/HE: We want the house, the furnishings, a new car every year, substantial alimony and, ahem, there's always the—um—problem of my fee.

WE: Well, I'm not sure we can agree to the house. It's owned jointly and should be sold. And your alimony request is too high; we might have to cut it by, say, 50 percent. But as to your fee, I want you to know that I appreciate how hard you've been working for your client, and as soon as we finish this negotiation amicably for both parties and reach what we believe to be a satisfactory agreement from our standpoint, my client will most gladly pay your fee in full.

Often, depending on the sophistication involved, all this is implied rather than said. But the message is there. What is the message? He expected his fee to be cut by two-thirds. Instead, we promise him his entire first request. All he has to do to get it is cut his client's demands—a great trade for us and a profitable decision for him. There's only one complication. He's done in his client, however subconsciously. (I have laid down an unbending rule for every lawyer in my office: When you represent the wife, there is to be no discussion whatever about your fee from the husband until all items involving her have been settled.)

You should be able to confide in your lawyer, and it's important that you do. Tell your lawyer the whole truth about everything to do with the marriage and breakup. Don't hold back and cause your lawyer to be taken by surprise. That is why it is important to have a lawyer you trust, and who is not a square. Nothing is more hypocritical than some of these stuffed-shirt lawyers who go into a state of shock when forced to deal with unpleasant reality.

I mentioned earlier that "blackmail" is a part of most matrimonial disputes. The good lawyer uses threat to expose secrets subtly. It gets casually worked into a discussion with opposing counsel: "Fortunately my client is not the type of person who would use this, but she has proof of such-and-such—and I'd hate to have to answer for her if she isn't fairly treated." When confronted with this, the other attorney is at a great disadvantage unless he has been told all the dirt by his client so he can separate the bluff from the threat. In short, if you've selected the right lawyer, use him to your full advantage; confide completely.

Just because you've told your lawyer all your dirt doesn't mean s/he is obliged to reveal it in your court papers. A lawyer should always be candid with any court and not misrepresent facts, but it is nowhere required that the official papers amount to your confessional. When it comes to your lawyer's estimate to the court of how much money your spouse has, and how much of it you need, it is almost unheard of not to exaggerate both, in the client's favor. Every attorney does it and everyone knows that everyone does it. The courts will almost invariably cut down the request, so the realities force you to ask for more than you expect.

Some people, both lawyers and clients, are not fit by temperament to play this game of fake and parry. Occasionally an attorney on his own, or more often on a client's instruction, will put all the cards on the table at the outset. In my experience such openness rarely works and often prevents the very agreement it is supposed to encourage. It's like a union negotiation; you never offer your top figure, because nobody on the other side will believe it is your top. They'll expect further concessions and will not agree unless they get them.

Several years ago we had a matrimonial case in which, against our advice, the husband took the initiative and went to court, fully and accurately disclosed his finances and said to the judge, "This is what I'd like to pay for alimony and support," naming a reasonable figure. Of course the judge awarded the wife more, much to the husband's chagrin. We have another client who always says precisely what he means and will not deviate from a position he regards as fair. He has authorized a multimillion-dollar offer in a pending matrimonial settlement. I wanted to ease into that figure, but he insisted on offering up front. When I presented it to one of the leading divorce lawyers on the other side, he was delighted and predictably treated our final offer as an opening figure and responded by tacking a zero onto it. But our client meant what he said, and, if anything, his next offer will be lower.

One common mistake which lawyers often make, especially in matrimonial cases, is to make all correspondence between the parties sound like a lawyer talking. In the period between separation and divorce, the exchange of letters between a wife and her husband should sound like a wife to her husband, not a lawyer to a court. Instead, letters and affidavits too often read in stilted legal style: "I, Nora Jones, wish to relate to the court the following circumstances which, taken together, have made untenable and unfeasible a continuation of any marital relationship, and which, taken together, establish a *prima facie* case for a legal separation. I have endured this relationship for ten years under the utmost hardship, suffering and humiliation." A judge reads three sentences of this and knows that Counselor X dictated it to a secretary from a form book whose page was entitled "Typical aggrieved wife's affidavit." It's much more persuasive if an affidavit, and all letters, are in the wife's own language and in layman's terms. Judges are impressed with sincerity and often can tell the difference between that and what the lawyer dictated—particularly in matrimonial actions, where exaggeration is the name of the game.

Now as to letters. If a letter goes from a husband to a wife or vice versa, I will always insist (even if I write it) that it sound the way the wife talks to the husband, or vice versa. I learn a little about the wife's style. I will then give a typed draft to her, and have her copy it over in longhand, perhaps accompanied by misspellings to lend artistic verisimilitude. "Harry, life with you has stunk for a long time, your a cruel and lousy lover, a terrible husband, and I can't stand watching you beat the kids any longer."

Another thing which applies to all legal situations in this book: If it should happen to be your misfortune to get into court and testify, *get your main point across fast*. Perhaps these comments should be addressed more to lawyers than laypeople, but if your lawyer doesn't present things well, you can help out. Frequently the legal papers in a divorce action begin with ten pages of dates —"This proceeding was commenced on June 24 . . ." Who cares! Finish with the required legal details, and in the meantime get right to the heart of the matter. In the first paragraph say, "This is an application by a woman married for seventeen years to the same man with three young children who has now been cut off from all support and has been forced out of the house to the point where she is living in a room in her mother's apartment and is asking this court to come to her aid by awarding a sum of ——, which would barely enable her to exist and would nowhere equal the standard of living which she enjoyed while living with her husband, who was a man of substantial means, earning in excess of $40,000." In other words, get it all in in the first page or two.

I would generalize. When asking for a raise, when negotiating a deal, when settling a dispute, get it out up front. Most human beings don't want to be bored. They want to be entertained. They want it short and sweet. Make it punchy and get it all up front.

Some couples attempt to split the difference between doing it themselves and each hiring a lawyer. Instead, they submit their dispute to binding arbitration. In my experience, this is a mistake. In my opinion the American Arbitration Association is a bunch of people who very seldom bring common sense to bear on a problem; knowing that no rules of evidence are involved, they usually take the gutless and easy way out by splitting the difference regardless of the merits. Sometimes one party is totally right and the other is totally wrong. The arbitrators' decisions rarely reflect this. Nor do arbitrators give reasons for their decisions. Their decisions are virtually unappealable except in the most extreme circumstances. My advice is to stay away from a bunch of cold strangers who are exempted from rules of evidence and law and have no review authority to which they ever have to answer.

PROPERTY SETTLEMENT

We come now to the division of wealth, which may or may not be tied to contingencies.

ALIMONY AND SUPPORT The wife—i.e., dependent spouse*—is not always entitled to alimony in the breakup of a marriage. The rule varies among the states. In some states, if the husband proves to a judge's satisfaction that his wife was at fault—through adultery, abandonment, cruelty, etc.—then the court may not award her alimony. In the other states judges as a matter of personal policy often will refuse to give alimony to the spouse at fault. In any case, in all states the husband must continue to support any minor child.

In addition to the spouse's fault there are other reasons why a court will in its discretion deny alimony. For example, there may be no alimony in the breakup of a brief childless marriage where a young wife is competent to earn her own living. Pressure from women's lib has resulted in many more men's being liberated from supporting their ex-wives.

While the rule precluding alimony to the party at fault is less stringently applied in some places than in others, it is a general rule. Therefore if you are a spouse who might someday in the future desire or need alimony, *do not admit fault*. If you are a spouse who does not wish ever to have to pay huge alimony, *do not admit fault*. Even in a moment of remorse do not send an apology letter to your spouse saying: "I have been unfaithful but I will try hereafter to deserve your love." That little note may cost one hundred times its weight in gold, when once again you have engaged in extramarital affairs and would want to deny them.

Good trial lawyers are trained to think how statements "will look on the record." They engage in two contests at once: They try to win the case at hand at the trial level, playing to a live jury, but all the time they are conscious that the important case will likely be on appeal and that the appellate court will judge by the written record. It's the last decision that counts. Matrimonial life is like that too. Remember, you leave a trail in living. Be

_____

* I suppose by this point it must be clear that I am using the term 'wife'' to refer to the financially dependent spouse, and the term "husband" to refer to the independent spouse, knowing full well that some wives are the source of wealth and some husbands are the dependent ones. For ease of reference it's easier to play the law of averages, and I trust even the liberationists will direct their efforts elsewhere.

conscious of your record. You may someday have to appeal to and from it.

How the amount of alimony and of child support is determined depends on many factors: the length of the marriage, the number and ages of children, the comparative financial conditions of husband and wife, the standard of living enjoyed by the couple prior to separation. A widespread rule of thumb is that a husband pay one-third of his income for support.

Thus the husband has an incentive to earn as little as possible around the time alimony is set. At one time he could defeat, or at least deflate, his wife's claim for alimony by getting fired. This was especially convenient in a family business situation in which money could be fed to him under the table. Recently, however, courts have begun to pierce the veil. Such was the case not long ago in New York, where the husband's father, who controlled the huge family empire, took the stand and candidly admitted that he had fired his son so that the son's wife wouldn't get any alimony. But the state judge imputed to the young heir what he should have been earning and made an award accordingly. Nobody can make a person work, but more and more if a husband refuses to work in order to defeat a claim of wife and child, he will be made to pay alimony nonetheless, out of capital. Not surprisingly, emotion has a great deal to do with the outcome of matrimonial disputes. The lawyers for both parties are supposed to assess things dispassionately and arrive at a fair, mutually acceptable settlement. But the clients, in the end, make the key decisions. If it is true that "hell hath no fury like a woman scorned," then it is true as well that the earth sees no more stubborn fighters than a man who suddenly realizes he's been made a fool of for years by a woman whom he loved and who has used him.

The point is that sentiment counts heavily in the size of the settlement. The lawyers, if they can, should keep emotion out of it as much as possible and attempt to arrive at a quick agreement. The longer negotiation drags out, the uglier and less agreeable it often becomes, heading inexorably into a drawn-out court battle in which both parties lose.

It pays to keep on good terms with the other party. If a husband dislikes a wife or comes to hate her, he's going to feel that any money he pays her is blood money and he's not going to want to do it. If the wife feels she's become a laughingstock, she will try to take him for all he's worth. So once again, it pays to keep things on an even keel emotionally. But, sadly, this usually breaks down at some point, unless it's been a very long marriage and the people approach the split from a decent common-sense point of view.

There are situations, however, in which a wife can adroitly handle a husband. For example, several of Alan J. Lerner's wives apparently could get him to sign anything they stuck in front of him. Owing one wife, Micheline, so much in back alimony that State Supreme Court Justice Gabel appointed her the receiver of his assets did not stop him from assigning to Nina, wife #7, from whom he is currently separated, 70 percent of all of his royalties for the rest of her life. Moreover, the agreement was drawn up by *his* lawyers. The Lerner story is a fascinating one, but I'll tell it some other place.

The point is, emotion can count for much too much. In a deal or negotiation, rational people seek to find an area of mutual gain through trade and to fashion an agreement by which each gains. On the other hand, in a fight, two people seek not so much to gain mutually as to inflict pain and suffering on the other person. Marital disputes all too frequently degenerate from deals into fights, and both parties lose.

If you're heading into a breakup, try to separate your bitterness toward the other person from your attitude toward him or her as a trading partner. Keep a cool enough head to recognize the areas of mutual benefit; settle quickly, and break as cleanly as possible. If your passion prevents your reason from searching out mutually profitable arrangements, leave the negotiation to your lawyer.

Alimony takes two basic forms: periodic and lump sum. The lump sum is, as its name suggests, a single large payment up front, whereas periodic alimony is a continuing obligation satisfied by regular smaller payments over time. Courts will rarely award lump-sum alimony unless the parties have previously agreed to it.

Often a wife will prefer a lump sum to periodic alimony—

especially when there are no children born of the marriage. With a lump sum, she has the money immediately and irrevocably, where periodic alimony customarily ends with her remarriage or with the death of either party. I say "customarily" because the parties can agree otherwise. Some husbands are willing to continue alimony payments even after their wives remarry. Other will offer incentives to ex-wives to remarry—for example, a lump-sum payment equal to a year's or two years' alimony as a wedding gift. The logic behind this is that otherwise a woman on easy street with fat alimony checks coming in every week will be reluctant to remarry.

Alimony may be readjusted to take account of changed circumstances of the husband, particularly if it was fixed by court order rather than by private agreement of the parties—the latter being viewed as a contract. And sometimes a wife who has agreed to forgo all alimony in return for a generous property settlement will later sue for alimony, alleging changed circumstances. If a husband wishes to protect himself against that, he should insist on a divorce being awarded in his favor, against his wife, on some ground of fault. As a matter of law, this will preclude her ever being able to collect alimony. Even in the growing number of states which have instituted "no-fault" divorces (by which a consenting couple can get divorced without the tedious delay of establishing who was at fault) there remains the option of a fault divorce. If a spouse wishes to protect himself against increased future claims, he should insist on a fault divorce.

REAL AND PERSONAL PROPERTY. When a marriage breaks, the wife is entitled to support as long as she is not at fault. A more complex problem is the disposition of their property. How property is divided varies widely among the states. There are three basic methods: (1) In *community-property states,* such as California, the wife is entitled to one-half the increase in her husband's assets from the date of marriage to the date of the breakup, on the theory she shared his life and contributed to his growing affluence. (2) In *traditional states,* such as New York was until 1980, property belongs to the person who has legal *title* to it. (3) In *equitable-distri-*

bution states, such as Michigan and, as of July 1980, New York, the court is empowered to make a property division between husband and wife in whatever manner it deems fairest. (The only property subject to any division is "marital" property. Typically, each spouse gets to keep all the property s/he brought into the marriage—plus any increase in value—gifts from people other than the spouse, and inheritances.)

Whether a party is better off in court or with an out-of-court settlement depends on the particular judge and the circumstances of the case. But in jurisdictions where courts must award property strictly according to legal title and can only remedy the lopsided result by increasing alimony and child support, the wife is generally better off with an out-of-court settlement. In a community-property or equitable-distribution state, on the other hand, if there has been a long marriage and the husband is unwilling to give any property, the wife may well do better in court. She can demand a financial examination of her husband to establish his assets, and if he conceals assets or undervalues them, a court can make its own determination and award her a share based on the judge's independent assessment.

Out-of-court settlements allow the parties certain other advantages. I've mentioned that alimony is tax-deductible to the one who pays it. (It is income to the one who receives it.) Property settlements—just splitting up the marital property—are not taxable. In order to get the husband tax benefits his lawyer will seek to have the settlement characterized as alimony and the wife's lawyer will fight to have it called "property." But here, things can get tricky. If you are the dependent spouse and the other lawyer too easily agrees to label future payments as "property," beware! The husband may have a legal ace up his sleeve. He may be preparing to go into personal bankruptcy immediately following the divorce. In that case, alimony payments would not be dischargeable. He would continue to owe them, whereas property debts would be canceled. Bankruptcy is a very complicated area that few lawyers have mastered and it gives rise to all sorts of intricate strategies.

Spouses often use insignificant things—wedding gifts or Aunt

Tilly's vase—as the bone of contention for venomous squabbles. It is a way of punishing, by preventing items of great sentimental value from remaining with the spouse who truly wants them. Sometimes a huge and complex settlement will break down over the most trivial of details. I take this as a sign that at least one of the parties doesn't want to get divorced, and will use a trivial squabble as one last resort to explore the possibility of a reconciliation.

Finally, there is that item of greatest sentimental value which, sadly, sometimes neither spouse really wants—the child.

CHILD CUSTODY

It used to be a foregone conclusion that the mother would get custody of the children, particularly when they were young children. This is no longer the case. The only criterion the court is legally allowed to use is the welfare of the child. If, on balance, the child is better off living with the father, then the court must award custody to him. The judge, before making this decision, will almost invariably interview the children to determine their wishes. Still, many judges continue reflexively to award custody to the mother without making an honest determination of the children's best interests. This is blatant sexism; it is also unfair and cruel.

Some judges who rigidly award custody to a mother will always and only award custody to the father if the mother has committed adultery or is a lesbian. But adultery does not automatically make her an unfit mother, and more judges are focusing upon the key question: Who can better bring up the children? In general, adultery and sexual deviance no longer eliminate a parent's chances of custody. Sexual deviance is a factor weighing against custody, but can be offset by other factors. The decisions regarding homosexual parents have been conflicting in recent years. Recent cases decided in Minnesota and New Jersey gave custody to mothers who were admitted lesbians.

A more difficult question is whether a mother's abandonment of the household necessarily disqualifies her from obtaining custody of the children—the question posed in the novel/movie *Kra-*

mer vs. Kramer. There are many, many real cases that involve the same principle. My experience is that what Mrs. Kramer voluntarily did at the end of the story—giving the child back to the father —is what a court will now usually do.

A real case of the kind is *Di Giardi* v. *Di Giardi,* which was decided after a lengthy trial in New York supreme court before the highly respected Mr. Justice Grumet. In this case, the father, an Italian immigrant who became a successful doctor, and the mother had been married about ten years and had two children. The mother had turned off to the father sexually and had bluntly told him she wanted out of the marriage. He was distraught, as he wanted to keep the family together and was still very much attached to his wife. She began an affair with another, older man, who lived in Texas but frequently came to New York, where he maintained an apartment. He had a wife and three children.

The evidence indicated that Mrs. Di Giardi had done just what Mrs. Kramer had: She had left the children with their father and gone off with another man, although she had kept in touch with the children from time to time. Then there came a time when she realized she'd made a mistake and she went to court to get custody of the children. The court awarded custody to the father, not because the mother had committed adultery, but because she had turned the children over to the father. The judge held that when a mother does that, dumps her children on the father in order to pursue what she thinks will make her more happy—women's-lib freedom or whatever—she then has almost certainly struck out in any future attempts to regain custody. Even if the mother suffers a nervous breakdown, or is physically incapacitated, the court should not dwell on her emotional needs. The sole criterion for custody is supposed to be the best interests of the child, even at the price of the health of one parent. The parent's feelings should never be considered as an independent ground for custody.

Most courts will respect arrangements worked out by both parents, arrangements sometimes referred to as "joint custody." It is the rage to say that joint custody is the rage, but in my experience, although real joint custody has been going on for years, the legal trend is more toward awarding custody to the father. Psychiatrists and social workers tell me that splitting a child's living arrangements between two homes often results in splitting his personality. The old Biblical story of Solomon's awarding custody to the mother who preferred relinquishing her child to splitting it in two could well be applied to our more modern setting. Judges who recognize that shuttle custody disserves the child will adhere to the more standard if less symmetrical award of physical custody to one parent and visitation rights to the other. In fact, "joint custody" is now often used as a euphemism for granting custody to the father. Sooner or later courts will abandon this face-saving label and call custody to the father what it is.

There is one more way in which children can be divided between parents: the cases in which the girl will go with the mother and the boy with the father. There is no fixed judicial policy here. It depends on the children, the age difference, how close they are to each other, and whether splitting them up is feasible under the circumstances. Moreover, when children get to be a certain age, about thirteen or fourteen, there isn't a judge or a parent who is going to tell them where to stay. Children by this time know their parents, know their own mind, and will in most cases ultimately make their own arrangements. This, by the way, is one of the many, many reasons why parents should never turn a child against the other parent. A spouse should be mature enough, no matter how much s/he personally detests the other spouse, to encourage a continued love between a child and both parents. A good relationship maintained with both parents will enable the child when s/he grows up to decide how to cast his or her lot, with the advice and consent of both parents.

JURISDICTION

Sometimes a spouse will move to another state where s/he finds the divorce laws are more favorable, and initiate proceedings there. This will work as long as the move is legitimate—i.e., it must be a move which contemplates permanent residence in the new state and not a sojourn to obtain a divorce before moving back. In order to institute matrimonial proceedings one must be a good-faith resident of a state for a certain period of time. If a spouse has reason to believe that the other party is attempting to move out just to get a divorce in some other place or that a just-completed move is phony, s/he should catch it as quickly as possible. Immediately go to the court where your action is pending and enjoin your spouse from proceeding in the other jurisdiction.

Once a spouse gets a divorce in any state in this country, such a decree, according to the Supreme Court, must be given "full faith and credit" by all states, as the Constitution provides. The only ground for attack on such a divorce is that the state granting the decree did not have jurisdiction over the parties, but that is often an impossible argument to make.

It is otherwise with foreign divorces. U.S. courts are not required to recognize them, but under a doctrine called "comity" most courts will usually recognize foreign divorces if there is jurisdiction over the parties and the foreign divorce doesn't look too fishy. Once again, if you get wind that a foreign quicky divorce is underway, go immediately to your court and obtain an injunction.

3.
COHABITATION

THE 1960s and 1970s, it is said, brought to the fore a new kind of warfare. Gone were the uniformed combatants clearly identifiable by their traditional emblems. Taking their place were informal fighters engaging in briefer skirmishes. It is no longer officially clear exactly who is in or out of the fight. Yes, the nature of the battles has changed. Ours is the era of guerrilla war . . . between the sexes.

The new morality, the sexual revolution, has hit. It has brought with it a new legality. Women's liberation has become women's litigation. Whether we are truly in the midst of a full sexual revolution may well ultimately depend upon whether we are on the brink of a legal revolution.

COUPLES OUTSIDE WEDLOCK

Between 1960 and 1970 the number of couples living together outside of wedlock increased 800 percent. Between 1970 and 1978 it doubled again. The 1980 census reflects a further increase. Refusing to exclude from the jury the "prejudicial" fact that an unmarried couple was living together, Federal Judge Whitman Knapp recently quipped, "Oh, come on now. These days practically no one gets married."

Cohabitation without marriage has become widespread. It was

only a matter of time before attempts would be made legally to protect it.

HANDS-OFF DOCTRINE:
MERETRICIOUS RELATIONSHIPS

Our story opens in California—politically, legally, and in several other ways the nation's weirdest, most unpredictable and most innovative state. The mother state of Proposition 13 which can somehow send to the Senate at the same time the liberal Alan Cranston and the conservative S. I. Hayakawa and successively elect as its governors Ronald Reagan and Jerry Brown can be expected to produce other significant offspring.

In 1943 the California supreme court answered with a simple no the question: "Does a woman living with a man as his wife but with no genuine belief that she is legally married to him acquire by reason of cohabitation alone the rights of a co-tenant in his earnings and accumulations during the period of their relationship?" With this answer California was in tune with the rest of the nation. Traditionally courts have deemed cohabitation a "meretricious" —an illicit sexual—relationship and refused to recognize any property rights arising out of it. Judges often coupled their reiteration of this rule of law with moralistic denunciations of unmarried cohabitation. One commented: "We are here confronted with a situation in which good morals would offer no brief in behalf of either party. In fact, if it were possible we would be inclined to dismiss them both with the Shakespearean denunciation 'A plague on both your houses!'"*

The traditional rule was simple: Without marriage there would be no share after the split. Live together, leave alone. The courts would not get involved in extramarital property affairs.

MARVIN DOCTRINE:
NON-MERETRICIOUS CONSIDERATION

In 1957 a lone voice in the legal wilderness, Justice Finley, ob-

---

* *Smith* v. *Smith*, 108 So.2d 761, 763 (Fla. 1959), quoted in Minnesota Law Review 62, p. 452, n. 14.

served that in practical effect a court's refusal to protect either cohabitant simply rewarded the cunning exploiter:

> Under such circumstances, this court and the courts of other jurisdictions have, in effect, sometimes said, "We will wash our hands of such disputes. The parties should and must be left to their own devices, just where they find themselves." To me, such pronouncements seem overly fastidious and a bit fatuous. They are unrealistic and, among other things, ignore the fact that . . . the party who has title, or in some instances who is in possession, will enjoy the rights of ownership of the property concerned. The rule often operates to the great advantage of the cunning and the shrewd, who wind up with possession of the property or title to it in their names, at the end of a so-called meretricious relationship.*

In the 1970s, further faults appeared in this otherwise rock-solid doctrine of hands off. A California intermediate appellate court held in 1973 that unmarried parties who have engaged in a "meretricious" relationship and have established "an ostensible marital relationship" as well as "an actual family relationship" and who subsequently break up are obliged to split equally all property which *would have been* community property had they been married. Two years later another intermediate California court followed suit.

There is a claimed logic to this. Alimony often terminates to the divorced ex-wife when by her life-style she holds herself out as the spouse of another person. If it makes sense for her to lose her property rights vis-à-vis her ex-spouse by living as if married to a new one, the argument can be made that it also makes some sense for her to acquire some property rights vis-à-vis her new quasi spouse. I find this fallacious to a large degree. The "holding-out" doctrine goes back to a right accruing from a formal marriage (alimony). In the "quasi" situation, there might or might not be legal assumption of responsibility.

It wasn't until 1976, however, that national attention sharply

---

* *West v. Knowles,* 311 p2d 689, 692–3 (1957).

focused on this new doctrine coming out of the California courts. The occasion was a suit by Michele Triola against actor Lee Marvin, with whom she had lived continuously for six years. Michele Triola Marvin—she had legally assumed his last name three days before they separated—claimed that they had agreed to be known as husband and wife and that Lee had promised to provide for her needs for life. Although all the property accumulated during their cohabitation was in Lee Marvin's name only, Michele claimed that they had orally agreed that while they lived together they "would combine their efforts and earnings and would share equally any and all property accumulated as a result of their efforts, whether individual or combined." In return for and in reliance on this agreement Michele had given up her promising career as a singer to devote herself full-time to Lee as his "companion, homemaker, housekeeper and cook."

Michele was represented by Marvin Mitchelson, the renowned California divorce lawyer. We've been on the same side often, but we disagree now and then—as in his representation of Saroya Khashoggi, who at this writing is trying for the equivalent of a second divorce (this time in California) against Adnan Khashoggi, the wealthy entrepreneur—despite the fact they were already divorced abroad in 1974, and she remarried on the basis of the previous divorce decree! She and her attorney, Mitchelson, are asking us for a mere $2.5 billion. Mitchelson is clever in that he never four-square stakes everything on one tenuous or novel issue, but combines theories. Thus, in the Marvin case he did not shoot everything on the mere living-together theory, but alleged an express agreement to support and share—making it partially a breach of contract action.

Lee Marvin defended by pointing out that they had made a deliberate choice not to formalize their relationship in marriage. Their living arrangement, therefore, was essentially outside the law and gave rise to no contract rights. To understand his position we need to recall some black-letter law. It is a basic principle in contract law that there must be some "consideration"—something of value which induces the agreement. It is also a basic rule of contract law that a court will not enforce any contract whose consideration is itself a violation of public policy. So, for example, an illicit sexual relationship, such as adultery, fornication, or prostitution, being against public morals, no contract the essential consideration of which was such a meretricious relationship would be enforced. It was Marvin's defense that any understanding he might have had with Michele was based upon their meretricious relationship and was therefore unenforceable at law.

In its headline-making opinion, the California supreme court rejected this:

> Although the past decisions hover over the issue in the somewhat wispy form of the figures of a Chagall painting, we can abstract from those decisions a clear and simple rule. The fact that a man and woman live together without marriage, and engage in a sexual relationship, does not in itself invalidate agreements between them relating to their earnings, property, or expenses. . . . Agreements between nonmarital partners fail only to the extent that they *rest upon* a consideration of sexual services.

Thus, a contract to share accumulated property would not necessarily fail because it was "involved in" a nonmarital sexual relationship. Only if it were "expressly and inseparably based upon an illicit consideration of sexual services" would the court refuse to enforce it. The court noted that to equate the nonmarital relationship of today to prostitution was "to do violence to an accepted and wholly different practice." Rather, "the prevalence of nonmarital relationships in modern society and the social acceptance of them marks this as a time" when courts should not automatically disqualify contracts made pursuant to them. The California supreme court held, therefore, that express contracts between nonmarital partners should be enforced "except to the extent that the contract is *explicitly founded* on the consideration of meretricious sexual services."

But the state high court took two giant steps beyond this. In the absence of an *express* agreement as to division of property accumulated during cohabitation, and as to responsibilities for support after a split, the high court ordered lower courts to scrutinize the conduct of the parties to determine whether there may have been an implied agreement of partnership or any other tacit understanding between the parties. Secondly, reaching the outer bounds of possible remedies, even if courts found that there had been no such contract, expressed or implied, they could fashion other equitable relief which seemed to them to be warranted by the circumstances of each particular case.

So, the court found in this case that there had been more to the Marvins' formal cohabitation than illegal coitus. But apparently there hadn't been much more. Michele won in principle but Lee kept most of the property. By the court's decision, Michele received only a little more than $100,000, but California received a new doctrine, and the other forty-nine states received a flood of litigation. Nor did all of it come from cohabitants of the rich and famous.

POST-*MARVIN* LITIGATION

There was, for example, the case of Irma Kozlowski, a Polish immigrant who barely spoke English and knew almost no one outside her own immediate family and ethnic community. In 1962, Irma, forty-eight, married and a mother of two, met Thaddeus Kozlowski, forty-two, also married and a father of two. Thaddeus, a "personable, sophisticated, apparently well-to-do businessman," immediately exhibited an amorous interest in Irma, soon expressed his love for her and insisted that they leave their families and set up a new household together. He promised her he would later divorce his wife so as to be free to marry her. She agonized for four months and finally capitulated, and the couple began living together. During the early years of their "illicit equivalent of marital bliss" three of the four children of their prior marriages joined them. Thaddeus sought out Irma's husband and arranged for her divorce. He, however, remained married.

During their cohabitation, his wealth increased but he kept his business affairs to himself. Title to all his assets, including houses in which he, Irma and the children had lived, was solely in his own name. She didn't know what he was worth and was completely dependent upon him for all her needs, maintenance and support. She had no possessions other than her clothing, personal effects and his gifts of jewelry and furs. She had on her part kept house, shopped, acted as mother to the children and hostess when necessary for Thaddeus' customers and business associates. To that part of his world Thaddeus and Irma were husband and wife. But relatives and close friends on both sides were fully aware of their true relationship.

Often an important indication as to whether a cohabiting couple are holding themselves to the outside world as husband and wife is that they assume the same last name. But by a remarkable coincidence, before she ever met Thaddeus Kozlowski, Irma's married name had also been Kozlowski. During their early years together, when from time to time Irma asked Thaddeus about marriage, he was evasive. After living together for six years, in 1968, they had a falling-out and separated. Before Irma left, Thaddeus had her sign a release by which she accepted $2,000 in cash plus the cancellation of a $3,000 loan he'd made her daughter for her education as "full satisfaction" of all claims she might have against him.

Within a week after that separation, Thaddeus was pleading with Irma to return. "He insisted they would be happy together for the rest of their lives, that he needed her, that he would take care of her and provide for her if she would only come back" and resume her life with him. But he was no longer evasive about marriage. It was out. Thaddeus countered her suggestion of marriage by observing that a marriage license was only a piece of paper and that "it's what is in the heart that really counts." They resumed their life together.

In July 1977 it became obvious that Thaddeus had another woman, no longer loved Irma and wanted to be rid of her. She was crushed, and left in a huff. Thaddeus, without Irma's knowledge, had finally sued his wife for divorce. Now he married his new flame, thirty years younger than he.

Irma, out on her own without means of support, sued Thaddeus, claiming she had been his "partner" for fifteen years and as such was entitled to a share of the assets accumulated during their time together. Her claim was not only that there had been a contract between them (express or implied) to support her for the rest of her life, but also that, whether or not there ever was actually an agreement, out of fairness she was entitled to support. The legal label is "quasi-contract," which is a fiction to reach a fair result. The law will assume that "whatsoever it is certain that a man ought to do, the law supposes him to have promised to do." The theory is that it's unjust to allow one individual to "enrich" himself at the expense of another. The California court in *Marvin,* recall, had stated that such a remedy was available.

But this was New Jersey. How did she fare? The court rejected her claim that she had become Thaddeus' partner, noting that she'd exercised no control over the business and had not expected to share in the profits and losses of the business enterprise. 0 for 1. Her second claim was for money owed her for past services. Here the court did find an express contract when they first reconciled, but any claim for services rendered during that period "was more than satisfied by the value of the weekly support, clothing, trips, vacations, medical benefits and jewelry Thaddeus had provided for her." 0 for 2.

Finally the court reached her claim for future support. Early in its opinion the court acknowledged that the problem was essentially the "long-range social consequences of the 'new morality,' its relaxed moral standards and the substantial increase in cohabitation by unmarried couples."

For this court, in this case, then, the question became simply: "Is there any remedy available under our law for a woman who has devoted 15 or more years living with a man, for whom she provided the necessary household services and emotional support to permit him to successfully pursue his business career and for whom she has performed housekeeping, cleaning and shopping services, run the household, raised the children, her own as well as his, all without benefit of marriage; a woman who was literally forced out of the household with no ongoing support or wherewithal for her survival?''

I guess it is no surprise that any court which is willing to ask the question this way would also be willing to answer it with a yes. There was a remedy. The court found that he had promised to support her forever, and since "she performed diligently and fully her part of the bargain" the court found a contract to support her existed between them and ordered him to do just that. Although basing its award on contract, the court hinted strongly it would have been willing to take up *Marvin*'s invitation and fashion relief on the grounds of simple fairness—"quasi-contract": "This court could not countenance the unconscionable result which would obtain should all relief be denied this plaintiff who was cast adrift at 63 years of age without means of support, assets, and with little hope of developing support opportunities." As the court also said, "She has foregone any chance to develop skills or to seek out opportunities which, in the revealing light of hindsight, may well have served her better." The judge calculated the present value of the future support Thaddeus had promised and arrived at a figure: $55,000. 1 for 3.

Thaddeus appealed to the New Jersey supreme court, which in June 1979 unanimously affirmed the decision and the award, thus locating New Jersey within *Marvin*'s gardens. It made very little difference to the court whether the agreement was designated "express" or "implied": "Parties entering this type of relationship usually do not record their understanding in specific legalese. Rather, as here, the terms of their agreement are to be found in their . . . acts and conduct."

And the court also stated: "We are aware that many young couples live together without the solemnization of marriage, in order to make sure that they can successfully later undertake marriage. . . . The mores of society have indeed changed so radically in regard to cohabitation that we cannot impose a standard based on alleged moral considerations that have apparently been so widely abandoned by so many." And then, of course, came the standard disclaimer, in support of the institution of marriage:

"Lest we be misunderstood, however, we take this occasion to point out that the structure of society itself largely depends upon the institution of marriage, and nothing we have said in this opinion should be taken to derogate from that institution. The joining of the man and woman in marriage is at once the most socially productive and individually fulfilling relationship that one can enjoy in the course of a lifetime."

Recall that in *Marvin* an obstacle to Michele had been the traditional prohibition of any contract based upon illicit sex. The California supreme court had overcome the obstacle and found contract rights in cohabitation by severing the sexual component from the other services rendered. The New Jersey legislature, however, allowed that state's supreme court to confront the problem directly. Effective September 1979, in the state's revised penal law, fornication was decriminalized. Therefore, "leaving aside one's moral or religious beliefs, there was no legal impediment to the parties cohabiting in 1968. Thus any lawful agreement made by them is enforceable." By this opinion, New Jersey officially removed "the judicial barriers that may stand in the way of a policy based upon the fulfillment of the reasonable expectations of the parties to a nonmarital relationship."

ILLINOIS: NO ALIMONY WITHOUT MARRIAGE. Mitchelson predicted in 1978 that *Marvin*'s "underlying philosophy will be adopted, legislatively or judicially, by every state in the union within five to ten years." His prediction received some support when in April 1980 a New Jersey businessman settled with his live-in mate for $245,000 on a *Marvin* theory. But I'm not so certain about the future. One always gets back to the fact that when we speak of morality, we are recognizing the commitment of our civilization to marriage and family life. The fact that it has been taken lightly in recent years has hurt countless children and innocent parties—and has been motivated in large measure by selfish personal desire and unwillingness to accept responsibility and the sacrifices necessary for family life. And, legally, one must return to the basic premise that rights to property and support stem from the legal relationship of marriage, and are voluntarily and knowingly assumed by both parties when they formally legalize their status. Thus, I think Brother Mitchelson's prediction is unrealistic at maximum and premature to say the least.

Take, for example, an important state like Illinois. Two of its citizens, Victoria and Robert Hewitt, had been college sweethearts attending Grinnell College in Iowa. Victoria became pregnant and Robert told her that as far as he was concerned they were husband and wife and would thereafter live together as such. No formal marriage ceremony was necessary, he assured her, and in the familiar pattern of things, promised to share his life, future earnings and property with Victoria.

Robert and Victoria immediately announced their marriage to both sets of parents; and to the outside world they became husband and wife. Their family life reflected this: She devoted her entire effort in assisting him to complete dental school—her parents even helped him financially through school. Victoria also worked with him at the office, and although he issued her a paycheck, it was always deposited in a joint bank account and used for family purposes. Together they had two more children. In short, Victoria Hewitt—she, of course, had assumed his last name —gave every assistance that a wife and mother could give. For fifteen years Robert represented to Victoria and all the world that they were husband and wife. For fifteen years he acquired property, and his income grew until it reached $80,000 a year. In short, "the parties lived, and for a time, enjoyed a most conventional, respectable and ordinary family life." The single flaw was that inexplicably they didn't formalize their marriage. In September 1975, after fifteen years and three children, Robert decided to call it quits.

On behalf of herself and their three children, Victoria sued Robert, seeking a division of property, support and maintenance. Robert acknowledged the children were his and agreed to pay child support, but he denied that he owed Victoria any support. She relied on *Marvin*. He replied that, as their relationship had been meretricious, and insofar as Illinois required that all rights must rest upon a valid marriage contract, she had acquired no property rights.

The trial court found for him. But in August 1978 a unanimous appellate court reversed. Whereas Robert had characterized his relationship with Victoria as meretricious, the appellate court pointed out that as defined in the dictionary the "precise meaning" of that adjective related to a "harlot" or a "prostitute." Victoria, the court said, was no prostitute and she was no harlot.

Calling the logic of *Marvin* "particularly persuasive" where the facts show "a stable family relationship extending over a long period of time," and reiterating that "the value of a stable marriage remains unchallenged and is not denigrated by this opinion," the court reversed the trial court and sent the case back to it to determine Victoria's share.

Victoria's victory was short-lived. On September 19, 1979, the Illinois supreme court unanimously reversed the intermediate appellate court, and held that her claim was totally unenforceable because it went against public policy as recently expressed by the Illinois legislature in passing its Marriage and Dissolution of Marriage Act. The legislature had "considered and rejected the 'no fault' divorce concept that has been adopted in many other jurisdictions." In being one of only three states to retain fault as necessary for the dissolution of marriage, the legislature's pro-marriage policy had reaffirmed "the traditional doctrine that marriage is a civil contract between three parties—the husband, the wife and the state." The policy of the state's elected representatives was to "prevent the marriage relation from becoming in effect a private contract terminable at will."

In its opinion the Illinois high court implicitly criticized other state high courts which recently "had reasoned that the rendition of housekeeping and homemaking services . . . could be regarded as the consideration for a separate contract between the parties, severable from the illegal contract founded on sexual relations. This court is not going to join that fiction." "The real thrust" of Victoria's argument was a plea to "abandon the rule of illegality because of certain changes in societal norms and attitudes. It is urged that social mores have changed radically in recent years, rendering this principle of law archaic. It is said that because there are so many unmarried cohabitants today, the courts must confer a legal status on such relationships." The Illinois court refused to display "the naiveté involved in the assertion that there are involved in these relationships contracts separate and independent from the sexual activity, and the assumption that those contracts would have been entered into or would continue without that activity."

The Illinois high court was willing to buck the *Marvin* trend because for it there was "a more fundamental problem . . . of substantially greater importance than the rights of the immediate parties" and that was "the impact of such recognition upon our society and the institution of marriage." Granting Victoria and others who deliberately chose to enter into "meretricious" relationships support would likely "encourage formation of such relationships and weaken marriage as the foundation of our family based society." A Pandora's box would be opened, basic institutions would unravel: "In the event of death shall the survivor have the status of a surviving spouse for purposes of inheritance, wrongful death actions, workmen's compensation, etc.? And still more importantly, what of the children born of such relationships? What are their support and inheritance rights and by what standards are custody questions resolved? What of the sociological and psychological effects upon them of that type of environment?"

Unless the legislature beat the path, the court was not going to lead Illinois into this thicket. And so, as the 1980s began, there was no palimony in Illinois.

NEW YORK: DISTINGUISHING *MARVIN*. I couldn't conclude this chapter without some mention of New York and its cohabitants. Until 1977 the McCullons had lived together as man and wife: joint bank accounts, joint tax returns, wedding rings, three children, etc. To all the world they were married. This went on for twenty-eight years, when Mr. McCullon found another woman. A New York trial court expressed its support for the *Marvin* principle of a "presumption that non-marital partners intend to deal fairly with each other." The court cited a national survey which indicated that 52 percent of the American public answer no to the question: "Is it morally wrong for a couple who are not married to live together?" There was, as could be expected, the standard support for "the sanctity of marriage as one of the bulwarks of American Society." But the court balanced its general support against "the untold physical and mental anguish which may be visited on one of the parties, in this situation, if no relief is afforded." Unwilling to "place its stamp of approval on every non-marital relationship," the court was happy to make an exception in this case. Why? Well, for one thing, here a woman in later years of her life is left abandoned with her minor child; she has forsaken employment and any independent desires of her own in order to care for the defendant and their children. She must now start over, only she is now twenty-eight years older, at a time for her when gainful employment is hard to find. Compounding this was the unpleasant fact that at least one of the children and perhaps all three were totally unaware of their own illegitimacy until their parents separated. As the court characterized it:

"Meanwhile, evidently with callous indifference to the feelings of his daughters, the defendant raises the issue of a valid marriage to their mother at the time he abandoned her to pursue a new life with another woman, a strain of cruelty which could result in their bastardization."

One last thing capped it off. The court had no problem overcoming the obstacle that illicit sex—fornication being a crime in New York—cannot be an essential consideration in Leonard's promise to take care of Susan. Recall that the Illinois supreme court had emphasized that in reality sex is always an essential consideration. How could the New York court ignore that reality in this case? Simple. Sex happened not to be among Susan's wifelike duties. The couple had had no sexual relations for the past fifteen years! Susan was awarded alimony and child support.

While palimony suits do not always involve the rich and famous, as we've seen, they often do. Whereas the Erie County,

New York, court had held that twenty-eight years of housework and bearing and raising children were enough to award Susan McCullon palimony, in April 1979 a trial court in Westchester County, New York, rejected the *Marvin* doctrine in a suit against rock star Peter Frampton by his ex-cohabitant of five years, Penelope McCall. Although Penelope asked for half the house, half his earnings during the period and support thereafter, the court fixed the figure at a nice round number: 0.

Why? The court distinguished *Marvin, McCullon,* and an intermediate case, *Hewitt,* on the grounds that here Penelope and Peter never held themselves out as husband and wife, she hadn't even changed her name, nor were they ever free to marry each other. Penelope worsened her own case by claiming that Frampton had promised her a partnership if she would leave her husband. This enabled the court to conclude that illicit sex was at the core of the claimed business partnership, and adultery being a crime in New York, the contract, if it ever existed, was held void and unenforceable.

More recently, in June 1980, New York's high court emphatically declined to go the whole way with *Marvin*. While allowing an action based on an *explicit oral agreement* to share the wealth, made by an unmarried couple who had held themselves out as husband and wife and had children, at the same time, the court unanimously held that a judge may *not infer* an agreement—may not find an implied contract—arising from a couple's living arrangements.

THE TROUBLE WITH *MARVIN*
So where are we now in the '80s? We are in a period of unpredictable flux. Let's leave aside for the moment the question of whether palimony itself is good, right or wise, and if so under what circumstances.

Without taking a stand for the moment as to which policy is by itself the wiser, taken together, there is clearly injustice which stems from inconsistencies among different states' laws. It could be argued that a person chooses the state of the union in which s/he lives. That may be true with many of my clients who are wealthy and well informed about the predictable ramifications of a particular choice of residence and life-style, but it is not true of the vast majority of the millions of people in this country who are presently living together. In a basic sense, there is across this nation no equal protection of the laws. But this is not unique to matrimonial situations. There is no uniform national code on these issues. But neither is there as to criminal law or many if not most areas of law. That's all part of federalism and states' rights.

But let's return to the question of palimony itself. Is the *Marvin* doctrine good, wise, just? I don't think so. To me it distorts reality to force cohabitation rights into a "contract" mode of analysis, especially for couples whose only conscious choice was probably *not* to enter into a contract. The actual expectation expressed by people living together is most often a "wait and see." Contract is wisely used to allow the fulfillment of promises mutually agreed to and understood by both parties. It deals easily with monetary equivalents. But here, the essence of the action is not really that the "wife" has not received the monetary value of her spent labor, but rather that she is uncompensated for her spent youth.

The *Marvin* court and others which have followed the doctrine assume that the parties meant to deal with each other fairly. But that's not always so. And, once again, this is not a contract. Love lost, life misspent, childrearing are emotional intangibles that should not be quantified: They have no market-price equivalents. Does that mean that cohabitants are worthy of nothing? On the contrary. There's nothing to stop unmarried folks who are living together from making gifts of money or property to each other, or from buying a house in joint names with the right of survivorship. If people were only a little more savvy, they could learn to protect themselves during cohabitation. Not only can assets be transferred or jointly purchased, promises as to the future can be put in writing. "But this is all so formal" is the response I hear. "People living together are unlikely to formalize such transfers." Just so.

The basic point to me is that the parties were free to marry or at a minimum to make property distributions to each other. In these cases it was their own voluntary choice not to do so. Having made that choice, the law should hold them to it. Without being sanctimoniously moral about the subject, marriage is the bulwark of society, and above all it protects children. There should remain substantial incentive to formalize the relationship, especially before having children.

I am also opposed to the *Marvin* doctrine because the possibility for fraud is enormous. I expect in the '80s a flood of cases, including some in which women claim they lived with men who deny ever knowing them. With this doctrine, how do you predict in advance what your legal rights and obligations are? The possibilities of fraud are overwhelming: the secretary of long standing who will claim she regularly slept with her boss and gave him her best years, turning down higher salaries and promotions, never marrying, etc. Soon the symmetry of the sexual revolution will seize us and men will claim alimony and property from women with whom they lived. This "equality" has already gained a foothold—men have sued their wealthy wives for alimony, and some have gotten it.

But these suits only begin to scratch the surface. After *Marvin* there was a case in California in which a man who claimed he'd been living in a homosexual relationship with an actor sued for a share of his friend's assets. There was a certain surface logic to his claim. If California will allow palimony for couples in spite of the fact that they chose not to formalize their relationship, *a fortiori* why should that politically peculiar state not protect a homosexual who does not have the legal option to marry his lover? But if, as is my opinion, the *Marvin* doctrine on a heterosexual basis is sheer baloney, then on a homosexual basis it is at best salami.

The law is a seamless web—a fine tissue. A change like *Marvin* in one area must and will disturb the rest. Rights other than alimony have traditionally depended upon the existence of a valid marriage. In most states a spouse may not legally disinherit the other even though their June romance has for years turned into separate hatreds. The marriage rite, however brief the marriage relationship, guarantees at least a one-third income share. On the other hand, parents are perfectly free in most states to disinherit their children. How can marriage after *Marvin* be the crucial guarantor for inheritance but not for alimony? New Hampshire, of all states, in 1968 passed legislation treating a *de facto* spouse as the decedent's surviving spouse provided cohabitation is established for the preceding three years. And, for the purposes of workmen's compensation, Michigan recently permitted a cohabitant of thirteen years to collect under the "dependent" provision. Where does it stop? Who knows? If the changes are taken to their logical conclusion, we may truly have the sexual revolution which so many have claimed is already upon us.

Ultimately I am against a court's substituting its judgment of the pervasiveness of the new morality for that of the people's representatives. Let the state legislatures, which fix the rules for marriage and separation, decide this question, and then we'll see whether the people want to legalize their own new morality. I seriously doubt it. The ERA, on the brink of success, was beaten back and soundly defeated in such liberal states as New York and New Jersey, and the Gay Rights Bill has never passed the City Council in "enlightened" New York. We are still basically a conservative people, and the *Marvin* trend, in my opinion, is not as strong as the return to basics and to conservatism in this nation, and others in the free world.

To me, Marvin and the cases which have followed it have twisted things up. These cases masquerade as a mature toleration of the freedom of adults to choose unconventional relationships outside the bounds of law. How ironic; while pretending to embrace freedom and informality they have ultimately done just the opposite. Suddenly those who chose to live outside the protections of marriage contracts are "protected" anyway. Like it or not, the law, which was to be a liberator, now presses in upon our living arrangements. In the future it may be that if you want to keep a relationship totally free of legal obligations and truly informal, you must sign an ante-nonnuptial nonagreement, formalizing your informality: "We mutually agree that we do not agree to anything by living together. We mutually promise that we promise nothing." How silly.

If there is no such mutual desire to share, if two autonomous people truly want to be left alone together to join as they wish for as long as either one desires, in a relationship outside the bounds and obligations of the law, for the sake of companionship, and not for economics, they should be able to do so. And if they wish to give each gifts or joint ownership of property, there is nothing to stop them. But I believe we are a long way from giving legal sanction to the economic benefits that flow only from a voluntary and knowing legal relationship such as marriage. I do concede there will be a barrage of *Marvin*-type suits. My point is that to win them, one must be particularly adroit and ingenious—because it is an uphill fight.

As ye sow, so shall ye reap.

GAY MARRIAGE

Before the passion for sexual equality swept the world these past two decades, it was traditional for a couple to be declared "man and wife." With women's liberation the rage, rarely today is that phrase consciously uttered. Now the blissful couple are pronounced "husband and wife"—perfect symmetry from which we expect more perfect harmony.

But there is a group who would be delighted to adopt the despised "man and wife" and apply it, not to the couple, but to one individual in a marriage. Can an individual be both man and wife, or for that matter both woman and husband? Does our society allow gay marriages? Should it?

The first question is easy to answer: No. Nowhere in the United States, as far as I know, has the law recognized a single homosexual marriage. Nowhere is a person legally allowed to be both man and wife. Several have tried. They have claimed that constitutional guarantees such as "pursuit of happiness," "equal protection of the laws," etc. entitle them to homosexual marriages. But so far, as far as I know, all attempts have failed, with the courts holding uniformly that a "marriage" contracted between two parties of the same sex is a contradiction in terms, and therefore a nullity. It is void not just because the state legislature has chosen legally to prevent it but because an analysis of the very idea of "marriage requires members of the opposite sex."

So, for example, denying Marjorie Jones' request that a clerk issue her a marriage license to marry another woman, a Kentucky court said: "Appellants are prevented from marrying not by the statutes of Kentucky or the refusal of the County Court Clerk of Jefferson County to issue them a license, but rather by their own incapability of entering into a marriage as that term is defined."

Rarely does a statute actually specify that one party to a marriage must be a male and the other a female, but courts have read in this requirement. Proponents of gay marriages claim, of course, that this constitutes discrimination on the grounds of sexual preference, which is the very ill that the Equal Rights Amendment was designed to correct. I don't happen to turn on to ERA. And neither, in this regard, do the courts.

II

BUYING
AND
SELLING
GOODS
AND
SERVICES

WE HAVE just discussed the legal problems of matrimony and related familiarities. But many important contracts are not concerned with long-term intimacies. There is also an outer world, and much of our lives is spent in the enjoyment of it and protecting ourselves from it.

In the next sections we move into that outer world. We'll travel it and insure against some of its hazards. We'll have a frank discussion about the one person who should stand ready to protect both our outer and inner lives—our lawyer. Unfortunately sometimes the lawyer to fear is our own, and occasions arise when we should make a change and move on to another counselor before our cause is lost.

And we'll begin this transition from the inner world to the outer at the threshold—the object which is for most of us the liveliest reflection of our own personality, our home.

4.
HOUSING

FOR MOST people, buying a house is their most expensive and important single lifetime purchase. Yet many otherwise penny-conscious consumers who clip supermarket coupons and comparison-shop for the most trivial of items will squander thousands of dollars on a single purchase either from laziness, embarrassment, or hope obscuring reason.

Anyone who's ever been through the experience of buying or selling a house has his own tips. And books have been written on this. I have been instrumental in many a purchase and sale of a house, cooperative apartment and condominium and have a certain perspective myself.

If I may be permitted to indulge the ego I am reputed to have —but which only occasionally surfaces—I definitely come under the heading of a person who quickly knows what he wants. That's why I order ahead of others with whom I'm dining at a restaurant —because by the time they decide what they want to eat, I am usually halfway through dinner. And I'm a salesperson's dream— while somebody else is switching decisions back and forth as to which one of five neckties to buy, I will be in and out of the store with five different items selected in a matter of seconds each. Nor do I have patience with incompetence. My buddy Russell Eldridge enjoys telling the story of how we went into Bloomingdale's to buy a birthday gift for a friend. It was quickly selected—but I couldn't get a salesperson to gift-wrap it. We were finally pointed to a gift-wrap area, but there was nobody behind the counter. I went behind the counter and wrapped the gift we had bought. As I put it in a bag, I looked up to see about ten people standing in line with gifts they expected me to wrap. I did the best I could until some obnoxious woman started to bawl me out for putting a stuffed animal she had purchased into too small a box. I quit on the spot! So it is when I participate in house selection. I make up my mind quickly, and act quickly.

When, as others had successfully done, our law firm decided to lease a townhouse, my partners were scurrying around for weeks unable to make a selection. It took me minutes to find and recommend one. I have great confidence in the taste and judgment of my famous friend Barbara Walters. When we heard that the famed century-old Milbank town house in Manhattan was back on the market—a sale having fallen through—I asked Barbara to meet me there. She did, and we started at the sixth and top floor, and in seven minutes had seen every room and the cellar. As we ended up back in the lobby, Barbara and I looked at each other, and said this is it. I put in a hurry call to those partners I could reach. They came over and shared our enthusiasm. The key person in real estate in our organization who was going to buy and then lease it to us was finally located, liked the house, and made an on-the-spot offer at $50,000 below the price of the sale that had just fallen through. Within an hour, the sellers suggested we split the difference—and the deal closed within days. Of course, we put much reliance on the excellent reputation of Thomas Fowler Milbank, the executor of the selling estate. As fate would have it, we later became Tom's attorneys. What's more important, we became close friends and I became the co-executor of his estate on his untimely death.

I was driven out of New York State by the tax structure—15 percent state income tax, 5 percent city income tax, 8 percent sales tax, 8 to 9 percent real estate tax (it is true buildings are deliberately underassessed), gross occupancy tax, etc., etc., etc.—to nearby Connecticut, with no state or city income tax at all. The

Nutmeg State began to look awfully good. To add insult to injury, New York taxes nourish such worthy causes as welfare rolls permeated with phony applicants, a slew of unnecessary bureaucratic jobs, and a pension system where after comparatively short service, still-young men and women retire at ranges of up to 120 percent of their on-job pay. So, to Connecticut. The minute I saw a little scrambled-up Tudor cottage hanging over a stream and waterfall with tall trees and no visible neighbors, I knew that was for me. Since leasing it and living there, and doing more and more of my work there, I have come to love it. This is the place to say, however, in the words of W. C. Fields, that "after New York, every place else is Bridgeport." Well, Greenwich is just about in between New York and Bridgeport!

A final note about my own personal habits. We have many clients in Acapulco—such as the Baron Enrico diPortanova, an heir to the Cullen oil fortune, and his beautiful baroness. Rick's father, Baron Paul diPortanova, and his also lovely baroness winter in Acapulco too, as does our client Warren E. Avis, the founder of Avis Rent-A-Car and a man whose inventive mind produces a new idea a minute, the best yet being his decision to marry Yanna. As a result, lawyers from our firm have to shuttle back and forth a number of times a year. This led to one of the strangest house "deals" in history. It started when Baron diPortanova called a meeting of a group of his attorneys in Acapulco. We rented a house on the Pacific side (which should be much more desirable—it is to me—because that's the "nonsocial" section). It turned out the owner was an affable, well-read former naval intelligence officer and prominent socialite named C. Russell Hurd. We became fast friends, although I think at the start Russell eyed with suspicion these sly lawyers from New York. From that friendship, a year later, there developed a deal involving the house between Russell on the one hand and a client of ours and us on the other. It is a sort of partnership in which each accommodates to the other's plans, and the arrangements would baffle any real estate broker—but it works.

The usual line is "watch what I do, not what I say." In this case, forget that. Don't do what we did in the above situations, but do what I tell you hereafter.

BUYING

Almost no one can afford to make major mistakes when buying a house, and yet almost everyone who has bought one has a story to tell of pitfalls into which he fell.

LOCATION

When you're considering a house, first rule: survey the area. It is a saying of the wise that there are only three things ultimately to look for in a house: location, location and location. The easiest house to sell is the cheapest house in an area. Investigate the zoning; where is it commercially zoned and where residential? Find out the location of all nearby unbuilt-upon land. Who owns it? What's it to be used for? Talk to future neighbors. They will generally give you an overall favorable account of the area, as they are eager for the houses in the immediate locale to sell well. But every once in a while you'll find one who is disgruntled and will list what he considers disadvantages of the particular neighborhood: too many young people, no children, all Buddhist, etc.

How do you know the neighborhood is right? This question often becomes an ethical, and ethnic, one. The best thing to do is obvious: Look at names on mailboxes, and hang around and see who gets off school buses, how many and where they go. Knock on a couple of doors and ask.

The best rule is to spend an entire day outside the house. A street which is represented as "not that main" may turn out to be a veritable highway. I had a friend who bought a nice house in a beautiful suburban neighborhood on a quiet street. There was no way to know it by looking at the house at midday or in the late evening, but that quiet street was a standard shortcut from one main street to another. For four hours every day a steady stream of cars and trucks turned this quiet street into a thoroughfare. The only way he could have known was if a neighbor had happened to tell him, or if he had tarried for a day and observed the traffic pattern. He didn't and regretted it. Or the location may be under an airplane landing pattern even though the airport is miles away. So spend a day there.

CONDITION: RESALE HOUSES

This brings me to another very important rule. Try out everything. Once again there is the problem of embarrassment. How can you walk around flushing the toilets and turning on the showers in a stranger's home? You can, you should. Move furniture and look behind it. Are the walls painted behind the furniture? What does the floor look like under the rug? What does the counter look like under the hotplate? Check the basement for evidence of water damage. If a defect would have been ascertainable to your carefully probing eye and you fail to pick it up, you'll be stuck later. Feel embarrassed? Get burned once and you'll never feel embarrassed again.

Hire a reputable engineer and get an engineering report. Failure to do this in order to save the money is penny-wise and pound-foolish. I know of someone who bought the engineer's report at half price from another would-be buyer and later regretted not having gone around with the engineer himself.

An engineer is, by and large, going to use his own two eyes. He is going to turn on the water and see if it's working; he's going to plug a lamp into the socket to see if it's working. He's not going to break through a wall to see how the inside looks, nor is he, most likely, going to remove the switchplate or socket to see the condition of the wiring. He's going to look at the roof and tell you that although it is not leaking at the moment, it could leak any day, as the house is more than twenty years old. The engineer performs a very valuable function for those who are embarrassed to try out everything. He is getting paid to do that. He also performs a valuable service for those who do not understand what they see.

But remember—an engineer is out to scare you. He must justify his fee and will therefore find things wrong with the house. Use his report to gain concessions, but keep perspective and don't get scared away from buying a house which is otherwise an excellent investment because the engineering report lists a litany of superficial blemishes and hypothetical horrors.

Take the engineer's report and go over it with the seller. If any negative comment within the engineer's report is denied by the seller, get that denial in writing as part of the contract of sale. Otherwise, use all the negative aspects of the engineering report to extract concessions during negotiations.

In my opinion, termite inspection can be even more important than an engineer. A termite inspector will tell you if there are rotten beams. He'll inspect the structure of the basement.

Write everything significant into the contract, down to the pettiest detail; if you want to make sure something stays with the house, list it. Do not take the seller's word for anything. What is the seller leaving behind? What is the exact structural condition of the house?

CONDITION: NEW HOUSES

If it's a new house in the process of being built, check out the reputation of the builder. Here it's a good idea to upgrade structurally while a house is being built. Spend a couple of hundred dollars extra now to enlarge the fireplace. Spend the couple of thousand dollars extra for more storage space in the basement now. It will cost five or ten times as much later to alter a house that's already built. Pour all your money into the structure. If you're short on money, save it some other way: Live without landscaping for a couple of years, hold off on expensive furnishings, or scrimp somewhere else in your life, but make all foreseeably desired structural changes while the house is being built.

Few people use an engineering report when buying a new house. The way most new-house buyers get burned is by inferior materials and shoddy craftsmanship. The reputation of the builder is important. Talk to people who have lived in that builder's houses for several years. Find out what they didn't like about them and discuss it with the builder.

Another thing to look at with new houses is the builder's

guarantee. Is it merely a corporate guarantee or is it a personal guarantee? The difference may be enormous. A corporate guarantee may not protect you much if the corporation is not substantial. It makes sense in various types of construction to insist upon personal guarantees from the builder. If the builder refuses, it might be a good sign that he has little confidence in his own work, and therefore that you should have even less.

When the builder is building your house, talk to other people already living in another newly constructed house of his. Ask them: Has the builder been fair? What are the particular shortcomings of the house? Maybe this builder didn't contemplate certain features of terrain, or builds peculiarly small fireplaces, or misplants shrubbery so as not to utilize the maximum. Maybe he skimps on storage space, or uses especially flimsy window slides. All good things to know before paying for your new house.

PRICE

Suppose you have picked the area and have zeroed in on a particular house. Now the game begins. In essence it's simple. The seller initially asks for far more than the price at which he's willing to sell. The broker wants his commission and is ultimately an agent of himself, secondarily of the seller, who pays his commission, and only lastly of you, the buyer. The object is to buy it as cheaply as you can, spending no more than you're willing to pay. There is often an emotional component to buying a house. You and your family "fall in love" with the house. Falling in love is wonderful; it's also costly. Before walking through a house for the first time there should be a standing agreement among all members of the family: Look doubtful about any house you see, no matter how much you really like it. The *worst* thing you can do as potential buyers is to make the seller feel that you desperately want this house at any price, that you've been looking all over for months and have not found anything which even vaguely fits your bill, but now you've suddenly stumbled upon the house of your dreams. Once you convey this impression to the seller, as the cigar commercial goes, "they got you." Some people feel that if they convince the seller they really love the house and will take care of it, they will do better, as the seller will want to sell to someone who will take care of and appreciate his beloved house. By and large this is nonsense. Once the seller gets the idea that you'll pay any price, it's cookies for you. If he's wrong, there will be no sale; you will have killed it by your initial enthusiasm.

NEGOTIATING Third rule: Know what you want. What would you be willing to pay for the house? Determine this without paying any attention to the asking price. It's no bargain to pay $30,000 less than an asking price which is $50,000 too high for you. Ask yourself what is absolutely the highest price you would be willing to pay. Once you determine that, make an offer about 20 percent less than *your* top price. The broker may try to talk you out of making such a "ridiculously low" bid. "I would be embarrassed to pass this offer along to the seller," the broker tells you. It's all right; he'll get over his embarrassment. You do not need to feel the slightest bit of embarrassment. You are bidding in the range you are willing to pay. Many times your offer will come at just the right time. Quite possibly the sellers have bought another house and feel panicky about carrying two houses at the same time. Their facade quickly crumbles and they go down significantly in price.

The name of the game from here on is to find out their real bottom price and offer no more than it. One way to get a sense of it is to know what they paid for the house and when. You can find this out by consulting the records of the local town hall. Either the purchase price will be listed, or the tax stamps attached to the recorded deed will enable you to compute the purchase price.

Actually, you should find out as much as you can about the seller's situation. Is he having trouble selling the house? How long has it been on the market without moving? Has the asking price been dropped? Has he bought another house or made plans to move out of the area? What are comparable houses going for in the area?

Don't fall prey to the psychology of scale. When you're spending $100,000 or more on a house, what's a couple of thousand dollars here or there? It's the same couple of thousand dollars which, in order to save, you spend a lifetime of coupon clipping, or years of second estimates on lesser items. Don't get swept up by the size of the total expenditure. Don't forget that to you a dollar is a dollar. Each time you go up in price in a negotiation, try to extract some additional concession from the seller.

Avoid a bidding war, real or imagined. If there is another party seriously interested, contact him if possible and decide between you. If you can't contact the other party, then decide on your highest offer and make it while announcing that it must be accepted within forty-eight hours or it will be permanently withdrawn. If the forty-eight hours pass, withdraw it and let them call you. In negotiations, hang tough. Get up and walk out. Don't second-guess yourself if the deal falls through. And if they do call you back, you might end up getting it even cheaper.

One of the final concessions you can extract comes from the agent, not from the seller. Regardless of what they tell you about company policy, almost every agent will take a cut of a few hundred dollars in a commission fee if and only if s/he sees it is necessary to bring the parties together. For that to happen, you must convince the agent that you have reached your top price and will budge no higher. It's helpful to make the top price a round number to make it more credible that you would not budge from it. Don't feel embarrassed at suggesting that the agent take a cut in fee. You're not cheating him out of a commission, you're enabling him to earn one.

CONSTRUCTION

Before agreeing to a contract for any type of construction, such as building an addition, always ask the contractor how many man-hours it's going to take. You always want your bill or estimate broken up—labor and parts (or materials). If a contractor gives you a single price, he can hide a tremendous amount of his profit in saying they're material costs. They'll almost always make more on you that way. But if a contractor says that to add this portion or redo this room will take two men six days, and materials are going to cost him $5,000, and he has said he wants $10,000 for the job, you now have a good basis to ask, "Why?" You can ask how much his men's time is worth. That, of course, depends on how skilled the labor is. It might be worth $50 a day or $500 a day depending upon the type and quality of the craftsman. Is it rough work or fine cabinetry? But whatever it is, it allows you to make a more intelligent determination of whether you are being ripped off.

If someone tells me it's going to cost me $5,000, I for one ask for a list of materials. Then I go or send someone to a supplier of those materials and price them myself. If there's a great difference I'll pay the supplier directly by opening up a charge account and instructing the builder to charge materials to my account. Contractors don't like this because they make some profit from buying the materials wholesale and charging you the retail price.

Since you must pay the retail price, whether it be from the lumberyard or the contractor, you might as well allow the contractor the profit on the materials. So often the mild suggestion of establishing a charge account for the job, coupled with a demand of an itemization of material costs, will cause a huge drop in price.

A friend of mine recently had some landscaping done. He hired an excellent landscaper who gave him an estimate of $8,000, whereupon he asked for an itemization by bush and coupled that request with the suggestion that he might obtain the bushes himself, utilizing the gardener only to design and plant them. The result was that the original $8,000 estimate became a final bill of $4,200.

Of course it shouldn't be necessary to point out once again that it is absurd for you to be too embarrassed to ask for such an itemized breakdown. It's your money. And if you show some concern for it, the contractor is more likely to show some concern for it.

This is a general rule for all types of construction. Get it broken down into labor costs and materials.

Let me give you another example where doing this saved quite a bit of money. I have a friend who became involved in movie theaters. He bought one with the idea of twinning it—i.e., making two theaters out of one. He went to the fellow who in this locality had been established as the "expert" in this type of work. The contractor gave him an estimate of $60,000, essentially to construct a wall down the middle. I told him he was crazy to spend that money. "What's really involved?" I asked. "I don't know, but that's what he charges, and he's the expert and does a lot of business, so it must be a fair price."

Of course that's ridiculous. I said, "Find out exactly what material goes into this wall—what is 'the special sound material' this contractor was touting so highly?" So my friend went to another job this contractor was working on, asked the laborers, and found out that the material was nothing more than standard household insulating plasterboard, and strapping steel beams. He priced the materials given his dimensions and they came to $11,000. So I said, "Warren, how does he justify $50,000 in labor costs?" And Warren continued to defend the $60,000 price tag he was willing to pay. "He puts ten men on the job." "For how long?" I asked. "He's quick; he gets it done in a week." "OK, figure it out," I said. "Suppose they work six days each, that's sixty man-days. He's charging you $49,000 above material costs. At $100 per man a day, that's only $6,000. The man has to make a profit—he's the contractor, he's got to pay insurance, etc.—and he's entitled to a profit on the job, say, of $10,000. Go to a general contractor, not a so-called expert, give him your requirements, and ask for his breakdown." My friend did that, and sure enough, he got a price of $22,000, which he accepted. He is the very proud owner of profitable twin movie theaters today. His couple of hours of inquiry saved him $38,000. It's the same principle again and again with construction. *Before agreeing to any job, itemize it and break it down into its bits.* After having the contractor itemize it, price it out yourself, and if it's in the ballpark, then and only then agree to the job.

WARRANTIES

So you buy your dream house and it turns out to be a nightmare. Is there anything you can do about it? Can you fight back? Yes. A hundred years ago the prevailing view in law was that no matter how "morally censurable," there was no duty on the seller or agent to disclose facts. Shaped by an individualistic philosophy based upon the freedom of contract and unconcerned with morality, the law was simple: Let the buyer beware.

Presently the mood has shifted. Courts tend to try to reach a just result as far as possible while at the same time maintaining "a degree of certainty" that attaches to the purchase itself. The general rule has become that the seller and the real estate agent are not only liable to the buyer for affirmative and intentional misrepresentations, but also for nondisclosure of defects known to them and unknown and unobservable to the buyer.

This bears repeating in other words. The principle of *caveat emptor* applies to sales of real estate relative to conditions *open to observation* where those conditions are discoverable and the buyer has the opportunity for investigation and inspection without hindrance from the seller. In such a case the buyer has no just cause for complaint even though the seller has misrepresented some things which are not in themselves so major or reprehensible as to amount to fraud. Therefore if you can observe the problem, you must investigate. Try out everything! Try out everything! Try out everything!

When you've been taken, and you want to sue for fraud, remember these elements necessary for an action for damages for deceit: There must have been *concealment,* of a *material fact,* with *knowledge* of the fact concealed—if the seller doesn't know of the defect no fraud—with *intent to mislead* you into relying upon such misrepresentations followed by your *reliance* resulting in an *injury* to you because you relied. If it's all there and you can prove it, you've got a cause of action.

In December 1972, Vincent and Joanne Neveroski purchased a modest home in New Jersey. Four months after they took possession they found the house was so infested with termites they had to vacate. They sued the sellers, the real estate agents, and the exterminating company which had represented to them that the house was termite-free. They sought to rescind their purchase, to cancel their mortgage, and to win damages for fraud and breach of contract. The court stated the "underlying settled rule" that all people connected with a fraud are liable for the full amount of the damages. That included the real estate agents who "deliberately concealed" from the Neveroskis the material fact of the termite condition. The Neveroskis ended up getting $15,000 plus attorneys' costs.

What about the builders of new houses? Are they responsible for the lemons they build? Yes. The mood has shifted here too. There is now an implied warranty of habitability. And so, for example, it has been held that where a builder sells a new house to its first intended occupant, he impliedly warrants that the foundations supporting it are firm and secure and that the house is structurally safe to live in. This implied warranty of fitness applies even if the builder was not negligent in his selection of a poor site on which to build.*

One last recent change in the law has occurred in several states. Not only is the builder potentially liable to the purchaser to whom he sells the new house, but he remains liable for a reasonable period of time to subsequent purchasers of the house. Once again this implied warranty protects subsequent purchasers against latent defects which are not discoverable by the subsequent purchaser's inspection and which become manifest after purchase. Not all states recognize this implied warranty but several do, more each year.

In September 1979, the supreme court of Wyoming extended the protections even further. Not only did it hold that the implied warranty of habitability extends beyond the first owner to subsequent purchasers for a reasonable length of time for latent defects which become manifest after purchase, but it took a next step and allowed the claimant to collect from the electrical subcontractor who had installed faulty wiring.

The opinion joined Wyoming to the list of states that have "abandoned" the doctrine of *caveat emptor*. It is "out of harmony

---

* *Morley* v. *Laramic Builders*, 600 P2d 733.

with more compassionate and understanding views. The mores of the day have changed and the ordinary home buyer is not in a position to discover defects in a structure.''

So, do your best to protect yourself and make your home your castle. But when the cracks in the foundation appear, don't bemoan your fate. Fight back!

SELLING

There are three parties in a typical house transaction: buyer, seller and agent. Sometimes it's the agent who rips off the seller and/or the buyer.

For example, Marvin Starkweather owned twelve acres of rural residential property in Josephine County, Oregon. He had been recently divorced and had custody of his small son when he fell seriously ill, was unemployed and desperately needed money. So he decided to sell his property. He contacted Shaffner Realty Company, whose representative listed the site for $15,000. Some advertising was done and the place was shown to three people, but no sale. Concerned, Starkweather called Shaffner, who came himself to examine the place and told Starkweather he'd have to reduce his price. Starkweather suggested a cut to $12,500, but his agent told him that better properties were on the market for less. He suggested dropping it to $8,000 and prepared an "earnest money receipt" by which Starkweather promised to sell at $8,000 less a $480 brokerage commission. Desperate, Starkweather agreed. What he didn't know was that the purchaser was the realtor himself, who turned around after buying the property for the $7,520, spent $1,277 cleaning it up and painting the buildings, split the property into two parcels, advertised more earnestly, and sold the properties three months later for about $20,000.

Starkweather learned of how he'd been taken by his own agent and sued. The jury awarded $5,000 compensatory damages and $5,000 punitive damages. The Oregon supreme court affirmed, holding: "The law is well established that a real estate broker stands in a fiduciary relationship with his client and is bound to protect his client's interest. He must make a full and understandable explanation to the client before having him sign any contracts with the broker himself.'' Furthermore, ''a fiduciary relationship exists'' between seller and agent which means that the agent in ''good conscience is bound to act in good faith and with due regard to the interests of the one reposing the confidence.''

Not all dishonest moves by brokers are so blatant. Sometimes there is a hidden third party involved. For example, Ryan Ulich and his wife, Ann Mitchell, wanted a vacant lot abutting Lake Pontchartrain's levee. They hired Dunbar LaPlace to find such a lot for them. He found it, but first sold it to a friend, and then had his friend sell it to his client, Ulich and Mitchell, of course at a profit. The Louisiana court holding that LaPlace had violated his fiduciary obligation awarded the couple the difference between the market price and the cost to them.

This situation is not unique. A broker may screw the seller, and actually prevent a willing buyer from making the purchase. For example, Stephen Azierski was president of Security Aluminum Window Manufacturing Corporation, which had fallen into desperate financial straits. Azierski decided to sell certain corporate property in Newark, New Jersey. To that end he engaged Lehman Associates, a realtor. The asking price was $65,000. The agent in charge of selling the property, Mark Gale, told Azierski of a $25,000 offer from one Sam Minkowitz. What he didn't mention was that Minkowitz was a good friend of his. Azierski declined the offer. One day while driving by the property he noticed the salesman showing it to three men. He was later told by one of his tenants that the man, Johnson, was introducing himself as the new owner. When Azierski asked the agent, Gale, about this and whether there had been any favorable developments, Gale said no, and with regard to Johnson, ''Oh, some kook, don't even think about it.''

Of course, he didn't want Azierski to think about it. Nor did he bother to inform Azierski that Johnson had offered $44,000 for the property, which the agent had rejected as insufficient, nor that he had on February 28 offered $50,000 with a deposit of $500.

Instead, the next day, Gale telephoned Azierski and told him that Minkowitz (his secret friend) was fast losing interest in the property and if Azierski didn't accept the $25,000 offer he might be unable to find a buyer. In a financial squeeze, having just received service of process in a foreclosure proceeding, Azierski reluctantly accepted the $25,000 offer. Gale rushed over to Azierski's house with an agreement, and Azierski again asked him whether Minkowitz might bid a little higher. Gale said no, and Azierski signed the contract, dated March 2.

Meanwhile Johnson, the buyer willing to pay $50,000 whom agent Gale had rejected and had refused to tell the identity of the owner, became suspicious and concluded that something fishy was going on. He spoke to his lawyer; they discovered Azierski's identity and phoned him to find out what was holding up the sale. It was at that time that Azierski first learned of the $50,000 offer that his "agent" had rejected in favor of his own friend's $25,000 offer, which the agent had forced to contract.

Azierski immediately sued to rescind the contract and at the same time negotiated the sale to Johnson at $44,000. Gale and the real estate firm which employed him now had the gall to counter-claim for commissions "due" them as a result of the Minkowitz contract and, in addition, "commissions on any future sale to Johnson," and to cap it off, they counterclaimed for damages against Azierski for "malicious interference" with the proposed sale by Minkowitz to Johnson.

Minkowitz himself accepted $1,000 to cancel the contract and exit the legal scene. The trial judge awarded Azierski only $6,000 in compensatory damages as the difference between Johnson's earlier $50,000 offer and the contract price of $44,000. Both sides appealed. The New Jersey appellate court found that the realtors' "wrongdoing has been intentional and deliberate, and has the character of outrage frequently associated with crime." Furthermore, the court observed:

> Once it has been shown that one trained and experienced holds himself out to the public as worthy to be trusted for hire

to perform services for others, and those so invited do place their trust and confidence, and that trust is intentionally and consciously disregarded, and exploited for unwarranted gain, community protection, as well as that of the victim, warrants the imposition of punitive damages. . . . Punitive damages are particularly apt in such circumstances because they both punish the wrongdoer, and offer the wronged a greater incentive to bring derelicts to justice, a process which can subject the victim to considerable expense and trouble.

The appellate court affirmed the compensatory damages and sent the case back to the trial court for additional punitive damages. Azierski offered to accept $5,000, but the realtors refused to negotiate. Their stubbornness eventually cost them $15,000.

One of the lessons from this is to keep tabs on your broker. Even after you sell the house, keep track and see if it is resold soon thereafter at a much higher price. It may turn out that the party you sold to was either a friend of the broker's or the broker himself. In that case, you may be due thousands of dollars in compensatory damages and thousands more in punitive damages. Little comes to those who, having sold their homes, now sleep on their rights.

We've seen some instances where a broker rips off the seller. But the opposite happens too. A broker's commission is usually a percentage of the sales price (5 to 10 percent depending upon the type of real estate and the customs of the locale). This can amount to many thousands of dollars, all for a "mere" introduction. Many buyers and sellers try to cut the broker out of the transaction. It's perfectly all right to sell your house yourself, and not to use a broker. If you decide to do this, one hint: Although you do not list with a broker, you might want to call a few brokers in to look over your house, suggest a selling price, and offer hints on how to make the place more attractive to potential buyers. For example, brokers will tell you to make inexpensive superficial changes like painting a few rooms. A fresh coat of paint will often pay dividends many times its price.

Of course as a buyer you should be aware of this and buy the house, not its trimmings. Many foolish people will buy a house for its insignificant details, or pass up a great deal because the house is "dirty" or the stoop is broken. Don't fall for either. Another broker trick to sellers is to empty out closets to make them seem larger and unclutter rooms for the same effect.

In any event, a broker's consultation is helpful primarily to enable you not to undervalue your own house. You may have bought it at $60,000 and be happy to get $100,000 five years later. But the market may in fact allow you $120,000, and a broker would know this. Remember that a broker's suggested selling price includes his commission. No obligation attaches to you from the broker's visit, but if you don't want the broker to list your house, *make it clear* and don't allow a broker's clients to see the house. You do not need to sign a contract in order for you to be liable for a broker's commission.

Some people decide to try to sell it themselves through newspaper ads as well as through a broker. You've got to be careful. Make certain you know whether the potential buyer has been sent by a broker. If so, you won't be able to deal directly with him and cut out the broker's fee. You've got to know this when you bargain.

The temptation is always there for both the buyer and seller to cut out the broker and divide the fee between them. But while states vary as to exactly when a broker is entitled to a commission from the seller, it is generally agreed that when the broker procures a buyer ready, willing and able to buy at or near the seller's asking price, then once there is a valid contract for sale, the broker is entitled to a commission. This may be true even if the deal later breaks down, especially if the seller is at fault.

One last piece of advice when you sell a house: Avoid exclusive listings. A broker will try to get you to list "exclusively." The broker will tell you how much harder he'll push your house this way. It's seldom true. Multiple listing has become a common practice; it benefits both the seller and the buyer. Beware before signing any agreement with a broker. Sometimes an "exclusive listing" will guarantee the broker a commission even if you should sell the house on your own.

It's unfair, although tempting, to cut a broker out of a commission. Suppose you're the buyer and can't quite get together with a seller who calls you on the Q.T. suggesting you work it out between you—morality aside, if you buy the house that way, make certain the seller guarantees in the sale to indemnify you for any brokerage commissions which may arise by this sale.

CONTRACT AND CLOSING

After a year of fruitless searching during which time you don't want the houses you can afford and you can't afford the houses you want, suddenly you come upon a house that fits the bill with some small compromises. You are excited and a little frightened as the agent informs you that this is one in a million, the house is greatly underpriced, has just come on the market and won't last the day, and unless you put a binder down on it you'll lose it.

Don't put a binder on the house: Binders don't bind. They are merely good-faith gestures. If the seller wants to back out he can do so even if there is a binder. Binders have no legal effect whatever. They do have a practical effect: They lead to lawsuits.

So what do you do? You huddle, decide you want to buy the house, try out everything, express serious interest, plan to spend the next day there, and immediately *contact your lawyer* to start drawing up a contract.

Ninety percent of what a lawyer does in helping you to buy your house is handholding, psychiatry and social work. The other 10 percent, however, can save you money and future irritation. The good lawyer makes certain that *everything* significant is written into the contract—down to the pettiest detail. Here's where having tried out things and obtaining an engineering report pays off. You should know mostly what's in working order. These things should be written in: "The plumbing, electrical work, heating are in working order." All representations as to the structure of the house should be written in. In addition, everything that the seller has promised to do to remedy defects you've perceived, and *everything* the seller has promised to leave behind, should be written into the contract. Don't be afraid that the contract will be too long. Paper is cheap.

An experienced lawyer will think of guarantees and contingencies you will never think of. Suppose, for example, the seller is in the process of buying another house and assumes that he can vacate because he'll have another place to live. Suppose the other house purchase is delayed or canceled. The contract should specify a rent the seller will pay you for each day he occupies past the promised date of vacating. A good lawyer will demand that an adequate sum be put into escrow to cover this and other contingencies.

Suppose a loss—fire or vandalism—occurs after seller has vacated and before you move in. Who's responsible? The contract should specify this. If you need a mortgage, you should specify in the contract that the purchase is "subject to obtaining a mortgage of —— at —— percent," or "at the prevailing rate."

There is a second way a good lawyer serves you at time of contract. If s/he is aggressively acting on your behalf, there's usually room to knock down the purchase price in small ways. The closing date—the day the title of the house formally is transferred —may occur in the midst of billing periods. Usually the bills are allocated proportionately. For example, the taxes. The aggressive lawyer will round off the taxes in favor of the buyer and will tell the other lawyer he's doing it. The other side will be embarrassed to chisel and will accept it. Or again, with the fuel remaining in the tank. The seller, having filled the tank and used some of the fuel, is entitled to a rebate for the fuel remaining. An aggressive buyer's lawyer will round down the fuel rebate. I know of one lawyer who routinely tries to embarrass the other side: "Ah, throw in the oil —you filled it last month—you used it, you already paid for it. What are you worried about getting back, a few pennies? My client is paying you $100,000, as it is." A seller eager to be finished, and an opposing lawyer eager to return to his more lucrative practice, often will yield. This lawyer has as his goal to save every buyer the cost of his fee. If no other technique has worked, this lawyer will make a last-ditch effort to reduce the purchase price itself, especially if it is something like $103,500: "I'm knocking off $500. They're good kids and they need it. Be a sport."

At closing the lawyer is also vital, but for different reasons. There's very little give in the purchase price or conditions of sale at closing. All this should have been worked out in contract. Thus the lawyer's role at closing is to make certain that the myriad of papers are in order.

The lawyer prepares the deed and the mortgage and makes sure everything is done properly. The seller is selling only what he has. If, for some reason—and there are many possibilities that I won't go into here—the seller has defective title to the house, then generally the buyer is buying that defective title. Title companies check out the title. In the western part of the country, the general rule is for title companies to act as guarantors of the title. But in the East, they do not guarantee the validity of the title, and it is up to the lawyer to make sure the title is good.

There's a lot that can go wrong unless a practiced alert eye is protecting the buyer. If a mistake is made, it can be a costly one. Let me give you an extreme example, in which the buyer and seller decided they didn't need a lawyer at closing. Together they prepared a standard-form deed. The buyer paid the money and the seller gave him the deed, which the buyer carefully stored in his safe-deposit box. The only problem is that unless the deed is *filed* you don't ensure your ownership. The seller turned around and sold the house again. The second buyer found a clear title. His attorney filed his deed. The rule is that the first deed filed owns the house. What happened to the first buyer who had paid for the house he now didn't own? He was free to sue the seller, if he could only find him. Use a lawyer at contract and closing.

5.
INSURANCE

THE PURPOSE of insurance is to guarantee that your worth will remain constant to you or your loved ones in every substantially possible contingency. You are *over*insured when, in the event against which you are insuring, you would be richer than you are now. You are *under*insured when, in the same event, you would be poorer than you are now. As a general rule, you should allocate your money between other expenditures and insurance so as to make yourself equally affluent in all foreseeable circumstances.

POLICIES

Have you ever had trouble understanding an insurance policy? It is reported* that during oral argument before the New Jersey supreme court the following colloquy took place in a "comprehensive homeowner's insurance policy" case:

CHIEF JUSTICE WEINTRAUB:	I don't know what it means. They say one thing in big type and in small type they take it away.
JUSTICE HANEMAN:	I can't understand half of my insurance policies.
JUSTICE FRANCIS:	I get the impression that insurance companies keep the language of their policies deliberately obscure.

* *Jury Verdict Weekly News,* January 13, 1963, p. 3.

129

Not in insurance is ignorance bliss except for those who play hit or miss with their own fortunes. For the rest of us, who like to plan rationally how to insure against disasters, it is vital that we know precisely how we've provided for emergencies.

CLAIMS

Perhaps the only thing more difficult than understanding insurance policies is collecting on them. From an insurance company's perspective it's very simple: You need the money, we've got it. If we hold out on you, you cannot afford to fight to get it, so you settle for much less than that to which you're entitled. If worst comes to worst, we have to pay you what we should have paid you in the first place, plus a few dollars for your lawyer's fees.

Most insurance companies keep their own lawyers on retainer. You feel helpless before these giants. Don't. Fight back; the game doesn't always work for them anymore. Here's one you can win big. The key: a sympathetic jury awarding punitive damages and the court's not materially reducing them.

WHEN COMPANIES REFUSE TO PAY

In 1963, U. L. Fletcher was a thirty-six-year-old scrap operator for a rubber company, married fifteen years and the father of eight children. Fletcher earned almost $300 a week by working seventy to eighty hours at hard manual labor. He purchased a policy from Western National Life Insurance Company which would give him $150 a month if he should become totally disabled from sickness or injury. If the disability occurred from sickness, the payments were limited to two years. In the event of injury, the maximum payout period was thirty years.

Fletcher had met all his payments when in January 1965, while lifting a 361-pound bale of rubber, he injured his lower back and legs. He underwent a hernia operation, collected some disability insurance and returned to work. But his injury gave him trouble, and he was eventually placed on disability and forced to retire. He filed a workmen's compensation claim, and was treated by several doctors, who were in unanimous agreement that he had been disabled by the injury caused by the work accident. Western National resumed payments.

Everything was fine until May 1966, when Thomas R. Amason became Western National's claims supervisor. Amason figured out a way to reduce costs to the insurance company at the expense of poor Fletcher. It was simple, really. Call the hernia an "illness" rather than an injury and pay out under the sickness provision for only two years, rather than for thirty. This cost-cutting wizard with a heart of jagged steel informed Fletcher that he would be paid only for two years. In August 1966 the company ran a credit investigation on Fletcher which confirmed that he was really disabled and had a total income of only $384 per month—$118 disability benefits from Social Security, $116 from the rental of a house, and the $150 from his insurance policy. As to Fletcher's expenses, the private investigation report stated: "All of his income is going out to upkeep on his two homes, food for family and expenses and medical bills. He is barely making ends meet."

And so, knowing Fletcher's back was against the wall, that he was slowly losing his battle on $384 a month, claims manager Amason, with the express approval of the president of Western National, wrote him a letter which read in part:

"We have just completed making an intensive investigation of your disability claim. We were quite surprised to find you had a congenital back ailment which was not disclosed in your application." (Only one doctor had raised the possibility that it *might* have been congenital, and there was no evidence that when Fletcher first obtained the insurance he had any knowledge of a congenital defect.) Western National's missive continued: "We consider such information material and quite frankly would not have issued you an Accident and Sickness Policy had we been aware of your true medical condition. Consequently we feel there is definite misrepresentation on your part in not informing us of this condition. Based on this, we are contesting the validity of your Accident and Sickness Insurance Policy." The company stopped paying Fletcher entirely.

Not content with this, the insurance company demanded the *return* of $2,250 from Fletcher (less the premiums he paid). No defense like a good offense, especially when a person's down. Lest you think for a moment that, although heartless, the insurance company was arguably within its legal rights to do any of this, be advised that the question whose answer was supposedly a misrepresentation asked: "TO THE BEST OF YOUR KNOWLEDGE AND BELIEF, have you ever had or been under observation for any disease . . ." Fletcher had honestly answered no.

The next letter Western National sent insisted again on the company's right to recover previous payouts but indicated its willingness, in order to "avoid the further cost of litigation," to "make a compromise agreement." In its infinite generosity, the company promised to let Fletcher keep the $2,200 in payments already made to him in consideration of the complete cancellation of the policy and an execution of a full release. This letter concluded: "Failure to return this signed agreement . . . within ten (10) days shall be considered a refusal to do so and an unwillingness on your part to compromise this claim and our offer will then automatically terminate and we shall once again demand full reimbursement. . . . It is only fair to tell you that if we have to, we are willing to take whatever action necessary to have this policy cancelled. The action, however, is expensive to both parties and it is only for this reason we wish to effect a compromise settlement at this time."

How many people live honestly, work hard, suffer misfortune and are broken by the cruelty and indifference of scheming heartless corporate bureaucrats! Fletcher fought back, or rather his lawyers did.

Seeing he wasn't going to go for their disgusting ploy, Western now offered to pay Fletcher an additional $2,850 in exchange for a cancellation of the policy.

The lawyer flatly rejected it and turned Fletcher's case over to another attorney who specialized in litigation. The day of the trial, Western National agreed in writing that they owed Fletcher $150 a month for the next thirty years. But the fight wasn't finished. Fletcher and his lawyer pressed on. At trial, Fletcher testified that Western National's suspension of payments had forced him to reduce his family budget, thereby subjecting his family to a diet of macaroni, beans and potatoes. His utilities had been shut off for nonpayment of bills, and he'd been forced to "gather" money from friends and neighbors to get them turned on again. His mortgage payments were delinquent, his wife was working two days a week, and he had to pull one of his daughters out of school to tend to him and one small child.

Did all this amount to an intentional infliction of emotional distress whose elements are a defendant's outrageous conduct manifesting an intention of causing or reckless disregard of the probability of causing emotional distress which causes the plaintiff's severe or extreme emotional distress? You bet it did.

The jury awarded Fletcher not only $60,000 in compensatory damages but substantial punitive damages as well—$10,000 against Amason, and $640,000 against Western National, for a total of $710,000. For the moment it seemed justice was done.

But the trial judge conditionally granted Western National's motion for a new trial on the ground of excessive damages. In effect, he gave Fletcher a choice—go to trial again and risk losing, or accept a total of $250,000. On the advice of his lawyers, who were afraid "to shoot crap again," Fletcher agreed to the reduction.

Western National appealed. On appeal the company conceded its conduct had been intentional or reckless and outrageous. But it maintained that it was privileged inasmuch as it was part of a settlement negotiation.

The California appellate court, quoting standard textbook language, said: "Complete emotional tranquility is seldom attainable in this world, and some degree of transient and trivial emotional distress is a part of the price of living among people. The law intervenes only where the distress inflicted is so severe that no reasonable man could be expected to endure it. The intensity and duration of the distress are factors to be considered in determining its severity. . . . Severe emotional distress must be of such substantial quantity or enduring quality that no reasonable man in a civilized society should be expected to endure it."

Had this strong but "not overly articulate" man Fletcher, with only a fourth-grade education, suffered enough to warrant collecting? As the court said, "It would not appear unreasonable that a person with a prior history of industry and concern for his family would suffer substantial emotional distress in the nature of brief humiliation, embarrassment, chagrin, disappointment and worry as a result of these occurrences."

In the court's view, the insurance company had breached a duty to Fletcher. "An insurer owes to its insured an implied-in-law duty of good faith and fair dealing that it will do nothing to deprive the insured of the benefits of the policy. Included within this duty in the case of a liability insurance policy is the *duty to act reasonably and in good faith to settle claims* against the insured by a third person."

And so, in a ground-breaking opinion, the court held that "actual bad faith refusals to make payments under the policy," coupled with "false and threatening communications directed to plaintiff for the purpose of causing him to surrender his policy or disadvantageously settle a nonexistent dispute . . . is conduct that may legally be the basis for damages for intentional infliction of emotional distress."

Scolding the insurance company, the court said, "The very risks insured against presuppose that if and when a claim is made, the insured will be disabled and in strait financial circumstances and, therefore, particularly vulnerable to oppressive tactics on the part of an economically powerful entity."

And so the appellate court affirmed the $250,000 reduced award. And the insurance company, after some further resistance, paid every cent of it. And what of Amason? Had he realized the error of his ways? Had he realized the basic unfairness of destroying a human being in return for a giant corporation's $50,000 saving to which it was not entitled? No, on the contrary. At the time of trial, Amason was still claims manager, and testified that he would act the same way in a similar situation.

This sad tale is not an isolated instance. Its happy ending also has been repeated. Many deserving claimants have fought back and won.

ADJUSTMENT SWINDLES

Mrs. Frances Neal was paralyzed in a car crash caused by an uninsured motorist. Unfortunately her medical payments coverage was for only $5,000 and her uninsured motorist insurance coverage was for a maximum of $15,000. Farmers Insurance Exchange delayed paying her for three months when she desperately needed money, and then paid only $5,000, contesting the remainder. Eight months later when a family friend, a lawyer, begged the company for a prompt settlement, as Mrs. Neal's son had contracted cancer, major surgery had taken place, and heavy medical expenses were imminent, Farmers delayed several more months and offered to settle for an additional $5,000.

Meanwhile, Mrs. Neal herself died of cancer, and her husband sued. The lawyer made a highly emotional appeal to the jury, continually contrasting the suffering and tragedy which had befallen the Neals with the vast wealth of the insurance company. And guess what the jury did to the company for having delayed its $15,000 payment? It awarded Mr. Neal over $1.5 million—one hundred times the original claim. The trial judge cut it in half, to $749,011.48. And there it remained, all the way up through the California supreme court, which affirmed it.

You might be interested to read an excerpt from Farmers' "Claims Representative Field Manual." It may not be unrepresentative of the industry:

> It is important for the claims representative to learn how to sense opportune times for settlement. This will apply whether or not claimant is represented by an attorney. Such things as a marriage or death in the family, the purchase of a home or automobile will present the ordinary claimant with a financial situation which will suggest to him the advisability of getting his money out of his claim. If the injury is such that

settlement may be tactfully approached, the claims representative should follow through with appropriate discussion.

In its final paragraph the manual concludes that "the psychology of settlement negotiations is a study in itself."

THE MEANING OF "ALL RISK" COVERAGE
There is a very successful contractor in Bridgeport, Connecticut, named Gene DeMatteo. He loves boats. Several years ago he traded in a nearly new motor launch for one of the first Chris Craft Roamer yachts to come off the assembly line. Named the *Counterpoint,* the yacht was specially designed by Chris Craft with engines by Detroit Diesel, a division of General Motors. Who could ask for anything more? Not Mr. DeMatteo. He happily paid $230,000 over and above the trade-in value of his previous boat.

The *Counterpoint* was a disaster from the word go. It was months late reaching completion, and once under way, its troubles were so numerous as to be almost comical. The first year, it spent 232 days under repair in shipyards. There was hardly a repair yard up and down the Inland Waterway that didn't know her. A shakedown cruise attracted such celebrities as the famous actor and former United States Senator from California George Murphy, as well as some of DeMatteo's customers. Imagine his chagrin, then, when just a matter of minutes underway, the fancy new Roamer blew an engine and had to limp back to port. Thus it went for two or three years. At first, Chris Craft was cooperative. Then the company stopped honoring its warranties, as did Detroit Diesel. DeMatteo, seething by then, sued Chris Craft and Detroit Diesel in federal court, alleging a defective and unseaworthy product. On July 3, 1976, DeMatteo and some key customers were standing on a dock, awaiting the *Counterpoint*'s arrival in New York to participate in "Op Sail," when he received instead a message that it had sunk off Cape May, New Jersey.

Now, obviously, when DeMatteo bought the boat, he insured it. This was done through the local agent of INA of Philadelphia, one of the biggest marine insurers in the world. It was insured for

$300,000. When the boat sank, a claim was made to INA, which politely responded that the "check was in the mail." In fact, INA went so far as to request a photographed ceremony of DeMatteo receiving the check—as soon as it arrived. All this time DeMatteo and his staff were cooperating with INA about the details of the past troubles with Chris Craft and Detroit Diesel—including the lawsuit he had filed. Months later, after DeMatteo had given all the information the company could extract from him, the envelope presumably containing the check for $300,000 finally arrived. DeMatteo shook it, expecting the check to slide out. But, lo and behold, instead of a check, out came a letter disclaiming liability, and saying that INA would not pay the $300,000 or any part of it because of the boat's history of troubles.

I heard this story over the breakfast table in the kitchen at Greenwich, Connecticut, where I live and work, one Sunday morning. Gene, of course, wanted to sue INA on the policy, and also move the case against Chris Craft and Detroit Diesel for the pre-sinking problems. He wanted me to represent him, despite the fact I had not previously tried an admiralty case. I agreed to try both cases.

The insurance-policy case was tried first. The judge was Federal Judge Milton Pollack, one of the most capable, no-nonsense trial judges in America. A case that takes a month before some other judges takes three days before Judge Pollack. He doesn't permit lawyers to waste hours arguing objections and having "bench conferences." He permits them to say two words: "I object." Then he rules, and thereby gives the lawyer the benefit of any ground for objection that might conceivably be available. In short, he just stops him from talking it to death. Another of Judge Pollack's long suits is guts. He is the judge who put an end to the ban on the Concorde landing in New York. His judgment was quickly vindicated when the noise tests showed that 707s made more noise on landing than did the Concorde.

We end this section as it began—because Judge Pollack's skeptical questions to the insurance company were very much like the colloquy of the New Jersey supreme court. When the evidence showed that INA had voluntarily waived its right to inspect the boat time after time, that DeMatteo had spared no effort or expense to repair the infirmities, and that the insurance company not only accepted his premium money each year but actually offered him higher coverage, Judge Pollack exploded. His thesis was simple: You took the insured's money for premiums for years, the boat sank, and now you don't want to pay. The top admiralty firm opposing tried to rely on the "exclusions"—about the sinking having to be from an "external cause," whatever that is. Judge Pollack, as did the Jersey judges, looked above the "fine print" and saw the words "All risk" coverage. "All risk" meant just that to him.

Judge Pollack rendered judgment in full for Gene DeMatteo —the $300,000 full value of the policy. The other side never went through with a threatened appeal—and that envelope with the check for $300,000 finally did arrive. We quickly and successfully moved to settle our suit against Chris Craft and Detroit Diesel, and with the guidance of another capable federal judge, Lawrence Pierce, we agreed on a figure, and Mr. DeMatteo received another check.

So watch out. Just because you pay your hard-earned money to make certain you will be protected if tragedy strikes doesn't mean that if tragedy strikes you will be protected. Your insurance company is supposed to deal with you fairly and in good faith. But if it doesn't, you must insist, sign nothing, stand up, and fight back. If you do, you may well win, big.

SMALL CLAIMS

If a person has a homeowner's policy and is getting a runaround, the law generally does not permit the costs of a suit against the insurance company to be tacked onto the recovery. For example, if I have a homeowner's loss, or a collision loss on my car, of $1,000, totally legitimate, and my insurance company is horsing me around, nitpicking, hinting that the claim is inflated, and offering to settle for $700, and if I go to a lawyer and ask for relief, the lawyer will take anywhere from one-third to one-half. So if I go to court and win the $1,000 to which I'm entitled, after I pay my lawyer, I end up with between $500 and $700. I'm forced, therefore, to accept my insurance company's $700 offer on a legitimate $1,000 claim, or to go it without a lawyer. The only redress in this situation is a complaint to the insurance department or resort to a small claims court.

Small claims courts used to be known as plaintiff's courts. But plaintiffs misused them by taking major corporations to court for $100, say, on the theory that the corporations would not expend their resources to defend piddling suits. Because of the volume of such litigation and the aggregate threat it posed, corporations will now defend such suits with high-priced lawyers. Their credo has become "millions for defense but not one cent for tribute."

So in most cases today, the corporations will no longer offer you a settlement just to save the time. They'd rather pay their lawyers. Moreover, it's difficult to recover punitive damages unless you can show an intentional or wanton mistreatment.

BROKERS

Most people deal with insurance brokers who don't protect them —who care only about their own commissions. There are valuable amendments to auto insurance policies, for instance, which increase your coverage for peanuts, but which your broker doesn't tell you about because they're not worth peanuts to him in commissions. Take, for example, the uninsured motorist provision. Presently, in New York and other states, every auto policy has a mandatory $10,000 provision. What that means is that if you get into an accident with a hit-and-run vehicle or someone who is uninsured, you are allowed to claim against your own insurance up to $10,000. You may have $100,000 or $300,000 in insurance protection against injuring somebody else, but when you're the one who is hurt, you're protected only up to $10,000. That's obviously absurd—it violates the basic principle of insurance that you be equally wealthy in every reasonably likely contingency.

For $15 or $20 a year, you can protect yourself up to the same limit as your protection against injuring someone else. There's also an amendment which protects you from the "underinsured" driver who injures you, which will make up the difference, up to some specified limit, between what s/he has in coverage and the actual cost of your injuries. But agents don't tell you about these amendments. It's easier for them to sell you your liability insurance; it covers you against *your* collision and that's it.

The same thing is true with brokers' treatment of homeowner's policies. In many states, insurance companies offer homeowner's insurance that compensates you for actual replacement value, rather than for cost less depreciation. This is a recent change. With inflation rates soaring, and depreciation allowances so large, if, for example, you buy a piece of furniture for $1,000 and insure it, and two years later a chandelier falls on it and destroys it, you're lucky under a cost-less-depreciation calculation to get paid half the money needed to replace it. You complain, but the insurance company shows you the fine print. Replacement-value insurance adjusts for inflation. And it's not much more expensive to buy. But, once again, insurance agents don't make you aware of the option, because it's extra work for them without much of an extra commission and they'd prefer to work off standard-form volume.

PROTECTING PERSONAL VALUABLES

In recovering for lost or stolen valuables, documentation is crucial. Before insuring each valuable item, an appraisal should be made, and a photograph of it should be taken. You need a professional appraiser, but they are not expensive. You do not need a professional photographer. Simply take all your jewelry, lay it on black velvet and, using slide film, take a photograph. Do the same for sterling, china, paintings, rugs, valuable furniture. If necessary, these slides can be blown up. Lock them in your safe-deposit box and forget about them. If you don't have a safe-deposit box, give them to a friend to hold.

You should have periodic appraisals made of valuable property. Many women have engagement rings which twenty or thirty years ago were appraised at $2,000 or so and today are worth more than $10,000. Without recent reappraisals, they could not possibly collect anything approaching the actual worth of the jewelry. A person who works for years to buy a ring and loses it, who is a W-2 employee who could never afford to replace it, may suffer a serious material lifelong loss. For him or her, insurance is wise and rational.

If you suffer a loss, contact your insurance company, and remember advice previously given. Sign nothing. It might be a release of your claim. Accept no check—same possibility. And make no statement of the facts until you have consulted an attorney and/or knowledgeable friend.

In certain circumstances, you may choose not to insure and instead to take the gamble. This may be a wise and rational decision for some people, if they make it consciously and knowingly. But to leave yourself vulnerable against a loss you cannot withstand is not to be your own best friend.

If you're not insured, however, in the United States there's one advantage. You can always deduct losses from fire or theft as a straight deduction from income on your income tax.

6.
TRAVEL

FROM OUTER space, the world must look like a beehive; things and people perpetually in motion. Whatever moves our hearts and minds, airlines, railroads, ships, trucks and buses move our bodies and possessions. Trade and travel all over the world is exploding. In business, in daily life, we depend so often without realizing it on things traveling on time without damage. And of all the precious things we move, the most precious are ourselves and our loved ones.

We travelers are of two types. In the last decades there has arisen a class of global commuters for whom oceans are merely hours in the schedule. In recent years, as my clients have become more mobile and scattered, I've been forced to join this class. Traveling means different things to different people—for some it's the pace of daily life, while for others, 355 days is the price to be paid for the once-a-year ten-day trip. But even for the business traveler, there remain places to go and trips to take for the rest and pleasure of going to and fro and being there. So, however much a person travels, he treasures the time set aside for "getting away." Yes, more of us are traveling more, and complaining more often about getting ripped off. The causes of disappointment are several, and preventive moves are diverse, but one culprit above all seems an always ready ally to ruin our times and compound our losses. And that obnoxious creature is—"the fine print."

FINE PRINT

Wherever you look, or don't look, somebody's designed fine print to strip you of your rights. Walking through a park and resting on a bench? Chances are there's some fine print on the underside that the Parks Department is not responsible for splinters, muggers, and bird droppings. Fine print does seem to be everywhere: on the face or back (or sometimes tucked inside) airline, bus or railroad tickets, or claims checks, on shavers, on cars, everywhere.

All this fine print is not there to give us any meaningful clue as to what is going on, nor is it written in tiny legalese because space is at a premium. What's it all about?

The legal theory of fine print is simple. With a very few exceptions two people can agree to just about any contract—they can allocate risks any way they choose—and courts generally will force each party to fulfill its side of the bargain. Therefore a carrier, hotel, manufacturer, etc. designs an agreement whereby it gets our money, usually up front, and in return promises in fine print to do much less than we would reasonably expect. That way, if necessary, with the aid of a magnifying glass, they can later point to qualifications in our "agreement" which oblige us to pay up but do not require them to deliver. But this is only half the function of fine print. The other half is often the more important. Not only does fine print enable them to disguise how little we're getting for our money; it also enables them to minimize their own liability in case they should foul up as to the tiny promises they actually have made. Manufacturers, storage companies and airlines most of all fear liability for the consequences to you from their negligent failure to do as they promised. Some airlines head the list of fine printers.

If necessary, airlines can tolerate refunding your money, but adverse consequences which flow from their foul-ups range from inconvenience and embarrassment to financial ruin and loss of life or limb. Above all, they don't want to make your troubles their troubles; so, in fine print, they disclaim "consequential damages."

The United States is a great country. It is a vital part of a free-enterprise system which essentially respects people's rights freely and intelligently to enter into contracts which the legal system will enforce. But in reality few people read the fine print and fewer still understand the microscopic legalese in which it is written. There has been no meaningful bargaining over the terms of the contract, and not only are you offered goods and services on a take-it-or-leave-it basis, you also have very little idea what it is you are taking. My philosophy is that those who are big enough to operate airlines and hotels can afford the theft and loss insurance necessary to protect us, the consumers, from their mistakes.

On their part they will trot out the black-and-white fine print. But you can fight back. The greatness of our system includes the fact that often the black and white is overcome by the red, white and blue.

TRANSPORTING US AND OURS

All concerned agreed that the death of Sir Michael Robert was tragic and avoidable. Northwest Airlines conceded that Michael had been worth a substantial sum and that in transporting him they had negligently caused his death. But the airline had erected three separate lines of defense to shield itself from claims by angry people like the Klickers, who sought to palliate their grief over the loss of their prize golden retriever.

The outer defense, the perimeter to be scaled before the airline would pay anything, was its standard fine-print rule, by which it sought to exempt itself entirely from any liability for the "loss, death, or sickness" of any live animal it transported. A court brushed this disclaimer aside, characterizing it as "void against public policy." * The Klickers had tried to buy a seat for Michael but Northwest forced them to ship him as baggage. With its outer defense having fallen, Northwest was going to pay something for its negligence in killing Michael, but how much?

---

* The Civil Aeronautics Board—CAB—in 1975 finally outlawed tariff provisions "which purport to exculpate carriers from liability for their own negligence in the carriage of live animals as baggage."

Next came barrier two: the $500 ceiling, which Northwest routinely placed on its own liability for loss or damage of "any personal property, including baggage . . . unless the passenger at the time of presenting such property for transportation, when checking in for a flight, has declared a higher value and paid . . . an additional transportation charge."

Let's pause for a moment in this story. This is an important theme that crops up again and again in fine-print situations. Where they limit their liability unless *you* choose to pay extra, if the item is worth more to you than the ceiling, *pay the few cents extra to insure it at a higher rate*. If they offer extra insurance to you, take them up on it!

Had the Klickers actually paid a higher transportation charge? Yes and no. Northwest had forced them to send Michael not only as baggage, but as excess baggage, not counted in their allowed weight. Therefore they did pay extra for him as excess baggage. In addition Northwest had demanded and received from them twice the ordinary excess baggage charge to ship the dog. So, yes, the Klickers had paid well above the minimum to ship Michael. But above and beyond all these extra charges they had not paid specifically to raise the $500 ceiling. Was this failure the Klickers' oversight, which, while making us feel sorry for them, also makes it fair to hold to the $500 mini-maximum? No! Informed of Michael's $35,000 value, Northwest refused to allow the Klickers to declare it or pay additional charges on that basis. Having been denied an opportunity to raise the ceiling, the Klickers now raised the roof.

The court kicked aside Northwest's mini-maximum of $500 and assumed for the purposes of its decision that the Klickers had insured Michael to the limits of ordinary excess baggage. Having scaled two Northwest disclaimers—first that of any liability, and second of any more than $500 liability—were the Klickers finally free to collect the full market value of their lost animal? Not quite. One more wall: The airlines have a ceiling to cover all property whatsoever. Northwest absolutely refused to "accept for transportation or for storage personal property, including baggage, the declared value of which exceeds $5,000."

This barrier held: The federal trial court awarded the Klickers $5,000, one-seventh the value of Michael. Both sides appealed.

All three defense barriers automatically popped up again to be attacked on appeal. In its 1977 decision, the federal appeals court once again kicked aside Northwest's first line of defense, the complete disclaimer:

> A carrier who stipulates not to be bound to the exercise of care and diligence "seeks to put off the essential duties of his employment." It is recognized that the carrier and the individual customer are not on an equal footing. The latter cannot afford to haggle or stand out and seek redress in the courts.

In holding that a common carrier could not totally disclaim liability for loss caused by its own negligence, the Ninth Circuit Court of Appeals rejected as "flatly wrong" contrary decisions of other federal appeals courts supporting such airline disclaimers. Instead, this court wholeheartedly adopted the dissenting views of the brilliant New York Federal Appeals Judge Jerome Frank, who in an earlier case would have disallowed Eastern Airlines from fine-printing away all liability for negligently mishandled baggage containing jewelry.

Next the court swept aside Northwest's rule requiring additional payments for anything in excess of $500. It had "no application because the airline refused to permit the Klickers to declare a valuation of their dog." As the court said:

> Carriers may partially limit their liability for injury, loss, or destruction of baggage on a "released valuation" basis, whereby in exchange for a low carriage rate, the passenger shipper is deemed to release the carrier from liability beyond a stated amount. The released valuation limitations bind the passenger-shipper to the restriction on liability, however, only if he has notice of the rate structure and is given the opportunity to pay the higher rate in order to obtain greater protection.

Finally the court reached the last defense, which had held up at the lower court level: the airline's refusal to accept baggage the "*declared value* of which exceeds $5,000." The emphasis was that of the appellate court, which kicked open the final door to full recovery. "By its own terms, this rule cannot apply to the Klickers because the airline refused to permit any declared valuation for their dog. If the airline erred in accepting the animal, the responsibility for the mistake falls on the airline, not on the innocent shipper." Otherwise, obvious injustice would have been done. Although in black and white Northwest seemed to have the Klickers "dead to rights," when the Klickers fought back, the black and white yielded to the red, white and blue.

Although in death Sir Michael Robert netted the Klickers a substantial sum because the airline negligently shipped him, Agnes Blair's remains turned out not to net her husband Graham very much at all. Graham sued Delta Airlines for physical damage to the casket, for the cost of attempted restoration of his wife's dead body and for great mental anguish. He claimed Delta had been grossly negligent in loading and unloading the shipment in the rain. Delta's standard rule: unless baggage was paid for at a higher rate for a higher declared valuation, liability was limited to 50 cents a pound. Graham had not paid extra for Agnes' flight. The court held, therefore, that "since Mr. Blair did not declare a higher value, the 'shipment'—casket and remains of Mrs. Blair weighing 265 pounds—even if negligently damaged by Delta could be worth at most $132.50." The court concluded that "for purposes of disposition of this case, a box of human remains is not significantly different from any other piece of freight." And "even if it were different, the same legal principles are applicable to such box as would be applicable to any other pieces of freight or cargo."

Not that we always love the remains we ship. While on patrol, David Gibson, a wildlife officer with the Florida Game and Fresh Water Fish Commission, was scratched by a raccoon. Gibson turned the raccoon over to the local health department, which packaged the head and shipped it via Greyhound Bus to Jacksonville for rabies testing. Typically, Greyhound's standard carriage contract limited its liability to $50 for any package under 100 pounds unless a higher tariff was paid. None was paid. The head got lost. Greyhound was notified for the first time of the significance of the package; even so, Greyhound refused to trace it.

Gibson had to undergo a painful series of rabies injections and suffered an adverse reaction, causing him "suffering, anxiety, and emotional distress." Gibson sued. To understand how to fight back we need to know a little black-letter law. Earlier in this section, I mentioned that merchants want to avoid all liability for adverse consequences caused by their negligence in failing to perform contracts. A person injured by the other party's negligent failure to perform as promised can sue under two different fields of law: contract, and tort.

Under a contract theory, the question will be what the parties have agreed to, including limitations of liability in the event of a failure to perform. Tort, however, is injury *independent* of a contract. For there to be a tort, in general there must be a legal duty to act in a certain way, a breach of that duty, and a damage or injury as a proximate result of that breach. Traditionally courts have been unwilling to allow for consequential damages in contract actions. As we'll see, this is changing. Entirely apart from any contract, if someone intentionally or negligently injures you by violating his duty toward you, you may be able to collect in tort for your pain and suffering.

Back to David Gibson, wildlife officer, suffering the effects of rabies shots because Greyhound negligently lost the head that bit him. Gibson sought to hold Greyhound responsible under its contract and for the tort of intentional infliction of mental distress. Citing *Blair* v. *Delta,* the court denied recovery beyond the $50 because the extra insurance hadn't been paid. Did Greyhound's refusal to trace the package after being informed as to the consequences of its loss show a "wanton disregard" for Gibson's welfare? No, the court said. "While it may have been considered good business for Greyhound to trace the package, not doing so did not amount to outrageous conduct." This highly debatable statement was followed by another which was either irrelevant or a non sequitur: "If no special duty of care attached to the shipment prior to its loss, it would not be fair to allow one to be imposed afterwards." Once again, the lesson is to declare a higher valuation and pay extra to insure it. You'll not only increase your payoff should they lose it, you'll put the carrier on notice as to the cargo's importance to you and make it more likely it ends up where it's supposed to.

These may seem like unusual cases, but they happen. The more usual mishap concerns luggage checked on airlines. Some people can go through a lifetime without losing a bag checked through on a plane. Others frequently are on the victim's list. Unfortunately I've fallen into the latter category.

Some years ago, on my first trip to Greece, I was to join friends on a boat at Figliomeni port in Athens. All my luggage was lost on the New York–Athens flight. After a few quick purchases, we set sail and returned to Athens a week later. Sure enough, the luggage had been retrieved—that is, what was left of it. The clothing bag was shredded. Anyway, with some reluctance but encouraged by the philosophy that lightning doesn't strike twice in the same place, we rechecked the luggage through to the next stop— Nice. On arrival, I rented an Avis car, and opened the trunk, waiting for a friend who was to pick up my luggage. He appeared and signaled me that the luggage was lost again! I thought he was putting me on. He wasn't; the luggage was gone a second time. They wanted me to fill out all sorts of forms—you know, where you draw a picture of the missing suitcases, etc. This time again, as it turned out, I got my luggage back—after having bought a second new set of clothes, for which I billed the airline. Since the amounts were not that great and the bags had been retrieved, we arrived at a satisfactory settlement, which may be the most unusual fact of all.

INTERNATIONAL CARRIERS. On international flights, the "fine print" is known as the "Warsaw Convention." It is remarkable how so many different countries which agree on little else have managed to unite in sharply limiting their own liability to the traveler for loss of life or luggage.

It seems to me that if a left-wing banana dictator in Panama can get the United States to hand over the canal it built and paid for, surely the innocent traveler should be able to get the full value of his loss from whatever carrier. The analogy fails to impress some of my liberal friends, but they cry the loudest of all when they lose their bags.

Let's take a look at some specific provisions of this international skyway ripoff known as the Warsaw Convention. First of all, by its own terms it "shall apply to all international transportation of persons, baggage, or goods performed by aircraft for hire." Much of it concerns the documents that the airlines have to fill out. But the interesting part is Chapter III—Liability of the Carrier.

Having sanctimoniously declared that an airline definitely *is* liable for loss of life, limb and luggage, the Warsaw Convention goes on to limit that liability for loss of life to $75,000 (including legal fees)—not a princely sum until you consider that as of 1965 the maximum was $16,600. (The United States government unilaterally threatened to dishonor the convention unless liability was increased to $75,000. Thus this increase applies only to flights which begin, end, or stop at some point in the United States.) The baggage liability limit of 1965—$20 a kilogram, or about $9 a pound —remains, however, unchanged. (There is one source of hope in all this. The convention actually pegs liability limits to the French franc, which it defines as "consisting of 65½ milligrams of gold at the standard fineness of nine hundred thousands." It goes on to provide that "these sums may be converted into any national currency in round figures." It seems to me that if the price of gold soars high enough, we may yet be adequately compensated. Long before this happens they'll probably change the rules.)

My education on how to beat this international conspiracy against secure possession of one's property all started in Sri Lanka, formerly known as Ceylon. As long as you avoid its summer monsoon season, Sri Lanka is a beautiful and inexpensive country to visit. I'll never forget what happened when one of my law partners, Tom Bolan, and I were at a little hotel there and were rushing to catch a helicopter flight. We gave the desk clerk an American Express card; the sign of its acceptance was prominently displayed. The clerk disappeared inside the hotel office, and didn't come out for what seemed an eternity. Tom and I finally knocked on the door, and walked into the office. There was the poor fellow poring over Amexco's book-length list of stolen and revoked credit cards. He looked up and told us that he was unable to accept the charge because he couldn't find the name on the card on the list! I've often wondered how many people with stolen cards have been the guests of the management!

Anyway, back to "fine print." On this trip, I had violated my own rule of never checking luggage because Tom Bolan had already decided to check his. Our plane set down at the Colombo airport and we went inside to watch the luggage being unloaded. When the process was about halfway completed, there was great commotion on the airfield. Marching bands appeared, replete with colorful flags. Another plane set down; photographers pushed forward, as did Sri Lankan dignitaries. On inquiry, we learned that the president of some African country had arrived on a state visit. How did this affect my life? Well, when all the commotion started, our airline decided to stop unloading luggage, and to take off for the next stop, Singapore, which by coincidence is where I am writing this particular chapter. I never saw any of my luggage again.

Here began a correspondence between the airline and myself. I was in perfect shape because the luggage was new and so were most of the clothes, etc., and I knew their exact replacement values. I sent the airline a list and asked for a check. As expected, its reply was the Warsaw Convention baloney, and an offer of the maximum amount of $400, which was well below my replacement cost. I replied by letter that either they pay every penny of the loss or I would be happy to make up for some past sins by serving humanity in suing the airline, and doing everything I could to knock out the self-imposed limitation on liability—Warsaw Convention or no Warsaw Convention. I still don't know if I'm pleased or not that my "scare" tactic prevailed. I was paid in full. But it doesn't always work that way. Sometimes you must go to court.

Not all courts are in love with the Warsaw International Skyway Ripoff. Consider the fate of Nasrollah Maghsoudi, on his way to Iran with mastertapes he hoped would someday top the charts of Tehran. Maghsoudi bought an around-the-world ticket from Pan Am and left Honolulu for Iran via a stopover in London. He did not declare excess value of his tapes nor pay a surcharge.

Maghsoudi arrived in London, but his suitcase didn't join him; so he put in a claim for $6,190, valuing his master tapes at $5,400. He waited around London for a few days, hoping for the return of his suitcase, and then flew on without it to Iran.

Four months later he got a letter from Pan Am asking for his baggage claim check and his ticket. He duly sent off copies. (Rule: Always keep *all* documents from any flight in which there is a dispute, including boarding passes, unused meal vouchers, etc. Rule: Always, always send copies; never, never send originals.) At this time Maghsoudi informed Pan Am that the loss of his tapes had rendered his trip to Iran worthless, and requested that his claim be settled for $6,190 plus another round-trip ticket to Iran.

Two months later he received a letter from Pan Am conceding the loss of his suitcase and enclosing a check for $400 in complete satisfaction of his claim. (Whenever you receive these paltry checks in "full satisfaction of the claim" do not cash them. Some people like to cross out the "full satisfaction" statement before cashing them, figuring they preserve their options to sue for more later. Your position is stronger, however, if you refuse entirely to cash the check.) Maghsoudi had had enough.

In January 1979 he filed suit in Hawaii. Iran by this time was in turbulence, shattering his dreams of success. He sued for damages in the amount of $192,790: $7,790 in actual damages, $50,000 for emotional distress and mental anguish, $100,000 for lost income because of the political changes in Iran and the remainder for punitive damages, costs, attorney's fee, and so on.

What of the Warsaw Ripoff? Well, for once the tables turned

and Pan Am got snared by its own fine print. "Because the Warsaw Convention was drafted with a bias in favor of the air carriers," the court would apply it only when its provisions had been *strictly* complied with by the airlines. Pan Am had failed to record the weight of the luggage on the claim check and tickets as required by the convention. Pan Am therefore couldn't adopt its limits.

Did this mean that the ascent of the ayatollah had netted Maghsoudi a cool $200,000? Hardly. With the Warsaw Ripoff not applying, liability would be determined under state rules. In computing actual damages, the court noted two legal principles which generally apply and which it is wise to keep in mind, in order to prepare to fight back:

1. Where two parties have made a contract which one of them has broken, as a result the other party ought to receive such damages as would be expected to arise "in the usual course of things" or such damages as were in the contemplation of *both* parties at the time they made the contract.

2. Where there are special circumstances in a contract and its observance would take the contract out of the natural or usual course of things, *damages* which result from *special circumstances* are recoverable if, and only if, those special circumstances were communicated or *known to* the *party breaching* the contract *at the time* he *entered* into the contract.

Occasionally there will be exceptions to these rules, but usually they will be enforced. So, if you are contracting, and you know there is something special about your needs, or you are particularly relying on the other person to perform his part of the agreement, let him know in writing at the time of the agreement the degree to which you are relying on him, and all expected dire consequences resulting from his failure to perform as promised. Occasionally this will scare off the other party. But that's probably just as well, although not always. More often than not, however, another person who has just promised to perform will be willing formally to be put on notice as to how important it is to you that he perform as promised. (Somehow this rule doesn't usually apply to marriage contracts, but I've already discussed those in an earlier chapter.) The point is, put the other on notice of your special needs *at the time* you make the agreement. Otherwise telling him later how much you really needed him to perform will not help.

Let's continue with some other ways around the Warsaw International Ripoff. We've seen that one way out for a sympathetic judge is to set aside the Warsaw Convention when the airline does not record "all the particulars set out" in the other rules. Then, as the convention itself says (Article 9), "the carrier shall not be entitled to avail himself of the provisions of this convention which exclude or limit his liability." There is yet another loophole (Article 25): "The *carrier* shall *not* be *entitled to* avail himself of the provisions of *this convention* which exclude or limit his liability, *if* the *damage is caused by his willful misconduct*" or by such default which by local standards is "equivalent to willful misconduct."

In July 1974, Charles and Hermaine Cohen, husband and wife, were on a twenty-eight-day tour of South America. They had departed from New York on an itinerary which included Bogotá, Lima, Asunción, Iguassu Falls, Rio de Janeiro, Manaus, Belém, Paramaribo, Georgetown, and the return flight to New York. On July 18 they boarded a Varig Airlines flight supposedly bound for Rio de Janeiro. After takeoff they learned that their flight would first stop in São Paulo, Brazil, and they would be transferred to another flight which would take them on to Rio.

When they landed in São Paulo, the Cohens expressed concern to the Varig agents that their luggage might not be loaded on the connecting flight to Rio. They were assured that everything was being taken care of. The agent left the waiting area, went out to the airfield and on his return told them he "had personally seen to it" that their luggage was actually placed on the flight.

When they arrived at Rio, they and the other passengers were informed that everyone had to board a bus which would carry them to another aircraft which would fly all of the passengers on to New York.

But the Cohens were not continuing to New York. They so informed the Varig representative in charge, were told to stay on the bus and were driven to the terminal building. When they asked about their luggage, they were directed to the baggage receiving area, where they waited; but no baggage. After a while, when it became obvious that their baggage wasn't coming, they protested to various Varig personnel, including Varig's lost-and-found agent, who couldn't locate it. When the final boarding announcement was made for all passengers bound for New York, Cohen, by this time quite indignant, demanded that his luggage be removed from the New York–bound plane. Varig's personnel refused and told him that they "would not go to the expense of unloading the plane" for him. The Cohens were told that the plane would be returning from New York City in two days and they could get their luggage back at that time. Mr. Cohen explained that they were leaving the next morning for Manaus, Brazil, that they had eighteen days left on their tour, which was taking them to the Amazon jungle and Georgetown, Guyana, where they had friends and expected to be entertained.

Cohen told the agent that he and his wife had no clothes other than those they were wearing, and the agent was once again asked to go out to the plane and get the luggage. Again he refused: "We will not do it. You will get it back on Saturday morning." The plane took off for New York. The Cohens' luggage was never seen again.

The next morning, according to schedule, they flew to Manaus, where they were unable to buy ready-made clothes which fit them, and after two days they left, again on schedule, for their journey by ship down the Amazon.

During the remainder of their trip they suffered the physical discomfort of being without their clothing and personal effects, including water-purification implements. They were distressed and embarrassed at being inappropriately dressed at prearranged affairs with dignitaries and friends of high social standing in the countries visited. For example, in Georgetown, at a dinner given in Mr. Cohen's honor, whose guest list included the Chief Justice, Cohen was forced to wear the same disheveled suit that he'd been traveling in. And, of course, his wife's predicament was no better. They had spent fruitless hours shopping for suitable clothing. Their trip had been seriously marred, if not ruined.

When the Cohens returned to New York, Varig had offered

them $640 in addition to $60 originally given to tide them over. When they protested, Varig's regional general manager replied: "Did you expect us to unload a whole plane just for the two of you? We don't do that." The Cohens fought back.

They sued Varig in New York civil court. After a trial without a jury, the court ruled that while ordinarily the Warsaw Convention would have limited the claims for lost baggage on this international flight to the $700 Varig had offered, the airline's refusal to unload the Cohens' baggage amounted to "willful misconduct" and therefore, by its own terms, the Warsaw Convention did not apply. The court awarded the Cohens $6,440.65, half for the value of their lost baggage and the other half for their physical inconvenience, discomfort and mental suffering.

The Cohens had won round one, but the fight was far from over. Varig appealed, and a divided appellate term knocked the award down to $700, denying that the airline's act amounted to willful misconduct under the Warsaw Convention. Round two to the airline.

Now the Cohens appealed to New York's intermediate appellate division. Each half of the trial court's original award which the Cohens sought to have reinstated presented a separate question. First, did the airline's refusal to unload the plane amount to "willful misconduct" so as to eliminate the $700 ceiling? And secondly, if the Cohens were to be reimbursed for the full value of their baggage, could they also collect for consequential damages from their lost baggage—their physical discomfort and mental anguish?

The appellate court first defined willful misconduct as "a conscious intent to do or omit doing an act from which harm results to another, or an intentional omission of a manifest duty. *There must be a realization of the probability of injury from the conduct, and a disregard of the probable consequences of such conduct.*" The burden of establishing willful misconduct rested on the Cohens. But by the fair preponderance of the evidence in this case, the Cohens had met their burden. As the court observed, the decision not to unload was motivated strictly by profit and loss and not by any doubt as to the whereabouts of the luggage. "The options available to Varig were either to satisfy its contractual obligations to plaintiffs, thereby incurring expense and perhaps delaying the flight, or insisting that plaintiffs take the loss. It chose the latter. The determination was purely a business one." Furthermore, Varig had full knowledge of the consequences of its inaction. Therefore the appellate court reinstated the trial court's award for the actual value of the lost luggage. First half of round three to the Cohens.

Then came question two: Were the Cohens entitled to collect for their mental distress, embarrassment, inconvenience, etc.? Were they entitled to collect for the *consequences* of Varig's willful misconduct? As you would suspect, airlines routinely attempt to insulate themselves entirely from any and all consequential damages. A fine-print disclaimer is part of almost every airline's tariff conditions. Varig's read that "carrier shall not be liable in any event for any consequential or special damages arising from carriage . . . whether or not carrier had knowledge that such damages might be incurred." (As of December 1979, under newly promulgated Civil Aeronautics Board regulations, air carriers may no longer disclaim all liability arising from negligence on the part of their employees.)

If you notice, the language quoted from the Warsaw Convention specifically referred only to consequences of "delay," and the Cohens' damages had resulted from lost luggage rather than delayed luggage. But this technicality did not deter the court: "Damage caused by delay, quite obviously, contemplates consequential loss. Neither law nor logic suggests any reason why plaintiff's damages should be any the less because their luggage was lost rather than delayed."

So, round three to the Cohens? Not quite. Although the convention posed no insuperable barrier to the Cohens' claim for consequential damages, the court felt constrained by the legal traditions of New York. "The law has been traditionally reluctant to extend its protection against the infliction of mental distress, even for intentionally inflicted wrongs. Courts, however, have been willing to allow damages where the mental anguish accompanies a slight physical injury." That's the rule in a nutshell. In New York you have to demonstrate some physical injury, however slight, to collect for mental anguish. States differ on this. And there are exceptions, recently in increasing numbers, even in New York. The New York courts have been willing lately to award for mental suffering unaccompanied by physical injury when a carrier's agent insults a passenger, or a hotelkeeper insults his guest. And, as we'll see in the section on torts, there are other exceptions. But here the traditional rule prevailed.

"Although the courts are at long last moving in the direction of recognizing one's interest to mental and emotional tranquility as an area entitled to legal protection, we know of no authority which sanctions a recovery against a carrier for mental distress and physical inconvenience where the gravamen of the wrongdoing is either loss or mishandling of luggage."

And so, although Varig's "callous disregard" for the Cohens' plight was "motivated by selfish economic interest and justifies a finding of willful misconduct under the provisions of the Warsaw Convention," the court found that "this is not the appropriate case for the award of special damages for physical inconvenience, discomfort, and mental anguish."

There were two dissents in this case. One would have limited the liability to the $700 Varig had offered: "The refusal to unload the 707 viewed in context with the surrounding circumstances is consistent with Varig's responsibility to the passengers on its New York bound flight."

The other dissent, by Justice Leonard Sandler, an outstanding jurist, would have reinstated the entire award, including the consequential damages, because there was willful misconduct coupled with specific and adequate notice as to the consequences. (It's unfortunate that the famous journalist William F. Buckley, Jr., didn't know the Cohens instead of the Cohns. In late 1980, when checking in for a Varig flight to Rio, he was given the astounding news that his excess baggage would cost close to three times the price of his first-class ticket. He switched to Eastern.)

The Cohens' attempt had partially succeeded. They did get

back the full value of their baggage. Some lessons can be learned from their story. Pay attention. Do not assume that the world is looking out for your best interests. The airlines have built impressive ticket counters and terminals magnificently constructed with electronic sensors, etc. But proper baggage handling still depends on human beings. If your situation is unusual, be aware where your baggage is, and make airline employees aware. Don't rely on your claim check. When airline employees refuse to accommodate your special needs, inform them several times, and in no uncertain terms, of the likely consequences of your damage. If you have a dictating machine with you, announce in front of them the expected consequences of their foulups and get one of them to acknowledge into the machine that he is on notice. Your composure and care in "making a future record" might well scare them into performing unpleasant expensive emergency acts to prevent your future suffering. Why? Not because they care how much you'll suffer, but because they'll be concerned about how much your suffering may cost them. Whenever someone is worrying about you, even from selfish motives, you've got the game half won.

By the way, before we leave the international-flight scene, I should mention that the Warsaw Ripoff's "willful misconduct" escape clause is not easy to raise successfully. For example, a Mr. Rymanowski arrived in Venezuela via Qantas and was to continue to San Juan on board Pam Am. A customs officer advised him that, although in transit, he would have to have his baggage inspected. This seemed odd to Rymanowski, who became suspicious and informed a Pan Am agent who was then checking him onto a San Juan flight. The agent took the customs receipt and assured Rymanowski that his baggage was on the plane, refusing to allow him to examine his own baggage. On arriving at San Juan, Rymanowski presented his baggage receipts; his baggage was gone. Pan Am invoked the Warsaw Ripoff and paid him $400. He argued Pan Am's "willful misconduct," and in an affidavit he swore that a Pan Am employee in Denver, Colorado, had informed him that "Pan Am at Caracas was notorious for bags disappearing" and that an unidentified official of an "official agency" had told him that there is much "corruption and collusion in this area of the Western Hemisphere." The court distinguished his situation from the Cohens' and invoked the Warsaw Ripoff.

HOW TO BEAT DISCLAIMERS Whether it's plane, bus or railway, the carriers have you coming and going, unless you're careful. To protect yourself, I repeat, pay the extra tariff. Paul Lovinger didn't, and when Greyhound Bus lost his color transparencies, recorded tapes and manuscripts which represented eleven years of work, the court invoked the *large-print* limits to its liability to $50 "unless a greater amount is declared in writing." Lovinger claimed he hadn't seen this provision, but the court rejected his claim: "Acceptance and use of the ticket sufficed to establish an agreement which limited carrier's liability." Again, this was large print which he had missed. And if you notice, on most airline tickets all the legalese about the Warsaw Ripoff is in tiny print and then again on another page there is a large-print disclaimer as to domestic flights.

Somehow United Airlines had failed to print the separate large-print disclaimer on the New York–San Francisco ticket of Bonnie Greenberg, a New York schoolteacher. She didn't read the fine print, whose bold large-print heading made it appear it applied solely to international flights. When the airline lost her baggage, it tried to limit its liability to $750, as provided in the tiny print. But the court rejected it, holding "a notice so elusive" cannot limit its liability. To be legally effective the airline's disclaimer "must be positioned and identified so as to penetrate the traveling public's reasonably focused consciousness. Instead the defendant has set before the traveler a morsel of nourishment hidden in a banquet of dust. Authority and principle combine to deny it effect."

The court therefore awarded Ms. Greenberg $1,869 for the value of her baggage and $80 for traveling to the San Francisco Airport for four days to recover her baggage, and reiterated that "inadequately communicated notice cannot alert a passenger to seek alternate protections such as insurance coverage." Again, the black and white was overcome by the red, white and blue.

This case teaches something else. You don't always need a lawyer. Bonnie Greenberg saved the expense by representing herself, and she didn't have an open-and-shut case. The problem is you don't want to have to go to court; it costs more than it's worth. Legal fees often eat up any recovery you might get. The airlines know that.

But this, too, is changing. P. W. Isaacs had checked three pieces of luggage with Delta on his trip from Atlanta to New York. He claimed to have received two pieces in New York. The value of the third, he alleged, was $750. Delta had limited its own liability to $500. But the airline refused to settle at all, vaguely hinting that it didn't believe Isaacs had really lost a bag, even though he still possessed the claim check. But Delta had no proof to the contrary, and if it thought Isaacs wouldn't bother to pay a lawyer's fee to sue for $500, they miscalculated. He sued, and the court awarded him the $500 *plus* $500 in attorneys' fees, saying that "a party may resist settlement of a claim without fear of future liability for attorney fees if the resistance is predicated upon a bona fide controversy. However, where a defendant has disclaimed *all* liability prior to litigation," a difference at trial as to how much was owed didn't justify their initial refusal to discuss a settlement.

Once again, a moral of these stories: Carriers can limit their own liability if there's a treaty to help them, or if they give you adequate notice and the choice to pay more in order to be paid more if the insured item never arrives or is damaged. If they'll allow you, declare the extra value and pay for it. If you've paid as much as you're allowed and your loss exceeds that amount, press your claim. Keep an active concern and awareness about your own situation. The law helps those who help themselves. Make your record; put the carrier on notice as to any damages that will flow from its error. Press your point with people in charge; deal with supervisors; get their names; record their statements. A pocket dictaphone will pay for itself if you use it only once to save your luggage or get paid for it. And remember, regardless of what the fine print says, regardless of what the agents say, if you know you were wronged and injustice is being done to you, fight back—you might well have a winning case. Most times you will want to avoid the expense of court, and knowing your legal rights will help you settle your claim at a fair figure. No matter what or how they have you on black and white, sometimes the red, white and blue controls.

One final word about this nagging problem with luggage. The best way I know to beat the baggage problem is to carry things on board. This applies to trips around the world as well as short hops. It applies to major airline carriers as well as to the minor ones. When I select luggage, I do so from the size standpoint, choosing luggage I can carry with me. Clothing bags are accepted as carry-on pieces, and if well designed with outside pockets, they hold a lot. Couple this with a large multi-zippered shoulder pack and a piece of flat luggage which fits under the seat, and you can be equipped for many days with what you've carried aboard. This is my standard set of luggage. Using it, I know I'll come home with what I departed with, and this method has the added bonus of saving lots of waiting time at airports for luggage. In international flights it also saves time going through customs. If you must have luggage checked, check it as late as possible: Last come, first served is the way it works in many major baggage departments.

TRIP TRAPS

There is much more to say about fine print in other situations, and I'll mention it elsewhere. But while we've found ourselves checking in our luggage, let's continue to take a trip and survey some major bumps in traveling to see if we can do anything to avoid them or at least to cushion the shock or smooth the way.

OVERBOOKING

Should we have booked our vacation with an agent? "Agency" denotes an entity acting on another's behalf. An agent does his master's bidding, carrying out commands. A travel agent is the agent of . . . whom? One indication of whom an agent really represents is who pays him. Do we? Yes and no. We don't directly pay him to make our arrangements; he gets his percentage from the suppliers. Whether or not we book through an agent, the price to us is the same. The agent's commission gets passed on to all travelers in their ticket prices, whether or not they use him.

A travel agent is also booking agent for hotels and airlines. He is not your agent. He is theirs, trying to sell you their travel goods and services. But a travel agent may be paid by so many different tour operators and charter organizations that, as an agent to all, he is an agent of none. Another caution: In most states travel agents are not licensed, which means they have not posted a bond guaranteeing they can pay judgments against them as a result of their foul-ups. Even in states where they are licensed, there is virtually no supervision. In New York, all it takes is $25 and "satisfactory proof of good moral character," which is to say all it takes is $25, for the agent to get his license.

Another protection for the public from unscrupulous agents is supposed to be their membership in NATA—the National Association of Travel Agents. But membership in an association is hardly a guarantee of honesty. This is no less true of lawyers and their bar associations, which we'll see later on.

Does this mean that you shouldn't use travel agents where at all avoidable? No, on the contrary, use agents! Your ticket price is paying for them; you might as well get your money's worth. An agent is a convenience and can perform many services. A good agent has "contacts" at the airlines which sometimes enable him to get you space on "booked-up" flights during peak travel times. And an agent can use his friends at airlines to handle emergency situations. So use a travel agent! If you try doing everything yourself, you'll end up with many hidden costs you couldn't anticipate.

An agent can also save you money because he can deal in blocks of seats and a number of bookings and thereby command lower prices from the hotels for tours. I have a certain sympathy for travel agents: Most of them operate on a very thin margin of profit. But, having said that, I hasten to add a word of caution. Never take a travel agent's word for anything. If you don't like the flight he's selected and he tells you it's the only one available at that hour, *you* call the airlines directly and check out the information. Often you'll find more convenient flights available, and sometimes you'll discover that the flight on which you're scheduled to travel has been discontinued or changed. Check carefully every hotel voucher to make sure the accommodations described are what you ordered. There's still no guarantee, as we'll see in a moment, that what you get is what you've been promised.

These are days of heavy competition and gimmickry in the travel business. There are charters, packages, tours. The advantage of a charter is price. If you book far enough in advance and as part of a group, you fly cheaper. But the most commonly registered travel complaint is the lack of refunds for canceled charter flights. Another major complaint concerns flight changes. The charter passenger seems to be low priority. I had a friend who got burned by one "charter" gimmick. As advertised, it was a real bargain fare in return for the traveler's "flexibility." You had to agree to be on call both leaving and returning during the charter trip's two-week period. You could leave anytime during week one and return anytime during week two. My friend hoped for a full two-week vacation but was willing to settle for a one-week vacation at bargain rates, and so he paid his money. Have you guessed what happened? He and his wife were flown out on a Saturday, the last day of week one, and returned the *next day,* the first day of week two. So much for the bargain. Sometimes it's worth the saving to fly charter, but there is a risk you'll be left with unpleasant memories.

A "package" is a vacation preassembled by someone else. You take it as it is. The disadvantage is that inevitably it will not suit your taste in some way. The wealthy look down their noses on these plans as the "polyester" of travel fabrications, but I have friends who have had good luck with low-cost package deals. They report no significant loss of freedom. You can go off on your own and do whatever you want, except choose your hotel. Don't confuse "package plans" with tours.

"Attention Group Z, your bus leaves in two minutes." "Today is Tuesday; this must be Belgium." All attest to the whirlwind experience of smoke-filled buses, crowded with people you can't stand, driven to insignificant out-of-the-way places with the lure of a "free" tropical drink, which you need by the time you get there. A tour can so cram a place into you that you miss the country for its "sights." Unless you're a sightseeing buff with a super-gregarious personality, forget tours. We're certainly not using one on this trip. Nor are we taking a charter flight.

AIRLINES. On the contrary, we book through our agent, pay full fare, show up at the airport a half hour before flight time with a confirmed reservation—and are bumped off our flight.

If bumping weren't so common, I wouldn't believe any reputable merchant could do it and stay in business. Not only is it not punished; it is officially permitted by the Civil Aeronautics Board (CAB), the federal agency which regulates the airlines. Let me give you its side first. The CAB was formed to promote the interests of the airline industry. Bumping is good for the airlines. In order to encourage more people to travel, they want them to make reservations to fly even when they are not certain they really want to go: Make it easy to reserve by not penalizing for changing your mind, even at the last minute. This way, many people who would not otherwise make the trip if they had to buy the tickets when the time comes to travel will, from inertia, use tickets they've already reserved and paid for. And those who don't fly and eventually get a refund have given the airlines an interest-free loan all the while. So travel is increased by easy reservations, and the airlines flourish accordingly. This trade psychology often results in airlines' happily changing reservations, even to other "competing" airlines, hassle-free.

Stimulating the traveler to make reservations early by permitting last-minute cancellations without penalty means that a plane fully booked will not necessarily fly full. There will be some "no shows." Every empty seat which could have been filled costs the airlines. So they predict in advance a percentage who won't show, and they overbook. If more people than predicted show up for any given flight, some will have to be bumped. That's their side. Now let's look at ours.

We pay them money now. In return, they promise to fly us to

point P at time T. It's a simple "executory" contract: We pay them now; they fly us later. By confirming our reservation we inform them of our serious intention to fly on the agreed flight. But when we show up, they inform us that they've made similar agreements with more people than there are seats on the plane and although they've taken our money they're now dishonoring their confirmed promise. It's fraud! If I were to get extreme about it, I'd say it's larceny by false pretenses: intentionally misrepresenting a material fact to get someone to pay money. They make us believe we are buying a guaranteed seat; what we are really buying is the substantial possibility that we will be allowed aboard the plane and that it will fly on schedule.

To a passenger who's been bumped, an airline's offer to fly him free on the next scheduled flight can be very attractive. It may afford him a couple of hours at the bar, or a chance to catch up on some reading at the airport rather than in an empty hotel room at the other end of the flight. But for others, to miss a flight can be disastrous. Important business may depend on a prompt connection, or, as with Sherri Roman, whose ticket from Chicago to Fort Lauderdale had been booked through a travel agent—no difference in getting bumped—the delay may mean missing a family reunion to celebrate her grandfather's birthday. Delta offered her a 9:00 A.M. flight the next morning. Sherri called her parents in Florida, and then declined Delta's offer to put her up for the night and fly her out in the morning. Instead, as instructed, she demanded a refund and a statement from the airline that her flight had been oversold.

Delta gave her more than she asked, or less, depending upon how you look at it. Airline agents explained to her the inner mysteries of "Denied Boarding Compensation," which they were offering her in addition to her refund—$78.70, an amount equal to the price of a one-way ticket. The Delta agents were, by her account, "very nice" to her as they presented her with a release to sign, accepting the $78.70 "in full accord and satisfaction of all claims and demands which she had or might have arising out of denial of confirmed passage." They explained to her, and for the moment she understood, that she "was signing something saying that she wouldn't sue and it would give her back compensation of one-way fare for not being able to go." Although she was "upset and not quite sure what she was doing," nevertheless, she endorsed the draft and received her money.

Afterward, when she tried to sue Delta for a much larger sum to compensate her for missing the reunion, a federal court threw out the suit because she had signed the release and no undue pressure had been put on her. The court also denied her parents' right to sue separately for consequential damages they suffered by not having their daughter at the reunion, holding that the elder Romans were "too remote" from the situation to be eligible to recover from Delta for any misrepresentation made in connection with their daughter's flight.

There is no hard and fast rule as to how closely tied to a situation you must be in order to collect for adverse consequences you suffer on account of another's wrongful act. The law is in flux, and is generally moving toward allowing a greater circle of people to fight back. Her parents were wise to try.

Sherri's mistake was to sign the waiver. Signing waivers on the spot is a mistake in $99^{44}/_{100}$ percent of situations. If someone with whom you've contracted is so anxious as to make you an offer on the spot in return for your dropping all possible future claims, it's usually unwise to accept the trade. He's not offering it out of contrition, or the goodness of his heart. And rarely will he revoke the offer if you sleep on it and later decide to accept it. The odds are you can do better by holding out. It is almost certain that Sherri herself could have done no worse.

I call actions such as signing releases on the spot, or confession before you see your lawyer, etc., "zero plays." A zero play never wins and sometimes loses. Not that you should never make deals on the spot. Many a good deal falls through because of a lack of courage in making a quick decision. But before you sign any release, you should feel that you are happy with the outcome, not grudgingly accepting a consolation prize.

Do not assume that airlines, when they make an offer on the

spot or through the mail, always act in good faith. "Typically, a claim will be made, the aircarrier will send a sympathetic letter explaining that it is not liable for all or part of the claim and offer a sum in settlement. Despite the fact that the offered sum is nowhere near the actual value of the claim, most consumers will believe the self-serving statements of the air carrier and settle. In fact, air carriers routinely send letters to claimants which contain misleading and false statements about the law and their liability thereunder. This practice is widespread and has generated a CAB Investigation. . . ." The investigation is still pending.*

What, then, is the solution to the overbooking problem? The rules for bumping should be designed to ensure that those who care the most fly when scheduled. The solution is obvious. Overbook, and then auction the alternative accommodations. "Who will give up his seat for $100?" If there are enough takers, then presumably everyone who agrees to the alternative prefers it to flying on time. If there are not enough takers, the airline has to sweeten the deal until there are.

HOTELS. Back to our trip. We're finally "up, up and away, flying the friendly skies on the wings of man, the way the world wants to fly." We land safe and sound, recover our baggage intact and are on our way to the hotel.

In my experience, it is usually wise to pay the extra money for a decent hotel. A good night's sleep makes a good day's fun. And, with a better hotel, you're likely to be better located. For example, a hotel right on the ocean is, for those who use the beach, incomparably more convenient than one located in pine barrens a mile away. It's so much nicer to tumble out of bed onto the beach, go upstairs for a nap or a snack in midafternoon, and generally relax during the day so as to be fresh and enthusiastic for the nighttime. I would rather stay at a better hotel right on the beach in a less fancy spot than a mile away from the posh beach. If I have to get into a car, I might as well drive fifteen minutes as five. You spend

---

* Thomas A. Dickerson, "Travel Law: Baggage Claims" Air Law vol. V, #3, 1980 p. 130

so much money on a vacation; don't be chintzy in choosing your hotel.

Paying a deposit for confirmed reservations at a better hotel and actually staying there are two different things. There's many a slip between the reservation and your arrival. Like the airline industry, the hotel industry commonly overbooks and "bumps" guests with confirmed reservations. Industry experts report that it is standard policy at many hotels to accept between 5 percent and 15 percent more reservations than there are rooms!* Hotel overbooking is one of traveling's most common disappointments and ripoffs.

Motives for overbooking include the problem of "no shows" but extend beyond it to out-and-out theft. For example, Mr. and Mrs. D. F. Dold arranged through American Express to vacation in Hawaii and stay at the Outrigger Hotel. But when they arrived, they were refused accommodations and transferred to the Pagoda, far from the same thing. For the next two days they demanded and were repeatedly refused accommodations at the Outrigger. During those two days the hotel had referred seventy-three parties holding reservations to the Pagoda. But wasn't the Outrigger being *somewhat* accommodating by finding its disappointed would-be guests alternative accommodations, albeit at a less highly regarded hotel? Hardly. Here's the way the scam worked: Having paid American Express, which in turn paid the Outrigger in advance, the Dolds were issued coupons certifying their prepayment for the accommodations. On referral by the Outrigger, the practice at the cheaper hotel, which hardly informed its new guests of its own inferior status, was to accept the Outrigger coupons as payment, and then bill the Outrigger for the lesser cost of the rooms actually provided. The Outrigger pocketed the difference between the coupon's value and the actual value of the cheaper accommodations. As far as I'm concerned, this ripoff is theft. It could and should be prosecuted. As far as the hotels are concerned, it's common practice, and good business.

---

* See Thomas A. Dickerson, "Travel Consumer Fraud: Rip-Offs and Remedies," Syracuse Law Review 28, p. 847

This fraud is really a variation of one of the oldest dirty tricks in the book: bait and switch. Advertise one thing, get the consumer into the store, conveniently run out of the advertised item, and sell him a higher-priced commodity. Here, instead of jacking the price, the management charges you the same but gives you less. Only with hotels the "store" may be thousands of miles away from home in a strange place where you are at their mercy. We differ, one from another, on how much money we have to spend. But a precious resource in scarce supply for each of us, rich, middle-income, or poor, is our time. Especially precious is our vacation time. Those people who are knowingly responsible for ruining our vacations should be made to pay for it. And by those who fight back, sometimes they are!

The Dolds were a shrewd couple who didn't take their lumps lying down. First, they refused to hand over to the Pagoda the travel coupons from the Outrigger, insisting instead on paying in cash. Then, when they returned home, they sued the Outrigger not only for the actual damages, but also for *punitive* damages. Punitive damages are the key to fighting back against all sorts of disgraceful practices. The idea behind "punitive" or "exemplary" damages is simple. Money may be awarded above and beyond what is necessary to compensate a plaintiff for his actual property loss when the wrong done to him was aggravated by circumstances of violence, fraud or malice on the part of the defendant. Punitive damages are intended to punish the defendant for his evil behavior or to make an example of him so that others will not do the same.

We have seen that there can be a suit in tort for mental anguish caused by a broken contract. I mentioned that courts traditionally have been loath to allow these actions; so too they are loath to award punitive damages. The Dolds won their fight for damages because the Hawaii Supreme Court had established for that state a "fusion of the doctrines of tort and contract." But the court disallowed any punitive damages and in the end the Dolds were awarded only $600.

Considering the consequences, an even more egregious case

occurred when Mrs. Edward Brown, who had a serious heart condition, was "bumped" from a San Francisco hotel at which she had a confirmed reservation. Traveling in a party of four, the Browns were returning to their home in Atlanta from Hawaii. Mrs. Brown's doctor had permitted the trip in the first place only on condition that she stop over at San Francisco. The Browns had the misfortune of arriving at the Golden Gate City the day before both a World Series opener between Oakland and Cincinnati and the USC-Stanford traditional football fracas. The hotel lobby was a madhouse, and although it had guaranteed reservations for two rooms, the management could provide only one. Nor could any other hotel be substituted; San Francisco was sold out. The two couples had thirteen pieces of luggage between them and, as they could not readily separate their belongings, headed back to the San Francisco Airport and flew on to Atlanta.

As a result, Mrs. Brown became ill; her general health and heart condition deteriorated and she was hospitalized for two weeks. The Browns sued for the tort of pain and suffering arising out of the contract.

A trial court threw out the tort action and the Browns appealed. For some reason the appellate judge who wrote the opinion thought the whole situation cute. His insensitivity to the Browns' fate was manifest from the opening sentence of the opinion: "No Room at the Inn! Titled thusly this tristful tale takes this tribunal into deciding . . ." Lest any reader of his opinion fail to admire the judge's fanciful play with words, he footnoted them with a clever conceit: "As an ardent alliteration addict afflicted by such auctorial activity, the writer opines this suits him to a T."

Having preened for the public, the good judge then denied the Browns' right to sue in tort, resulting from a breach of contract. Things are changing, but slowly.

RUINED VACATIONS

Often we regret "roads not taken." But in the case of ruined vacations, in which half a loaf seems worse than none at all, there are often better moves than merely to compound your discomfort with disappointment. There are ways to make your present loss your future gain.

CRUISES. The tale of passengers in the grip of a callous and indifferent line putting money above duty can now begin. Beguiled by a brochure heralding "The Mediterranean 1971 Sailings . . . Italian Line's Ocean Travel—A New Touch in Class and Luxury aboard the 'Fun Ship' *Cristoforo Colombo*," William V. Owens had booked first-class transatlantic passage for himself and his wife at a cost of $1,456. The "unique appeal" of this pleasure cruise was that it was to last thirteen days and make stops of from three to seven hours in no fewer than seven Mediterranean ports, in Portugal, Spain, Greece and Italy, before final disembarkation in Trieste on August 17. Owens' expectations, and indeed the very core of the bargained-for passage, were soon shattered. On August 10, a few hours before reaching the first stop, Lisbon, moving in a dense fog, the *Colombo* collided with another ship. As a result, the entire Mediterranean itinerary in effect was canceled. The *Colombo* spent the next three days in Lisbon undergoing repairs and did not steam on again until August 13, heading for Naples.

The Italian Line told the passengers they would be deposited in Naples and assured them of first-class rail passage to Trieste. With six full days to prepare, on August 16 the Italian line took more than 150 first-class passengers off the air-conditioned ship—which remained in port for another seven hours after that—and transported them to a third-class hotel in Naples. The hotel had no rooms available, only a small lobby with seats for thirty. The outside temperature was ninety degrees, cooler than the inside of the non-air-conditioned lobby. Eleven hours later, at 9:00 P.M., the passengers were taken by bus to a railroad station. All of the first-class passengers were ordered by an Italian Line employee into compartments in three third-class railway "sleeper" cars—the most inferior type of sleeping cars in use in Italy.

How bad were they? Each car contained fifty compartments. Each compartment contained two vertical tiers of three narrow shelves each. The word "shelves" is used advisedly. "There was no bedding provided except a single sheet, and no ladders or footholds for climbing to the upper shelves, no individual plumbing, and of course no air-conditioning." Owens and his wife were forced to share a compartment with two other men and two other women. They were lucky. There weren't enough shelves to go around and some of the first-class passengers stood up all night!

Each car contained just three tiny toilets. Because of the communal living arrangement, and because their baggage was piled with all the rest in a separate car without any prior warning to them, Owens and his wife remained in their clothes throughout. This train, which left Naples at 10:50 P.M. and arrived in Trieste more than twelve hours later, had no dining car, and no food was provided at any time.

If this is what happened to the first-class passengers of the ill-fated *Cristoforo Colombo,* imagine what happened to the service crew. "Apparently responding to its own code of the sea, the Italian Line crew somehow secured markedly *superior* accommodations on the same train!"

When the Owenses sued, the Italian Line did not deny any of these facts. Instead, it first issued a self-serving statement that the collision at sea wasn't its fault, and it therefore couldn't be held responsible for the accident's aftermath.

Nonsense, declared the court. "In failing to transport plaintiff and his wife to four of the eight scheduled European ports, and in foreshortening the number of days at sea, defendant substantially breached the contract of passage."

"More important, the shabby treatment accorded plaintiff after the *Colombo* docked at Naples not only compounded the breach . . . but was itself independently actionable. First-class passage means precisely that, and it most certainly was not provided." The court continued in the right direction: "Indeed the law has evolved a liberal rule of damages where a passenger has been subjected to humiliating indifference and has been accorded treatment inferior to the class of treatment that he had bargained for." Furthermore, the court held that "damages arising from a breach of the contract to carry, which results in inconvenience and indignity to the passenger while in transit, are not limited to the price of passage.''

But the Italian Line trotted out the fine print. It claimed that the court was powerless to afford Owens any relief because of the existence of ''terms and conditions'' contained in the ticket booklet it had furnished. The court characterized this position as ''graceless and without merit.'' In a classic blast at ''fine print,'' the court expressed ''difficulty in ascertaining the existence of any reference to the terms and conditions.'' At the risk of considerable eyestrain, the court finally detected that, under a sentence in microscopic Italian script, there was a parallel, virtually unreadable, collation of English words, which appeared to state: ''Subject to the conditions printed on the cover of this ticket which form part of this contract.'' The court commented:

> This reference is so tucked away, so camouflaged by the surrounding Italian text, and so minuscule in presentation that it is literally a trap for the unwary. There is no legend, in contrast to the legends utilized on every other segment of the ticket, calling attention to its existence. It can only be located, after the most diligent search, if one knows beforehand that it actually exists. . . . And when one turns to the terms and conditions which defendant seeks to integrate into the contract of passage, the strain of detection is further increased. Fully 35 ''terms and conditions'' presumably are designed to relieve defendant of liability, and to place the passenger at the mercy of the Line.
>
> In a nutshell, defendant urges that the court is bound (a) by the covert statement on the face of the ticket, and (b) by the virtually indecipherable ''terms and conditions'' that the statement springs upon plaintiff.
>
> Justice is not that easily handcuffed. Patently, the contract of passage is a contract of adhesion. And vis-à-vis such a contract the law frowns upon any effort, by a carrier such as defendant, to expose a passenger to risks and detriments without fair notice or fair play.

Continuing to pile it on in this avalanche of criticism, the court repeated established anti-fine-print doctrine from the turn of the century. The U.S. Supreme Court held that "when a company desires to impose special and most stringent terms upon its customers, in exoneration of its own liability, there is nothing unreasonable in requiring that those terms shall be distinctly declared and deliberately accepted."

Furthermore, "recent teaching of the airline cases" is that courts "consistently reject" efforts of airlines to limit their liability under the "exceedingly fine print" of the Warsaw Convention. And, finally, this same Italian Line had "previously been called to task" by a federal court for the format of its ticket.

Taking it all together—ruined vacation, crammed into a sweltering lobby of a third-class hotel for twelve hours, crammed overnight into a horrific train without basic amenities while the crew relaxed in superior accommodations, unconscionable fine print, previous warnings, and a doctrine that liability can *exceed* the total price of the ticket— the court concluded: "Plaintiff's rights are clear. That he was damaged is clear. That defendant cannot be exonerated from liability is clear." How much was the judgment? $20,000 for each? Too much? Take a guess. "I find and determine that plaintiff has been damaged in the sum of $500. The sum so awarded represents approximately one third of the total price of passage." $500? Why so little? Why didn't the judge's actions match her words? It's a mystery. Even the judge tacitly conceded her award was less than full. Converting a mountain of Italian Line inconsideration and inconvenience into a molehill of damages, the judge herself noted: "This modest recovery makes more than due allowance for what defendant actually supplied, and indeed, affords defendant a dispensation which the court would be warranted in withholding."

What's going on here? I don't know. Why aren't those who are fighting back winning when they're definitely in the right? For some reason legal principles are not being translated into monetary practice. Sadly, so far, this seems to be a pattern in travel cases.

TOURS. As was their custom, the Paterson and Majewski families planned their joint vacation over the Christmas holidays. They worked through a travel agency with which they'd previously dealt. This year it was to be the Canary Islands. The retail travel agent suggested to the Patersons and Majewskis a package tour prepared by Odysseys (a wholesale agency), entitled "Xmas Jet Set Sun Fun/Canary Isle," which included a stay at the "Deluxe Semiramis Hotel." After traveling and waiting thirty hours, the two families, along with over two hundred other "weary but expectant guests," arrived at the "Five Star Hotel Semiramis," to be greeted with a letter from the hotel advising them that there were no accommodations available to their group. They waited for about four hours in the lobby of the Semiramis and were divided into groups and directed to other hotels. They were sent to the Porto Playa Hotel—a four-star hotel. What difference does one little star make? Generals in the army make a big fuss over it, but seasoned travelers . . . Well, perhaps ordinarily not much, but the Porto Playa was far from ready for occupancy. The lobby looked like a construction site. And during the travelers' stay, work was done in their rooms to hook up water and to complete electrical connections. Furthermore, no recreational facilities or other conveniences were provided.

Once again, the court made noises suggesting the potential of a large award, in tort as well as contract. "When a passenger sues a carrier for a breach of their agreement concerning accommodations the 'inconveniences and discomforts which a passenger suffers . . . are to be considered in the assessment of the damages' and damages arising from a breach of the contract to carry, which results in inconvenience and indignity to the passenger while in transit are not limited to the price of passage."

And so in this case a "realistic view for awarding damages to Majewski and Paterson would include not only the difference in the cost of the accommodations but *also compensation for their inconvenience, discomfort, humiliation, and annoyance.*"

The court gave each family over $1,000, which was the *total cost* of their trip, and indicated it might have awarded more.

The case of the large court-ordered payback for inconvenience and lost precious time, irritation, etc. is not yet. But times, they are a-changing, and the case is coming. If they bait-and-switch you, if your vacation is ruined because of terrible hotels, call up the travel agent. Make him understand that you are well aware that the law in many states allows you to collect for the intangibles over and above the total cost of the package. Although a majority of states still limit recovery to a full refund, don't ask for a full refund as your initial request. Demand substantially more than your money back. A full refund should be your fallback position.

The substitution of inferior services and failure to make events match the promises in the brochure are the most common travel traps. So far, the cases we've looked at are easy to prove: I was promised hotel A, I got hotel B. But other disappointments are less easy to prove. The glistening white sand was covered with trash and tar. The "gay night life" turned out to be two homosexual drug addicts lolling about the lobbies accosting the guests for a fix at all hours, the gourmet cuisine may have been relished by the roaches, etc., etc. How do you prove these shortcomings? It's difficult.

Furthermore, in one key respect, the game is stacked against the traveler, and the agents know it. Especially in those states which limit the recovery from breach of contract for travel services to the cost of the package, it may be economically infeasible to press a suit. Lawyer's fees and court costs may more than eat up any potential recovery. The agent may call your bluff and tell you to sue, knowing that you won't do it. What is the answer?

There are two: class actions and true grit. With an eye toward future litigation, when your vacation is busting, save all indications of your disappointment. Trap the roach in your food and bottle it with a sample of the food. Take photos of the litter-strewn beach. Keep all receipts for extra out-of-pocket expenses. Think about making your case *during* your trip.

I know a family whose vacation was an abomination. Everyone was in a terrible mood until they began to plan the lawsuit during the vacation. They vied with each other to see who could come up with the best and most creative evidence for a future lawsuit. This turned into a family sport, and they began to root for everything to go wrong so that they could document it. They even suffered a sense of disappointment at the few things which were delivered as promised. They returned home armed to the teeth and the travel agent gave them most of their money back, for a "ruined" vacation, which in retrospect was one of their most successful and fun-filled.

For a single family, considering court costs and lawyer's fees, fighting back against a ruined vacation may be more expensive than the expected fruits of victory. To succeed, you must sometimes band together with others similarly aggrieved. An up-and-coming way around the economic infeasibility of hiring your own lawyer to fight for a few hundred dollars is the class action. The theory is simple: If a large group of us is injured in the same way by the same company on the same occasion, we pool our claims and hire a couple of attorneys and sue on behalf of the entire group.

A class action is a potent threat to a travel agent. So when you find yourself stuck in a sweltering hotel lobby with 250 other angry travelers, stay calm and begin to prepare for a group fight.

A problem with class actions is that some jurisdictions, especially the federal courts, frown on them. For example, not long ago TWA advertised "mini-plans," which allowed travelers cheaply to visit one European city. The discount package included hotel accommodations, a rental car and other services. It sounded great in the ads, especially to people strapped for money. Fine print of TWA's brochure required the traveler to check in at his lodging before 6:00 P.M. *on the day of arrival;* otherwise the hotel voucher would be invalid for the entire stay. All right, perhaps a bit inconvenient; but the traveler makes it his first priority to check in at the hotel before seeing any sights of the city.

The catch in this case was that the guest houses were not located in the heart of the arrival city, nor in the suburbs, but were so far away that it was virtually impossible to check in before the 6:00 P.M. deadline. The "London" lodging, for example, was located in a town in Scotland some 350 miles away. As a matter of fact the distances between the "mini-plan" city and the guest-house sites varied from a low of 185 miles (Zurich, Switzerland, to Nauders, Austria) to a high of 480 miles (Athens to Karola, Greece). As a result, all passengers forfeited their free guest-house accommodations and were forced to fend for themselves.

In spite of the fact that there was some indication that TWA devised the mini-plans knowing full well that the participants would never be able to avail themselves of the free-lodging offer, and in spite of the fact that the CAB had issued TWA a cease and desist order, the federal court nonsuited the whole *group* of plaintiffs and directed them instead to their individual state courts.

Occasionally a court will overcome its shyness, however, and allow a class action by a group of disappointed travelers. For example, recently, in what the court described as a "nightmare," hundreds of passengers who had gone on a seven-day cruise and become seriously ill because of exposure to contaminated food or water on the ship were permitted by federal court to have six of their number band together and represent the class in a suit for over $3 million. There are all sorts of technical problems with class actions which a lawyer must handle, but often it is the only feasible road to recovery.

Another trap separating you from being made whole after a ruined vacation is the instability of the travel industry. I mentioned that many agencies work on a razor-thin profit edge. Often they post no bond, or one not large enough to compensate a class of disappointed travelers. What this means to you in practical terms is that even if your vacation is ruined and you have carefully documented proof, there may be no one solvent against whom to fight back.

Often when you book a charter flight through your local agent, he deducts a very small commission and forwards the bulk of your payment to a wholesaler. You're issued tickets, and before the scheduled departure is canceled, the wholesaler goes bankrupt and you're left with ruined plans and a worthless piece of paper for which you have paid plenty. Enraged, you demand a full refund from your travel agent, who instead offers to return his commission on your ticket. You want to sue, but your prospects depend on what state you are in. Most courts will focus on how the travel agent is paid, and many courts have held a good-faith travel agent liable only to the extent of the commission.

In a well-publicized incident, a wholesaler organized a charter from Pittsburgh to Miami which included air transportation and tickets to the Super Bowl. Nearly a thousand Pittsburgh fans contacted local travel agents and signed up, only to find, when they arrived in Miami, that the wholesaler hadn't purchased any tickets in advance to the sold-out game. The disgruntled travelers were forced to watch the game on TV in local bars; the wholesaler disappeared.

Sometimes you can fight back even when the wholesaler is bankrupt. Early in 1979, a federal appeals court permitted individual travelers and retail travel agencies who had made deposits to reserve places on defunct charter tours to band together as a class and sue the bank in which the tour deposits were kept and the bank officer who handled the deposits. The suit was for $740,000.

Especially in states which hold the local agent acting in good faith liable only for his commission, perhaps the best way to protect yourself against the unscrupulous bankrupt wholesaler is to inquire when you make your travel arrangements whether the local agent is booking through a wholesaler. If the local agent says no, get him to put it in writing. If he says yes, tell him you trust him, but you are wary about the wholesaler. He will assure you that he deals only with reputable people who never would do such a thing. "Fine," you say, "then you won't mind putting in writing your assurance of the ticket and guarantee of a full refund." If he refuses, go elsewhere. If no one in your town will put it in writing, then a concealed recorder which memorializes an oral promise ought to amount to a binding contract.

Let's return to our vacation. We book through a travel agent, we're issued a ticket for a flight that exists, we don't get bumped from our flight, we recover our baggage intact, and we go to a hotel which is essentially as promised. Eagerly we prepare to dash to the beach. But there's the nagging problem of valuables. What do we do with them? This question sends us back into the fine print and is a section in itself.

HOTEL THEFTS

Once upon a time innkeepers were liable for the property of their guests. The theory was that it was good for the new United States to have people travel among them. Strangers had to be able to rely on the honesty of the innkeeper and his employees. It was easy and tempting for the innkeeper to conspire to rob the guests. Therefore the old Common Law rules were changed to make the innkeeper in effect the insurer of the guest's property. Only in cases in which the property was lost through an act of God, war, or the fault of the guest himself was the innkeeper relieved of liability.

Times, but not temptations, have changed. Leather and oak lobbies have been replaced by brass and stainless stealing lobbiests. Many state legislatures, on behalf of the hotel industry, have enacted legislation limiting hotels' liability for guests' stolen property.

Most of us are familiar with the prominently displayed, large-print signs in hotels, motels and inns: "Management will not be responsible for valuables left in your room." These words are followed by others to the effect that safe-deposit boxes are provided for safekeeping. An obvious inference to be drawn is that if we follow these instructions and store our valuables in a safe-deposit box provided by the hotel (usually located in the area of the cashier's counter), we are assured that our valuables will be restored to us, or, if they are lost, the hotel will make us whole. Forget it. No way.

Once again we are victims of the "fine print"—the tiny print at the bottom of the sign that typically says the hotel is liable in any event only up to $500. The different limitations among the states vary in three key respects: money limits, the effect of the hotel's own negligence on its liability, and how negligence can be proved. The dollar amounts ($500 is typical) may be raised at the hotel's discretion by permitting a higher valuation in writing up to some fairly low limit, say $1,000. So, for example, if your box is robbed of a couple of million dollars' worth of unmarked jewels, the hotel's position is that you will be adequately recompensed by a check for $500. No more supposing; we're not in the realm of theory.

There has been an epidemic of Raffles-like burglaries of hotel safe-deposit boxes that has netted millions in jewels and money, and if any thief has been captured, I haven't heard about it. The thefts from New York hotel boxes have become as ritualistic and insoluble as kidnappings in Italy. The Pierre Hotel has been hit. So have the Plaza, the Sherry Netherland, and others. But the classic bust-in occurred at the swank Regency Hotel on Park Avenue late one Saturday night in November 1977.

Apparently, the day before the robbery, two men checked into the Regency as guests. Late the next night—Saturday—they emerged from the elevator nattily clad in tuxedos and proceeded toward the cashier's desk. As they did so, they were joined by a compatriot or two. When they reached the desk, they flashed guns and threatened to use them if their directions were not heeded. From the hotel employee behind the counter they demanded certain cards indicating the numbers of safe-deposit boxes held by well-known wealthy guests at the hotel. He complied. The robbers then broke open those particular boxes and removed the contents.

Most remarkably, the heist occurred while literally dozens of guests were returning from various dinner parties and after-theater suppers. As they entered the lobby, they were politely filled in on current events by one of the robbers and then—believe it or not—ushered into the bar and dining room opposite the desk and served coffee and soft drinks while the robbery continued. This went on for hours. Who would believe such a scene at a New York luxury hotel—on one side of the lobby the guests' safe-deposit boxes being broken into and contents filched, while on the other, next to the Park Avenue entrance, the robbers were serving coffee and refreshments to the entering guests! But the most amazing part of the whole thing was that, located behind the cashier's counter and the main desk were five concealed foot buttons which, when stepped on, would have alerted a protection agency and, through it, the police. The buttons were never pushed. The man behind the counter was afraid.

The defects in the hotel-safe security system were patent. The boxes were right out in the open for all to see, and there was very limited space for private handling of the boxes. When the space was occupied by one guest, the next guest's only alternative was to wait or openly display the contents of his/her box in front of whoever happened to be lurking about the lobby. Actually the hotel had some electronically wired safe-deposit boxes which, for some inexplicable reason, were left empty rather than being placed at the disposal of guests known to have extremely precious valuables.

I first heard of this brazen hotel heist the next day, Sunday, on the car radio on my way to a New York Jets football game in Queens. I mentioned it to my friend and partner Tom Bolan, who was joining me for the game and who had also heard the report. We agreed that none of our friends was affected or else we would have been called. After the game, I stopped by our law office in New York. As I walked into the foyer, the phone was insistently ringing. It was a friend, shaken and frantic, informing me that she and other friends had been principal victims of the heist—to the tune of millions, uninsured. Incredibly the management had never bothered to notify them that they had been robbed. The Baron and Baroness Enrico diPortanova had learned of it only after another friend, Doloris Bosshard, had called the hotel later Sunday afternoon, had related what she'd heard on the news, was assured that she and her friends had not been among the victims, and, after pulling teeth, was finally told by the desk downstairs that her priceless jewelry, much of which had been specially designed by her husband over the years, was gone. Among the other victims were Cadillac czar Victor Potamkin and his wife, Luba, who is a familiar figure on television. Interestingly and helpfully, both the diPortanovas and the Potamkins had made special advance inquiries about the safety of their valuables, and had received specific assurances in this regard.

To my law firm, all of this added up to a case of gross negligence. We therefore rejected the hotel's most generous offer of $500 per box and, instead, filed suit in our clients' behalf for the substantial value of the lost jewels and other valuables. As a result in 1981, after a jury was selected to try the issue, the hotel (or its insurance carrier) made a settlement offer, which was accepted. We agreed not to reveal the terms of the settlement, an agreement I do not choose to breach. But my enterprising research associate checked court records, and asserts without comment from me that the amount of the settlement adds a few zeros onto the $500.

The legal effect of negligence in this situation differs from state to state. The best rule is that if a hotel is negligent, all hedges are off; the loss is the limit. This makes obvious sense. If it's the hotel's fault, why should we suffer? In some of these states this rule is modified to require that the guest use a safe-deposit box or else the hotel is not liable, even if it is negligent.

Some states have further modified the rule so that even if a guest has used a safe-deposit box and the hotel was negligent, in order to collect the full value of the contents deposited for safekeeping the guest must have previously notified the hotel in writing of the value. This has its own unfair twists, as Barnard Simon, president of a small jewelry corporation, learned.

Simon was on the road, selling. One day he checked into a hotel and deposited with it for safekeeping his sample case containing diamonds worth more than $90,000. That evening he was accosted in his room by two men who bound and gagged him, took his safe-deposit box key and emptied his box. Simon had not given the hotel staff written notice of the value of the sample case, but they were aware of it. A Missouri federal court held that he couldn't recover its value as long as he hadn't formally given written notice. This result was, to the court, "perfectly consistent with logic and sound public policy." For "the hotelkeeper is not a banker; and he is not in the business of operating a safe deposit vault except as an incident to operating a hotel. Those who carry with them large amounts of money or jewelry must take other measures for their protection."

Perhaps this result seems not so unfair. After all, it can be argued that a guest ought to inform the hotel before he asks it to hold items of great value, and if he doesn't, the hotel shouldn't be responsible for what it doesn't know it has. The problem is similar to that with baggage. The upper limits of excess valuation are ridiculously low. If the guest informs the hotel as to the item's true value, the hotel will either reject it, or if it does accept it subject to the low limits on its liability, the guest, by putting employees on notice that there are items of great value in the box, increases the chances that a dishonest employee will set up a theft. His protection is, by his precautions, decreased. How do courts abide by these unfair results?

There's some economic theory behind this. In the words of the Missouri court: "The added cost to the hotelkeeper of providing for such protection even as against the willful act or negligence of an employee, is in the last analysis one of his costs of operation reflected in the rates charged to all. Why should those guests who do not need such protection pay for the cost of those who do?"

If this argument has some surface plausibility, remember it's a favorite of economists, whose new "science" has brought us simultaneously inflation and recession. Think about it for a moment: They say a person with valuables shouldn't be made whole by a negligent hotel because otherwise we'd all have to pay to cover the risk. What's wrong with the argument? What's wrong with it is that it gives the hotel no incentive to hire honest employees and to supervise them carefully. But, they say, by making a hotel pay the full value of losses when it is negligent, inordinate costs will be passed on to the consumer. The obvious answer to that one is that those hotels which are not negligent—which are well managed—can operate at lower costs and therefore at lower rates, by passing on savings from security to their guests, thereby driving out higher-priced competitors and leaving only the careful and honest in the hotel business making their well-deserved profits from their secure and satisfied guests. Two can play the same game of economic theory.

It is impossible to discuss this question of a hotel's negligence intelligently without also mentioning the problems of proof. How is a guest to prove the hotel was negligent? Once in a while, as with the heist at the Regency with many witnesses and an unpushed alarm button, the gross negligence is flagrant. Here it shouldn't make much difference who has the burden of proof. But ordinarily, a guest is unfamiliar with a hotel's internal procedures and encounters an icy uncooperative curtain from the hotel employees when he seeks to determine exactly how the loss occurred. For the typical victim, it is nearly impossible to prove the hotel was actually negligent.

To relieve this unfairness, many states provide that once the plaintiff has proved that he was a guest, and that he placed his valuables with the hotel for safekeeping, which valuables were not returned to him, there is a presumption of negligence which the hotel must disprove. On the other hand, the game is so stacked against the guest in other states that the low statutory limits apply notwithstanding the hotel's negligence!

Sometimes hotel liability may be established because of a particular circumstance. Not long ago there was another case before Judge Sandler in New York. Cyreld Spiller had used the hotel's safe-deposit box without incident, but now, ready to leave, she had packed her jewelry in her suitcase along with her clothing. After her two bags were brought to the lobby floor, she asked a bellboy to take them to the cab area and to watch them while she checked out. When she returned to the cab area, the bellboy had vanished. So had a suitcase. Sandler easily held the hotel liable for the luggage and clothing due to its negligence. But the statute which protected the hotel against loss of jewelry except when a safe-deposit box was used was more troublesome—especially because in New York the guest who fails to deposit property for safekeeping may not recover for the loss even if the hotel was actually negligent. But what's a guest supposed to do when it's checkout time? Judge Sandler, a compassionate realist, understood that the statute "was not designed to apply to a loss occurring under circumstances of this case." Having found that the loss resulted from the negligence of a hotel employee, he allowed Spiller to recover the full value of her lost jewelry as well as her other property. But a Judge Sandler is rare, and, despite the fact that any substantial hotel undoubtedly does or should carry its own insurance—and thus is in a position to make good to the wronged guest at no cost to it other than insurance premiums—the hotel game so far is stacked against the guest. Perhaps in the Regency case, however, the diPortanovas and Potamkins have done some trail-blazing for the rest of us.

In the meantime, the lesson to all of us who don't have a fortune in valuables and also care very much about them is simple: The best way to beat the problem of checking valuables is not to. Does that mean you should design some secret hiding place in your room? No. At best you can leave the valuables home. And use credit cards and numbered traveler's checks rather than cash. If you must carry valuables, insure them yourself if you can. If you can't, inform the hotel of their worth, put them in a box for safe-keeping and pray.

HIRED CARS AND DRIVERS

On this vacation we've taken together, we've seen people get issued nonexistent tickets, get bumped from flights, have their baggage lost, get bumped from hotels, have inferior accommodations substituted, place their valuables in hotel safes only to have them disappear. Could anything more go wrong? Of course; we haven't even left the hotel. Perhaps we want to go touring and rent a car for that purpose.

The Kermisches planned a vacation in Rumania and through their local travel agent reserved a French-made Renault. When they arrived in Rumania, no Renault was available and they were given to drive a Rumanian-made Dacia 1300, which proved to be defective. When they tried to return the car, they learned that their American car rental company (wisely) had no representative in Rumania and that the car had been rented from the Rumanian government, which doesn't pride itself on trying harder. Using the car in its defective condition had put a small dent in their plans. On schedule, they returned the car to the airport, to discover that they had put a small dent in the automobile, which was fully insured.

After the parents and their two children had cleared passport control and were waiting to enplane, a uniformed militia colonel forcibly took their passports, airline tickets and boarding passes from Mr. Kermisch and removed him from the passengers' lounge. He was "threatened" by representatives of the Rumanian government and advised that he wouldn't be able to leave the country until he had paid for the damage. It probably beats being held hostage in Tehran, but not by much.

The Kermisches didn't find the experience amusing. They sued the rental company for $145,000 in compensatory damages and $130,000 in punitive damages.

The trial court threw out the case on the grounds—get this—that New York was the wrong place to bring the action—*forum non conveniens,* the law calls it. What was the correct, "convenient" forum, where the New Yorkers should have instituted suit? You guessed it—Rumania.

The Kermisches declined the court's invitation to take that trip again. Instead they appealed the court's dismissal. The appellate court found that, considering the alternative, New York, while not the perfect forum, was adequate. It turned its attention to the Kermisches' five causes of action. In July 1979 the court threw out two of them, both concerning the false arrest by the Rumanian officials, "because there is no direct connection between the rental company and the purported detention by the officials of the Rumanian Government."

But it allowed the other three causes of action: (1) Rental company had induced plaintiffs to believe that they would be dealing with it rather than a communist government. (2) Rental company misrepresented the make of automobile to be rented. (3) And, most apt, rental company was negligent in making careless representations to plaintiffs and in failing to warn them that an inferior car would be rented from a communist government whose policy is to "detain, harass, threaten and arrest people" who fail to return rental cars in "mint" condition.

There are definitely hazards connected with touring, and problems with who is responsible for foul-ups. Sometimes a court will force the local travel agent to take responsibility. For example, a Texas court decided that a Texas travel agency was liable for injuries caused by a Mexican driver who hazardously drove a couple of travelers from Mexico City to Acapulco on winding mountain roads at over sixty miles an hour, refusing to slow down, although requested to do so in English and Spanish. The driver had crashed the car and hospitalized its occupants. The court held the Texas agency liable because it hadn't disclosed to the travelers that it was in effect only the booking agent of a Mexican travel agency, which had employed the driver. Courts go different ways on this.

Our trip comes to a conclusion. We land safely but a little late and say goodbye. I'm fortunate enough to have a ride, but you have arranged with the travel agent as part of your payment to be picked up by a limousine which never shows, and you pay a cab $45 to take you home. This happened to Faith Ostrander, who later represented herself in court, suing for the $45. She won. The court held that "a travel agency is the agent of the traveler."

If that's true, I've been fooled.

What lessons have we learned from our trip together? Be particular, use an agent and check up on him, get all guarantees in writing, use carry-on luggage, don't carry valuables, keep records and gather evidence of a vacation in shambles. Join with others in class actions and fight back. If you don't, the time that is ruined is definitely your own.

7.
LAWYERS

JUDGE LEARNED HAND, one of our country's greatest jurists, once wrote that "next to death or fatal illness, the one thing I fear most in this world is being a litigant in our courts." Shakespeare's Dick Butcher said, "The first thing we do, let's kill all the lawyers." Our society has had a love/hate relationship with its lawyers. And for good reason.

My personal feeling has always been that there is nothing wrong with putting your mind in the service of another person's best interests. I have agreed with the profession's Code of Ethics, which requires the lawyer to represent the client "zealously within the bounds of the law" and "resolve in favor of his client doubts as to the bounds of the law." Although others disagree, it seems to me that, for the good lawyer, the interests of the particular client are all. Law is an adversary proceeding. One side wins; the other loses.

A century ago, Lord Brougham expressed this credo as well as anyone:

> An advocate, in the discharge of his duty, knows but one person in all the world, and that person is his client. To save that client by all means and expedients, at all hazards and costs to other persons and amongst them to himself, is his first and only duty.

In my humble opinion, perhaps the largest, most organized set of scoundrels in this society is my profession: lawyers. In what way is this so? Too often lawyers don't deliver, too often they are incompetent, and many of the most competent don't give you their all. They pretend to represent your best interests and instead represent their own. They often keep one eye on your problem and the other on your pocketbook. Some are never satiated in demanding their fees, and to make it worse, they are incompetent. To me, these lawyers are the real problem of the profession.

Much of this book is devoted to giving you a sense of the kinds of things lawyers think about when they represent you, so that you can participate meaningfully in your own case. Any book which has as a major objective helping you help yourself, fighting back, getting what you deserve, should include a discussion of how to protect yourself against lawyers, especially your own.

Let's start with the criminal law and, initially, with what steps you can take to protect yourself from sometimes overzealous law-enforcement officers before you have retained a lawyer. The first rule is: silence is golden.

CRIMINAL LAW

We have seen that talking at the wrong time in the wrong place can come back to haunt you. That's true in many, many situations. Getting a client to shut up is about the most difficult, if not impossible, task that a lawyer handles. Almost never at a time of crisis does it pay to talk and thereby go on record as to events you may later have reason to want to obscure. This applies to people from the top down. If Nixon hadn't talked his head off into a tape recorder, he might well have served two full terms in the White House. If Teddy Kennedy had made but one call to save Mary Jo Kopechne's life rather than many to his lawyers, PR men and others to save his public image, he might have won the Democratic nomination for President of the United States. By remaining silent at the right time, he could have avoided or mitigated his career nemesis.

But let's take a group about which there is no question it should know better than to make statements. Some call it organized crime. (I call it disorganized crime.) This group has as a common denominator a penchant for getting arrested with alarming frequency. Its members don't even have to listen to their lawyers—all they have to do is watch *Perry Mason*—to know that the cardinal rule is to say nothing, not one word, when arrested. Whatever is said will inevitably come back to haunt them. But do they listen? Usually not. A man in his seventies who has been arrested more times than most people have been kept out of Studio 54, despite required legal warnings that he need say nothing, insisted on proclaiming his innocence to the prosecutor. In the course of doing so, he denied knowing one of his co-defendants when, as was later easily proved, they were old friends. If you must say something, let it be: "I'm innocent of this charge, but I want to talk to a lawyer," or "my lawyer." Always promptly have your lawyer notified. S/he knows what to do—or at least s/he's supposed to.

Let's turn now to an automobile or bus accident. You're hit or knocked down or you hit another car or bus, etc. The police arrive to take statements. Give none. Never bravely say, "I'm OK. I'm not hurt." At that point you don't know whether you are or not. And never say, "It's my fault." You don't know the law on the subject of proximate cause, contributory negligence, or last clear chance—so you don't know if it's your fault or not. And above all, *sign nothing.* Insurance companies just love to come around with a box of chocolates, a small check and a fountain pen with which all you have to do is sign a little paper. Don't. That paper might be a release in which you are giving up a cause of action worth a hundred times the amount of the check they can't wait to give you.

From time to time, you may be called on to testify in a lawsuit, perhaps your own. This process commences with "depositions," "examinations before trial" or "written interrogatories." You don't have to worry about the written interrogatories, as your lawyer will undoubtedly write out the answers for you. That's why

I think they are of dubious value, unless the lawyer is an idiot—a not uncommon occurrence.

But live oral testimony is another thing. A few basic rules: Be thoroughly prepared! Success at most things is 90 percent preparation. Rise to the occasion. When you have a lot at stake is not the time to slack off. I've had friends who normally pay great attention to detail, but who when the time came to make their biggest, most important moves, when things really hung in the balance, not only didn't pay careful attention but actually paid less than usual. Sometimes you get away with it, and sometimes it costs.

Being prepared is easy to preach and hard to practice. It takes patience and it hurts a little. A lawyer friend who jogs says the experience of adequately preparing is like not stopping until well after you first want to. I don't know. I don't jog. Some people have accused me of being unprepared. Often it is someone I've beaten, someone who claims I've stolen it all at the end by a slick summation. Actually I always try to win at the beginning, by picking the right jury.

But be prepared. Know every fact, conversation and document that is likely to come up. The one little detail you overlook may be just the one they press you on, and pound and pound away at, rendering absolutely useless all your other preparation. Remember, *they* ask the questions. A general rule in all games, including war and law, is that the attacker picks the spots. The defending blockader must be prepared to parry everywhere. But, having said that, I should also point out that defense, too, has its advantages.

Second rule: Relax and listen. Say as little as you can and say it in the way that helps you most. You should be a witness to your own self as a witness. Don't merely react to their questions: Consider them. What exactly is it that has been asked?

Don't be scared. Don't rush to interpret a perfectly innocent question as an embarrassing probe. It is amazing how easily some people cave in to the slightest pressure when they are scared—how they help their attackers. Stay calm. Once you've done your best to prepare, remember, no one knows your world better than you do. You're on home ground when you're being examined, especially when you're telling the truth. Use the advantage.

I knew a fellow who used to be his own worst enemy. He hid his house key under some leaves deep in an obscure hollow of a tree. I don't think a squirrel could have found it. Nevertheless, Jerry, we will call him, used to agonize over the prospect that a burglar would find it and silently sneak upstairs to kill him, his wife and his children. In holding himself hostage to his own self-intimacy, he had forgotten a very important thing. *They* don't know nearly as much about you as you do. Every one of us who has ever lived has privacies and personal embarrassments, at the very least intimacies, that we don't want or expect to be pried into.

But they don't know your past as you do. As I said to Jerry, "Only you know where your back-door keys are." Camouflage and cover-ups pervade the world. You alone know your own intimate affairs, they can only fish and paint portraits.

Listen to the questions they ask. Listen to the *actual* questions they ask. Don't play "fill in the dots" for them. Don't answer questions they should have asked if only they knew enough. And do answer questions you want asked, even if they're phrased a little differently. Answer the questions in the most innocent way consistent with honesty. There's more give in that word "honesty" than you would imagine, as Samuel Bronston, major movie magnate, found out.

The president of Bronston Production Companies, which made some costly European epics that flopped, filed for bankruptcy. His creditors examined him under oath to determine the location of his assets, to which they were entitled. The following brief but critical examination of Bronston was conducted by a creditor's lawyer:

> Q: Do you have any bank accounts in Swiss banks, Mr. Bronston?
> A: No, sir.
> Q: Have you ever?

A: The company had an account there for about six months, in Zurich.

Q: Have you any nominees who have bank accounts in Swiss banks?

A: No, sir.

Q: Have you ever?

A: No, sir.

It was later established that Bronston personally had had Swiss bank accounts for several years and knew it at the time he said, "The company had an account there for about six months," in response to the question "Have *you* ever . . ." Bronston was convicted of perjury and his conviction was upheld by a divided federal appeals court with the majority of the judges saying that "willfully giving false and evasive testimony" is perjury. They said that "an answer containing half of the truth which also constitutes a lie by negative implication, when the answer is intentionally given in place of the responsive answer called for by a proper question, is perjury."

But that court was overruled by the United States Supreme Court, which held that answers "may be shrewdly calculated to evade." "Literally true but unresponsive answers, even if the witness intends to mislead his questioner by the answer and even if the answer is . . . 'false by negative implication' are not perjury."

Not only can your answers be misleading, shrewdly calculated to evade, without being perjurious; they should be short, preferably yes or no. Why? Because if you dribble on, all you are doing is furnishing your examiner with new names and facts upon which he can frame additional questions—while a yes or no answer closes the subject. Let me give you an example. In the course of a debate in Philadelphia between me and the late Richardson Dilworth, a member of the audience asked me a ten-minute-long loaded question the substance of which was: "Don't you think it was your obligation to see that witnesses were given full rights during interrogation when you were engaged in a 'witch hunt' as chief counsel to the Senate Investigating Committee?" I was expected, of course, to give a ten-minute defense, which in turn would have fanned a meaningless shouting match, which is just what the questioner intended. Instead, I replied to his ten-minute question with one word: "Yes." After a second's hushed silence, the audience broke into applause and laughter, and that was the end of that.

Sometimes it is wise to minimize losses by cutting them quickly and conceding a damaging fact. When you fight over it, the little sharp angles of argument begin to cut you in different ways. There are times to concede and not fight for propositions we might want to establish in an ideal world. Know what's important to deny and don't yield from it.

This is all a function of *preparation,* to which I return. Be prepared, stay calm and listen to the question. Respond minimally unless you want to drive home a point. Drive home a favorable point. Be very contentious about ground over which you feel sure. Sidetracking, half-truths, unresponsive answers are all legal, the Supreme Court has told us.

Play the game not so much with your mouth as with your mind and your ears.

WHEN YOU NEED COUNSEL

At some time or other, almost every one of us has had a confrontation with the police. S/he may have been a victim, s/he may have been a complainant wishing to press charges, s/he may have been a witness, or s/he may have been the object of a policeman's search. The purpose of this section is to concentrate on the last. You find yourself eyeball to eyeball with the person in blue. What do you do? You find yourself accused. What do you do?

I couldn't write a section on criminal defendants without a few preliminary deeply felt disclaimers. The police have a difficult job. Every day they put their lives on the line to protect us, the citizenry. They are frequently harassed and abused, often blamed, and rarely credited for the split-second decisions they must make. They perform many community services, from giving out helpful information and helping the elderly cross streets to apprehending vicious criminals. In short, they are our primary guardians of law and order, without which a free society cannot exist. The vast majority are honest and decent, deserving of respect.

Nevertheless, there are some, whose number may be growing, who display a kind of arrogance toward the public. They think they owe absolutely no respect to any citizen, apparently believing themselves the law, rather than its guardians. It is unlikely, but possible, that you will find yourself subjected to unwarranted abuse after having been stopped, say, for a minor traffic violation. The consequences can be frightening, and fighting back can be difficult, as Lillian Shore found out.

On October 8, 1972, Mrs. Shore had taken her seven-year-old daughter Andrea boating at Lake Havasu, Arizona. Some months earlier, Andrea had undergone open-heart surgery. A California resident and registered nurse, Lillian Shore was at the time upset about her pending divorce action in Los Angeles. She chanced to hit a car from the rear while it was stopped at a stop sign. She offered on the spot to pay for the damages, but they were too minimal to consider, and no claim was ever pressed. Robert Rathbone, a lieutenant in the Mohave County sheriff's office, arrived at the scene of the mini-accident at approximately 10:45 A.M. He observed Mrs. Shore and promptly arrested her for driving under the influence of alcohol. Mrs. Shore vigorously protested her innocence. Although she made no move to escape or resist arrest except to protest her own sobriety, the arresting officer handcuffed her and forced her into his car. There is a certain type of cop who will not stand for anything but meek submission. Her daughter also was forced into the car but was not handcuffed.

Still protesting her innocence, Mrs. Shore was then taken to a police station, where she demanded to be given an alochol test. None was administered, as the station had no facilities to perform either a breath or a blood test. When she insisted she be given a test or freed, both mother and daughter were driven sixty miles to a hospital, where a blood sample was taken for eventual analysis. The Shores were then taken to the Mohave County sheriff's office, where the mother was put in jail and her daughter transferred to a "foster home."

Mrs. Shore was confined in a stinking unlit cell. Although she had more than $200 in cash, she could not obtain release because the local justice of the peace had a standing order that DWI cases should post $240 bail. No effort was made at the sheriff's office to arrange for a bond, nor was Mrs. Shore allowed at that time to make a telephone call to her family in California.

After several hours in the "tank," as the isolation cell was called, Mrs. Shore was transferred to another cell, which had two pairs of bunk beds. Two other female prisoners were already there, and Mrs. Shore was assigned an upper bunk without an adequate ladder to climb up or down. The toilet was in the center of the cell in plain view of the hallway of the jail, and when Mrs. Shore started to climb down to use it, the inmate in the bottom bunk reached up and fondled her legs. When, later, Mrs. Shore tried to climb down, she lost her balance and fell to the floor, hitting her head on the bed and gashing her eye.

Mrs. Shore was taken to the emergency room of the Mohave County Hospital, where the wound was stitched up, then returned to the jail, where she remained until about 10:00 P.M., when finally bail was posted by her family in California. The authorities refused to tell her where Andrea was, but a deputy sheriff overhearing the discussion between her and the others in the sheriff's office volunteered to drive her to the foster home to recover her child. The deputy then drove her and the girl to a local motel, where the Shores spent the night.

The next morning, Mrs. Shore hired a cab to transport her sixty miles back to Lake Havasu City to recover her car, which she planned to drive back to California. But when she entered the station to claim her keys, she was again confronted by Lt. Rathbone, who refused her possession of her own car. Understandably upset, she then demanded her keys, whereupon she was told to "shut up and sit down." At this point, Mrs. Shore and her daughter fled the substation to locate a telephone in order to call California to have her family drive to Arizona and fetch her. Lt. Rathbone followed in hot pursuit in his car. And, believe it or not, he once again handcuffed Mrs. Shore, and with the seven-year-old Andrea crying and beating him, took mother and daughter back to the police station. Mrs. Shore was returned to the tank and Andrea again taken from her mother. But this time Mrs. Shore's family flew out with an attorney.

The alcohol tests finally came back negative, and all charges against Mrs. Shore were dismissed for lack of evidence. Some months later she underwent plastic surgery to reduce the scar on her right eyebrow.

Lillian Shore fought back. In federal court, she sued the cop, the sheriff and the county for false arrest and malicious prosecution. On June 20, 1979, the judge awarded her $101,051.24, and awarded her daughter an additional $25,000 plus costs.

In considering whether there had been probable cause for the police to arrest and prosecute, the court reiterated black-letter law that

> circumstances known or believed by the accuser may be incriminating to the accused and yet may not so clearly indicate guilt that a reasonable man would initiate criminal proceedings without investigation. In determining whether an investigation should be made, the following factors are important: the necessity of prompt action to prevent escape; the availability of information other than that in the possession of the accuser; the existence of a ready opportunity to obtain an explanation from the person accused or to ascertain his reputation. . . . He may even be required to distrust the accuracy of his own observations when they are made under such circumstances that they may be suspected of inaccuracy.

The Shore case is an egregious instance which doesn't often happen. What happened to Marvin Budgar is more typical. Some cops think they own the road rather than merely policing it. On the evening of July 7, 1974, as Budgar was approaching the tollbooth at Exit 46 of the New York State Thruway, a state police car suddenly and without warning made a U-turn in front of him. He slammed on his brakes and blew his horn, shaking his fist in anger at the trooper. The cop pulled him over to demand why he had blown his horn. Instead of acting contrite, Budgar upbraided the cop for making the U-turn without signaling. The cop demanded to see Budgar's license, registration and insurance ID. All but the last were produced. Probably with some satisfaction, the cop began to write Budgar a summons when the latter located the insurance card and tossed it at the trooper. Believing that Budgar had held back the card initially to make him do needless work, the cop ordered Budgar out of his car. Budgar refused. The cop repeated his order. A heated exchange followed and Budgar was arrested, handcuffed, frisked and forcibly placed in the police car. He was taken to the state police station, photographed and fingerprinted, and charged by the arresting officer with disorderly conduct, resisting arrest and refusing to comply with a lawful order of a police officer. The charges were later dismissed for failure to prosecute.

Budgar turned around and sued for false imprisonment and false arrest, assault and battery, and malicious prosecution.

The court found that there had been no probable cause for Budgar's arrest and therefore there had been a false arrest. Regarding the charge of assault and battery, the rule is that "any use of force during the commission of an unlawful arrest is actionable" and "since the arrest was unlawful, a technical assault and battery occurred when [Budgar] was handcuffed and forcibly placed in the State police car." The court also found that there was malice, that the arresting officer had instituted the criminal proceedings "out of spite, rather than to see that the ends of justice were served."

Budgar had not sought punitive damages, and the court indicated it would not have awarded them in any case, but the spontaneous expression of righteous indignation at discourtesy from the cop and the inconvenience which followed did net him $2,000.

What is common to these situations and to many, if not most, confrontations with cops is that they occur on the road and involve cars. You're driving along on your way to an appointment, happily daydreaming, when you happen to glance in your rear-view mirror to see that ugly whirling red light right behind you. You immediately slow down to allow the car to pass, but it doesn't. You utter an expletive under your breath. What's the best thing to do?

The best thing would be for you to be a cop yourself or a cop's wife. Check the records and you will see that an infinitesimal number of police families get tickets. The next-best thing is to work for a public utility, like a telephone company or lighting company. For some obscure reason, cops are very sympathetic to persons in such occupations and routinely let them off. It is also helpful if you happen to have a PBA sticker prominently displayed on your car indicating that you are a supporter of your local police department.

Suppose, then, that you fall into none of these categories and you've been pulled over. What do you do? If you don't care about getting the ticket, then you can respectfully but firmly insist that if the cop is going to give you a ticket, then he ought to do it quickly without unnecessary delay as you are in a terrible hurry for an important appointment. An air of respectful firmness will generally save you time, but not money. In my experience, it is easy to force these confrontations to a speedy conclusion. My friends claim and my enemies complain that I have an intimidatory power that most people lack. Whatever the case, I've found that a simple "If you want to write a ticket, do it, but please *do it,* because I have to make it to the airport," or "because people are waiting," shortens the unnecessary twenty minutes to about five.

Suppose, however, you don't want to force the issue. Suppose you don't want to be given a speeding ticket with all the hassles that entails. (I don't drive usually because of vicious falsehoods circulated by my friends that I drive unsafely. So, while I'll pay the driver's fine, it's not my time that will be wasted.) What's the best approach in order to beat the ticket? Don't be arrogant, don't even be nonchalant. Be upset and concerned, with a touch of fear and apology: "Oh, my gosh; was I really speeding? I can't believe it; I'm usually so careful. I never do this. I feel terrible. How fast was I going?" Try to keep up a conversation. Usually the conversation will be a monologue with the cop punctuating, "Give me your license and registration." It's a good idea to fumble for your license and not immediately locate your registration, thus indicating that in the years you've owned the car this is the first time you've ever had need of it. If you've been stopped by a local cop whose job is not highway patrol, a cop who gives out two or three tickets a week, you have a much better chance of successfully evoking sympathy. Such cops use a lot of discretion, which is also a key point: In dealing with police, there is often great room for discretion. It is important to get the cop to use his discretion in your favor.

If the cop is a member of the traffic unit whose job is regularly to give out speeding tickets, your odds of beating it are reduced. Again, try to get his sympathy. Your attitude should be that he's right and you're wrong. That does not mean that you admit your guilt. It means that you express regret and fear about the situation and try to get the cop to feel sorry for you. Do not say: "Oh, my gosh, I was doing seventy-two; I'm terribly sorry." If you have to fight the ticket in court, you have made an admission which can be used against you. The cop now can put down at least that figure on his citation, confident that you can never beat it.

Most often you won't go to trial. But suppose you have two previous recent violations and this third will result in your losing your license, which you cannot afford. What do you do? *Never* give the patrolman the sense that you will go to court to fight the ticket. If the cop assumes that he is writing just another ticket that will be pleaded guilty, he won't make many notes. If, however, he gets alerted, tipped off that he has an arrogant, annoyed citizen who will fight the ticket and possibly make a complaint about his behavior, then he will be very careful to make detailed notes the better to testify against you at trial. Give the cop no way or reason to remember this incident. When a trial comes up in the future, let his memory be hazy. Don't give him any reason to remember you. That is a general rule of all confrontations with police which may someday result in trials.

Before we leave speeding tickets, I should say a few words about radar. You should understand basically how radar works. It uses a principle of physics called the Doppler effect. Unlike military radar, which operates on a pulse system, the police speedometer radar transmits a continuous beam of microwaves down the highway. An oncoming vehicle reflects these waves, which bounce back to the unit. A chart records the reflecting vehicle's speed in miles per hour.

While a radar unit will work with receding traffic as well, it is usually used on approaching traffic. In general, the unit is installed in a police car to throw its beam backward from the back left-hand window into oncoming traffic. First rule: By the time you see him it is too late. The unit is generally recording objects several hundred feet away. Typically, other police cars are stationed a quarter of a mile beyond the radar unit. A description of each speeding car is radioed down the road to the arresting troopers. If there happen to be two red Plymouths going by at the same time, you may escape, but the more unusual your car, the more likely you are to be unambiguously identified.

Is radar reliable? Can you fight back? Those are two different questions. Yes, radar is fairly reliable, and judges around the country are accepting it as an adequate proof of speeding, provided it has been recently tested. But, yes, you can fight back. Radar has its flaws. Power lines, neon signs and two-way radios sometimes cause false readings. Not long ago a Miami television station ran an exposé on the problems with radar. It was reported that a standard Florida Highway Patrol radar gun clocked a stationary house moving at twenty-eight miles per hour, and a swaying tree at eighty-five. And so, in January 1980, Florida Judge Alfred Nesbitt, citing the above mistakes, dismissed charges against fifty drivers because of the inaccuracies of police radar systems. Also, as radar technology advances, more and more drivers are looking to radar detectors to counter speed traps. Many states have responded by making such detection devices illegal, and these statutes so far have been upheld. A radar detector is only as good as the advance warning it gives the motorist.

The purpose of these comments is not to encourage speeding on the highways. That takes many innocent lives. But police don't only go after genuine speeders. Often communities use their radar units as sources of revenue. It is reported* that one year East

---

* *Penthouse*, January 1980.

Cleveland collected $565,000, which amounted to 11 percent of its total municipal budget.

There may be some relief in sight. If the United States, as reported, is developing a stealth bomber which is invisible to radar, how long will it take a smart car manufacturer to incorporate that technology and give us the 'stealth car'?

One last word, and then we'll move on to more serious matters than speeding tickets. Radar works only during the day, because the speeding object must be identified by sight. The standard police shifts are 8–4, 4–12, and 12–8. It takes some time to set up and test a radar unit. When shifts change, therefore, it is less likely that the men in blue are lying in wait. Thus, if you must exceed the speed limit, you are probably least likely to get caught around four in the afternoon, midnight, and eight in the morning.

Suppose you are threatened with charges of a more serious nature. Many teenagers, otherwise responsible law-abiding citizens, find themselves stopped for using drugs. Take a common situation: the kids go to a disco, and four of them go out to the car to smoke a joint. A cop walks over to them. What's the best way to react?

Once again, almost without exception, the only way you can get anywhere with a cop is by being nice and passive. Try to get him on your side. If the cop follows the rules, he's going to arrest you. But many cops are Vietnam veterans who themselves have smoked marihuana. It doesn't hurt to plead.

Suppose that fails and you are about to be arrested for something serious? First rule: Remember, don't make waves. Don't make waves because people remember where waves are, and if you are going to go to trial months later, you want cops' memories to be fuzzy. You don't want them to be able to focus on any specific incident which will jog their memory.

Second rule: Try to get the cop on your side. Niceness can pay big dividends, not least in physical comfort. The first objective after being arrested is to get out on bail as quickly as possible. You want to be released in your own custody, and not remanded to jail. Everything you do should be done with that in mind.

The cop will often have an input into the bail decision. A kid can have committed a burglary once and still be a good kid. Most often the prosecutor before making a decision as to what bail arrangement to request will talk to the arresting officer. When the DA is evaluating the case, what the cop tells him will be significant; if you haven't given the cop a hard time, that's likely to reduce bail. So the watchword is to come across as a nice inconspicuous first-time offender.

Third rule: Keep your mouth shut! If people in trouble understood the reasons behind this rule, perhaps they would follow it. First of all, there is no obligation to say anything. And, second, you have every reason to remain silent, as we have already seen. But the two reasons may sometimes conflict—i.e., how do I get a cop to like me if I don't admit my guilt? Don't I get him angry by not acknowledging his right to arrest me? Yes, to an extent. There's a tension between being palsy and being self-protective. If you don't think there's a reasonable possibility you can avoid arrest on the spot, then you must be minimally protective by not saying anything self-incriminating while trying to avoid angering the cop.

The best solution generally is to play the middle ground. Be honest without being self-defeating: "Look, I'm afraid to talk to you without my lawyer. Let me get a lawyer and then I'll talk to you." Asserting a know-nothing innocence in the face of an arresting officer who is sure of your guilt doesn't pay. So don't say anything about the crime. Just say, "I'm very frightened. I can't believe this is happening. I can't believe what this is going to do to my parents, my wife, my children." The trick is to beg for mercy without either confessing or protesting innocence.

Do not give your side of the story. You don't know what they're going to find in your car. You don't know what a friend may have left there. You don't know what someone may have planted there. So don't go into details. As prosecutors admit to their friends and among themselves, "It's better not to speak until things go down," because you never know what the prosecution has. A good district attorney will keep any exculpatory statement out of a trial, and any statement, no matter how innocent, may actually later serve to disadvantage you. Moreover, suppose, as in a case previously mentioned, the statement isn't quite true. One lie is enough to ruin a person before a jury. A witness' credibility before a jury is like a chain—no stronger than its weakest link. A judge will instruct a jury that if they disbelieve anything a witness has testified to, they may disbelieve everything a witness has said. Don't give a statement which will later come back to haunt you, even if it seems harmless at the time.

This leads to the next and most obvious rule: Don't confess. You laugh. How obvious. No one confesses, really, unless coerced. Right? Wrong. It may astound you but prosecutors and police report that more times than not people voluntarily confess. You're very tense and depressed, and you've been caught and you give up. If your objective is to avoid going to jail, it's a stupid move to confess. You'll almost never win at trial once you've confessed. So if you need to get it off your chest, just hold it in a little longer, until you see your lawyer.

OBTAINING COUNSEL

We've now dispensed with the preliminaries. You need a defense attorney. Let's take the speeding situation again. You've been stopped in some small town which has posted a twenty-five-mile-per-hour speed limit sign fifteen feet beyond a state fifty-mile-per-hour sign. Seeing the out-of-state license plate, the cop has taken you to the station house. You have demanded to see a justice of the peace, but it's late at night; he cannot be awakened. There is no need to spend a night in jail. You need a lawyer. If you don't know where to start, don't know what lawyer to call, you can almost always find out by asking people around the courthouse— be it the bondsman, stenographer or court clerk, or just hangers-on. They can steer you to the "right" lawyer.

What difference does the choice of lawyers make? Lots. Who is the "right" criminal lawyer? In an ideal system, where there is truly a rule of law and not of men (and women), the lawyer should make no difference to your case. But ours is a rule of laws *and* lawyers.

The first and most important rule: Get a *local* defense attorney. For local problems, get a local lawyer. Don't bring in Edward Bennett Williams or me. Very, very few cases actually go to trial. Ninety-nine percent of the time there is a plea bargain. If you are arrested for speeding, or theft of services for refusing to pay your restaurant bill, get a local criminal lawyer who deals with the DA all the time, who's before the judge constantly. It's just common sense. A person who knows the DAs professionally, who deals with them all the time, with whom they have a rapport, is likely to get you a better deal.

Obviously the best way to find the right local attorney is through recommendations. But if you don't have any personal contacts, or friends of friends, then a very good rule of thumb is to get as your defense attorney someone who was recently prosecuting that same type of crime in that same district attorney's office. If it's a federal case, it's a good idea to hire a former U.S. Attorney who's just finished a stint prosecuting the same kind of case in that district.

These lawyers know the system, they know the people, they know the ropes. And they know the cops; they know the ways things happen. On a mundane level, they know the forms and procedures. They will be sensitive to the weaknesses of the case, and they will know the office policy on plea negotiations on that type of case. They will have credibility in bargaining. Their representations will be accepted. If you have a truly mitigating circumstance, your local lawyer will be able to communicate it more effectively and make it count. S/he will know whether, when and how far to push in plea negotiations.

S/he also will know the weaknesses in the prosecution's case and can point them up to the prosecutor without offending in such a way as to foreclose a more lenient offer. The choice of defense attorney may make only a marginal difference, say six months more or less in jail. But that's an awful lot to some people. The lawyer may enable you to plead guilty to a misdemeanor instead of a felony, thus enabling you to keep your civil rights, or your liquor license or other professional standing.

When choosing your criminal lawyer, there's a common trap

to avoid. Just because a friend or member of the family is a lawyer doesn't mean s/he knows anything about criminal law. Get a *criminal* lawyer. And get one who is not afraid to negotiate. A good defense attorney will not take the first offer, nor will s/he force the case to trial. Like any other negotiation, there's give and take.

How about the DA? You can't control who your prosecutor will be but there are some general things to look for in order to make a decision as to whether and when to plead. In general, younger DAs are more aggressive, more concerned with justice, with getting "bad" people. Older DAs have seen everything. They're tired of bickering and don't care that much about the end result's being just, just as long as the case is disposed of. So I would say that in plea bargaining, you're generally better off with an older DA.

If you must go to trial, get an excellent trial lawyer. If you can afford him, Edward Bennett Williams is worth the money. A great defense attorney can hang a jury in at least 80 percent of his cases, often when the evidence is stacked against his client.

Your trial lawyer need not be a local lawyer nor a specialist in the particular type of crime being tried. I remember a fellow who was charged with a very sophisticated white-collar crime, involving selling commodities futures. I was recommended to him by one of the top men on Wall Street, and a couple of friends of mine. At our initial meeting, I took an instant dislike to him and decided not to represent him; apparently the feeling was mutual, as he didn't seek to retain me in the end. I think it is perfectly appropriate for a client to ensure that s/he's comfortable with the criminal lawyer and to ask probing questions before hiring one. Few of my potential clients actually do this, but I would not resent it. This person, however, was offensive. He challenged me to tell him all I knew about the sale of commodities. I told him I didn't know anything about the legal sale of commodities, to say nothing of the illegal sale. So he wondered aloud whether he shouldn't hire somebody who was an expert in the commodities market. I said: "I'll give you some advice. I don't think you want me and I know I don't want you. But if I were you, I'd be less concerned about what my lawyer knows about the sale of commodities futures—you can teach him in a half hour—and more concerned about what a lawyer knows of the courtroom and lawyering.'' Some lawyers are obnoxious and are total turnoffs to juries and judges. They object constantly and make interminable speeches, and by the end of the few days of trial the jury hates their guts, and through them, their client's guts.

Other attorneys are masters, but they are few in number. I had the good fortune of having three successfully defend me the three times I was a defendant. The first one was Frank Raichle of Buffalo, New York, past president of the American Trial Lawyers College. Raichle's a silver-haired, beautifully spoken man, with a great sense of humor and charm which endears him to the jury. Once he was cross-examining a key witness in my case; the witness happened to be a lawyer who was trying to place me at a certain location by virtue of a luncheon he'd had with a certain client. It turned out that this lawyer had charged the client for the time of the lunch and the client had also picked up the luncheon check. This sounds a little greedy, and Raichle brought the point out beautifully on cross-examination—whereupon the judge, thinking he could one-up Raichle, leaned down and said, "Now, Mr. Raichle, let's be frank. Haven't you done the same thing?" Raichle looked up and quipped, "How do you think I knew to ask the question?" The jury roared. Would that the bar as a whole had a fraction of Raichle's wit.

CIVIL LAW

You, your spouse, your child or someone you care about is injured in your presence. The actions you take at the time of the accident may ultimately be worth thousands if not millions of dollars to you.

First principle: Seek medical assistance immediately, always! The policeman on the scene of the accident asks, "Does anybody need medical assistance?" You do. Always request a hospital. There are several reasons for this. The first and most important is that you may be in shock and not realize it. You may have suffered serious head injuries and be unaware of them; you may be missing a piece of your body and not realize it. Always accept—indeed, insist on—medical assistance.

The second function of going to a hospital is to document your injuries as close to the time of the accident as possible. The insurance industry tends to place great reliance on medical reports made at the time of first treatment, right after an accident. That becomes the "authoritative" history of the accident. Therefore, it is very important carefully to relate the story of your injury to your doctor in a manner which will enable you to collect. The fact that you choose to go to a doctor indicates a severe injury. If you go to a hospital, the first report you make immediately afterward is generally assumed by a judge and jury to be the way it happened. The assumption is that a person is most concerned at this point with his own treatment and will therefore not have the time or inclination to distort and will rather tell it as it happened. Try, therefore, to keep enough presence of mind to relate the details in a favorable way.

If, for example, you've been in a car accident and neither car has passengers, if there are no eyewitnesses, the chief witness will probably be a cop. He asks, "How did it happen?" If you are certain how it happened and the other party is totally to blame, you can relate it: "I crossed the intersection on a green light; he must have run a red." Or, "He had no lights on and was stopped at a green light." Or, "He ran a stop sign." If you think it might be your fault, shut up! To the question "How did it happen?" say: "I can't think; my head hurts too much; I'm too shaken up." If you were partially at fault, you probably are too shaken up to give an honest but helpful account of the event. I knew of a situation in which a pair of cars collided, each with a driver and his wife. The key witness was a police officer who testified that the defendant had admitted to him at the scene that he had "lost control." By this statement, the defendant had also lost control of his case.

Of course, the layperson doesn't always realize which details will ultimately have legal significance. For example, a friend of mine, when he was a child, broke his ankle while running in a relay race at summer camp. Apparently he fell into a hole. His family sued the camp for medical expenses, etc., and claimed negligence in the camp's having failed to inspect the field and keep it in good condition. My friend was to be the witness in his own case. During the preparation before trial, his lawyer gently jogged his memory. "The hole had very light-colored dirt around it, didn't it?" Actually my friend didn't remember what color the dirt was, nor did he care. After enough suggestion, however, his memory agreed that the dirt was light. He asked his lawyer what difference it made. "All the difference in the world. If the dirt was dark, then the hole was fresh and might just have been made by a woodchuck. The camp, even with diligence, could not be expected to discover it. If, however, the earth was light, then the hole was old and the camp was negligent in not having discovered it and filled it in." The case never went to trial, but had my friend told a doctor that he'd twisted his ankle in a hole with dark-brown dirt, his case would have been worthless. The general rule, then, is to see a doctor, and describe all the pain you presently feel. But do not make detailed statements as to how you think the accident happened. "I fell down an elevator shaft" or "I twisted my ankle in a hole" is enough.

I've mentioned the importance of seeking medical assistance immediately after an accident. Often it is almost as important immediately to seek legal assistance. Here's why. A good negligence attorney, having been brought an accident case, will immediately dispatch a trusted and experienced investigator to talk to potential witnesses. The first person to interview a witness can skillfully produce favorable testimony from which the witness will not later diverge. For example, the question "How fast would you say the car was moving when it *crashed?*" will likely produce a faster figure than the question "What would you estimate the speed of the car at the moment of collision?" Each party is expected to remember the accident most favorably to himself and to testify accordingly. But the testimony of "neutral" eyewitnesses has the greatest impact at trial. It is absolutely vital sometimes that your side be the first to interview those witnesses. Otherwise by the time you get around to getting a lawyer, you'll be disgruntled to find that all three eyewitnesses have already signed statements which give a very unfavorable picture of your conduct. So find a lawyer quickly.

I do not mean in any way to encourage inaccuracy or slanting. I do intend to warn against what experienced people on the other side may well be doing, and how to avoid the pitfalls. As Omar Khayyam put it in his *Rubaiyat,* "The moving finger writes, and having writ, moves on. Nor all your piety nor wit . . ."

FEES

Like criminal lawyers, trial lawyers in the civil field come in all shapes, sizes and prices. The most common complaint against lawyers probably is that they charge too much. Of course there are clearly extreme situations, as we'll see. But how much is too much is a difficult issue. I have on occasion charged *substantial* fees, when the actual results have been most rewarding to my client, but I have never knowingly charged an excessive one. What constitutes an excessive fee? A lawyer charges for his expertise, his experience, his savvy, his feel for a case, his ability to know when to push and when to yield. These intangibles don't show up in time charts.

HOURLY. Let's start with the stuffed-shirt large and prestigious firms. They are the concern, by and large, of large corporations and banks, from which they derive most of their business. So the average person doesn't have to worry too much about them unless, of course, he is a shareholder of the company paying their fees. (For example, a few years ago, Ford Motor Company paid over $13 million in legal fees in one year, and that was when things were quiet—*before* I came along with a stockholders' derivative action.) The first problem with the most "prestigious" lawyers is that they seldom have guts. They are too concerned about maintaining their "ethical" reputations and upper-crust bar association standing to fight effectively. Ethics are fine and important, but to me an ethical lawyer is one who honestly presents choices to his client and

doesn't steer him into those which help the lawyer, such as pro-
longing litigation which could be satisfactorily settled or rapidly
concluded in court, in order to keep running up "hourly charges."
Another favorite fee-padding technique is to send two, three, four
or five lawyers to a meeting or to court when one good one would
suffice and avoid quadruple billing.

I understand the temptation; every successful lawyer does.
When business is booming, and other matters are pressing, quickly
settling a client's case, yielding on a key point in a negotiation,
may seem very attractive. When things are slow, fighting the same
dispute to the end, and running up the fee, may seem more attractive to the same firm. But this is unethical. Above and beyond the
lawyer's own best interest vis-à-vis the client, the client's own best
interests should be paramount. Many "Wall Street"-type law firms
are more concerned with the appearance of gentility than the reality of a genuine concern for their clients' welfare divorced from
their own.

In a number of large cities—Houston and Philadelphia, for
example—many of the leading law firms are so buddy-buddy with
one another that they are more interested in country clubs, cock-
tail-party circuits and college football games, which they share
with their "adversaries," than in giving their clients' particular
matters the full adversary treatment they require. The "fight" on
behalf of the client becomes a charade, just vigorous enough to
keep the meter charging away. This antique oak-and-leather "chi-
cane in furs" is no less wrong than its more modest Formica-and-
vinyl counterpart, about which more later. The Wall Street lawyer's awareness that today's adversary may be tomorrow's co-
counsel serves as an additional deterrent to going all out for a one-
shot client.

Legal ripoffs among the rich as well as the middle-income and
poor vary all the way from the simple failure to pursue a case
vigorously to an out-and-out sellout of a client. The rich sometimes
seem most ripe to be taken to the cleaners by "establishment"
lawyers.

For example, a large bank in Houston supposedly was acting

as guardian of the property of a wealthy young heir to the Cullen oil fortune—Ugo diPortanova, whose annual income is well in the millions. After going through a series of Texas lawyers, exasperated and furious, his father and guardian, Baron Paul diPortanova, came to me and told his tale: Out of the multimillion-dollar trust growing by millions each year, his son, the sole income beneficiary of the trust, got $120,000. It seemed impossible: A simple savings account would have done better than that. My partner Tom Bolan, who is a whiz in this area, reviewed the accounts with me. Texas law permits, though it by no means requires, a bank to charge up to 5 percent on incoming funds and 5 percent on outgoing funds. This means that on every single transaction—the sale of one bond and the purchase of another—the bank could and often would take 10 percent. It would sell a bond, charge 5 percent, deposit the proceeds, withdraw them and buy a different one—another 5 percent. Believe it or not, if this bank got a check for oil royalties, deposited it, and then wrote out a check to the Internal Revenue Service from the funds, these two thirty-second transactions cost the beneficiary of the trust 10 percent of the amounts involved.

Next we examined the hourly legal fees with which the bank was favoring its own Houston law firm. *Their* hourly charges for a year exceeded the total income paid to the beneficiary himself! I happened to notice that a person had been hired to do special accounting work. The name was familiar but I couldn't place it. Then it finally clicked in my mind: The name was oddly similar to that of one of the partners in the bank's law firm. I checked, and sure enough, it was the same person. Thus, together, the bank and its top-drawer law firm, as administrators of the trust, drew from the trust more than double what the beneficiary himself received! The icing on the cake is that the only lawsuit the bank's lawyers actually worked on was their own suit against, among others, the beneficiary's brother, who had helped to support him over the years. As this is written, a Texas court has ordered the beneficiary's income increased substantially. This beneficiary's brother is a fight-back man all the way—and one of the inspirations for this chapter.

He is Baron Enrico diPortanova, a man whose quiet generosity to charitable and patriotic causes around the world has won him the respect of those who know the story. A grandson of Hugh Roy Cullen, the billionaire Texas oilman, and the brother of Ugo, Rick is heir to one of the great fortunes in this country. By complex arrangements, the senior Cullens had provided for their grandchildren at a staggering level. An Italian citizen, he designed and sold jewelry in Rome while certain other members of his family and their well-paid associates cut up the pie. We are now at war in Texas—trying to get behind the iron curtain of the privately owned company that has been handling Rick's investments and those of his brother. It was a Herculean task even to discover who ran this private company and owned stock in it, and what jets and cars and political contributions flow from it directly and indirectly. This private company has Exxon Corporation as its partner in Texas and Louisiana oil and gas leases, but the diPortanovas, the Cullen grandchildren, don't have a clue as to the way in which the pie is being cut up. Indeed, key oil and gas properties are carried on the balance sheet at a value of zero or $1! Most people like Rick diPortanova would be happy to pocket the annual royalty check amounting to countless millions—but Rick and his father are fighters-back and they have taken up the gauntlet to fight the Texas legal and family establishment.

Although Houston is a banner place for things like this, it is not alone. One of our clients, a very shrewd and competent individual and the head of a family widely recognized in the sporting, charitable and business worlds, is the beneficiary of multimillion-dollar trusts which were administered by a bank in another city. In analyzing how the bank and its lawyers were handling his and his sister's accounts, he discovered that substantial amounts had been invested in companies with which the bank's long-time lawyers had interlocking relationships. Some were counsel, and others were directors of companies in which his trust funds were invested, some with unsatisfactory return. Our client's shrewdness resulted in our drafting legal papers in a federal court, seeking removal of the trustee bank and additional money damages. We went to the bank's president and personally deposited our legal papers on top of his desk. He read them, and, whether pretending or not, at least seemed unconcerned. He casually buzzed the intercom for a young lawyer who had recently joined the bank's staff. This young fellow was smart and practical. He read our legal complaint, put it down, turned to me and said without emotion in the presence of the president, "How can we keep this out of court?" Having anticipated just this possible question, my client and I had prepared terms and changes which were promptly accepted.

What this firm did to my client pales in comparison to what a different top-drawer law firm had done to his sister, who spends most of the year abroad, and had made the mistake of entrusting her affairs to this firm. A plan was devised whereby she would "borrow" $5 million (which she did not need) from her own trusts, which stocks she would then sell. She would owe the $5 million back to the trusts, repayment of which would have to come from after-tax income. Obviously she would also have to pay capital gains taxes on the sale of the stock—most of which was IBM bought decades before at a fraction of its current value. It made no sense. For what conceivable reason did she have immediate need for the $5 million?

Her brother, who discovered this move in the works, was on the next plane to France, where his sister was residing at her enchanting chateau in the wine country. The next day, Tom Bolan and I received an urgent telephone call. The "consent" she'd signed had been totally misrepresented to her; she had no idea where the $5 million was to go, and she'd been assured by her lawyer that there would be no adverse tax consequences.

I immediately checked with the court and discovered the order permitting all this had not yet been signed, but would be any day, as there was no opposition. I sent someone from our office to get the minutes of the "hearing" before the court. Sure enough, this giant firm had advised the court that there were probably no significant tax consequences to the deal, and that they supported it. A quick check of the tax law by our office produced a case right on point that held this transaction was fully taxable, and that almost

$2 million in taxes would have to be paid if this $5 million loan-sale occurred. Tom and I were on the next Concorde to Paris.

Within hours, the client executed the appropriate papers revoking the "consent," and directing withdrawal of the court petition. After the American consul decorated the papers with appropriate ribbons and seals, Tom and I were homeward bound on the Concorde (you depart Paris at 11:00 A.M. and arrive in New York at 8:45 the same morning!). By the time court opened, I was on the telephone with the presiding judge, and advised him the petition was being withdrawn, and asked him not to sign the order. We rushed down the appropriate legal authorizations to the judge to confirm the withdrawal of the petition.

Now hear this. The very next day, this premier law firm that had approved the deal and given the opinion on no tax consequences quickly dispatched a letter to the judge doing a complete about-face, conceding enormous negative tax consequences, and withdrawing its prior approval. After this disgraceful performance, they still refused to turn over the client's files, claiming some "hourly charges" were due—forcing us to go to court again.

Another caution about top-drawer law firms: They view criminal cases, accidents and matrimonial disputes with distaste. They take these cases only as an accommodation to large business clients; they are generally incompetent at handling them, and they charge exorbitant fees, in no way tied to the result they get in a case. These thoroughbred lawyers would tell you that tying the size of the fee to the result is distasteful—they might have to produce. So they politely charge you an arm and a leg for their failures. This fee perspective is linked with their practice of charging "by the hour," which invites padding of bills. Young associates, whose time is billed at a lower hourly rate, and who are striving to make partner, routinely hand in time sheets which are a measure of how hard they are working for the firm. The incentive is, then, to put in as many billable hours as possible, rather than to solve legal problems quickly and effectively. If the clients are large corporations or wealthy individuals, they rarely complain. There is no consistently workable way to check hourly charges; the client is at their mercy. The hourly-charge racket is often carried to the extreme of charging time for each telephone call. The big firms clean up millions a year this way. Without it, many of them could hardly support their overhead and lavish habits. On cross-examination in a fee case, I was able once to establish that a senior partner in one of the leading law firms had been charging more than twenty-four hours of time per day to one client, while working on other cases at the same time.

But if the large, powerful and wealthy law firms look down their noses at matrimonial and estate work, there are more than enough smaller firms waiting eagerly to take up the slack. The hourly-charge gimmicks, and ploys of all sorts, are practiced upon people with more modest means by lawyers occupying more modest offices.

Many widows' deceased spouses accumulate modest but substantial estates from lifetimes of hard work. Often these widows are unaccustomed to handling their own legal or financial affairs. Their lawyers can deplete the estates by insisting on personally getting on the phone each time the client calls for some help in filling out the myriad of forms and papers which follow the death. Many of the questions could be answered fully by a competent legal secretary, but under the care of shameless lawyers, charging for each "telephone consultation," modest estates and decent pensions are quickly devoured. The clients feel trapped, frightened to start over again with a new lawyer—the devil you know is better than the one you imagine. And they resign themselves to the inevitability that their husbands' dreams and responsible provisions for their family will simply be eaten away by "legal costs." That resignation is coupled with bitterness toward the whole legal profession. And who can blame them?

CONTINGENCY. The professional code of responsibility, which is rarely honored even in the breach, precludes lawyers from charging excessive fees. Given their incompetence and venality, some lawyers ought to pay to serve their clients. Others are only semi-competent, and having them perform their lawyering without payment on either side would be fair. But lawyers don't see it that way. They charge and they charge plenty. Earlier I suggested that contingent fees are often preferable to hourly fees because they give the lawyer an incentive to produce. But they also give the attorney an incentive to shave the time spent on a case and often to defer paying attention to it. And contingent fees give the attorney a strong incentive to be unavailable for discussion, as s/he cannot charge per phone call or per hour.

With this caveat, however, in my experience the bottom line is that most times you're better off with a contingent fee. The lawyer wants to earn, and the more s/he earns, the more you earn. It seems to me, if we've learned anything from the failure of Communism and the welfare state, it's that the best way to ensure that somebody else will perform competently is to give him a financial stake in his own success.

Yet sometimes fees, whether contingent or not, are unfair to the client. You can fight back over the fee if you've been taken. Aristotle Onassis did it with some help from me when he believed that he'd been overcharged by a major law firm which was handling Jackie's suit against a photographer who was making her life miserable. You snicker; "Onassis can do it." But he's not the only one successfully to fight back over fees.

Theodore Pietz's mother died. Pietz, a night clerk at a New York motel, was not aware of fees typically charged by attorneys to represent an estate. He employed Leonard Moriber to collect all monies due him as a result of his mother's death. Moriber agreed on condition that he be given a contingent fee of one-third the gross recovery if the matter was settled without suit and 40 percent if suit was filed. Now, it might strike you as unfair that an attorney should get one-third of what a person works a lifetime accumulating in order to be able to pass on to next of kin. Add to this that the bulk of the estate consisted of a mutual trust fund in which the client was the sole named beneficiary and that there was no will to be probated, and here is one really unfair legal fee.

So, by doing little more than sending a letter, the lawyer collected $23,126.10 due his client from a mutual fund. He also collected $444 from Blue Cross, $255 from Social Security and $124 from a savings and loan association account. He calculated the amount due him for his "legal work" on Mr. Pietz's behalf to be about $8,000 and advised his client that he would send him most of the remainder of the $24,000 estate as soon as Pietz first executed a general release for the $8,000 due the lawyer. Pietz balked and the lawyer persisted.

Pietz fought back. He filed a complaint, alleging that the lawyer's fee in this instance was excessive. A referee, after noting that a standard minimum fee for an estate of this nature is $500 for the first $10,000 and 5 percent of the excess up to $100,000—which would have come to $1,200—gave the lawyer "the benefit of the doubt" and more than doubled standard to $2,500, recommending the lawyer pay back the client the difference between that sum and the $8,000 originally charged.

The lawyer refused to comply. An additional recommendation of forty-five days' suspension was added on. The lawyer continued to refuse to reimburse the client.

The supreme court of Florida finally got the case and noted the difficulty in establishing just what constitutes an excessive attorney's fees. "The answer turns upon multiple factors including the difficulty of the case [here it was easy]; the contingencies if any upon which the fee is based [here it was automatic and uncontested]; the novelty of the legal issues presented [there were none but the most routine]; the experience of the attorney; the quality of his work product, and the amount of time spent in preparation and litigation." Commenting that the lawyer's role "frankly could have easily been performed by a layman," the court said the "use of a contingent fee arrangement under the circumstances of this case was manifestly improper." So the bottom line concerning fees is this: Fight back. If the fee is "clearly excessive," you may well get a rebate. Pietz did.

There is one kind of case in which contingency fees are standard. In personal-injury cases attorneys generally work on a percentage: 50 percent of the first $1,000, 40 percent of the next $2,000 . . . If the injury is serious and the potential recovery is large, there will be some flexibility in the fee. Remember, you, the injured, are the buyer. You are the scarce commodity. You have the case; the lawyer wants it. Don't be embarrassed to negotiate the fee.

A good negligence lawyer will work hard to establish a reputation as a person who is not afraid to go to trial. When the insurance company's lawyers know this they will more readily believe the attorney when s/he appears to hang tough by rejecting offers of settlement which appear too low. It is important, therefore, when hiring an attorney in an accident case to find out if your lawyer is also a trial lawyer or if s/he is going to refer the matter out if it must go to trial. The latter type will look for a quick settlement in order to avoid having to split the fee with a separate trial lawyer. So avoid an attorney who looks to settle a case because it's cheaper to him or her to settle than to refer to another attorney to try. Most formidable negligence firms have both "negotiators" and "trial lawyers" on their staff.

AVOIDING CROOKS AND INCOMPETENTS

There are subtle ways to sell out a client, and it may be very difficult for you, the victim, to be aware that your lawyer has in fact sold you out. An excessive fee is one instance, but in that case you usually know what you are paying, but have no comparative basis for knowing it's out of line! Other times it may not be so obvious that a lawyer is placing his or her own interest above or in direct conflict with the client's. You may never know that you were sacrificed.

One of the more common and most serious sellouts occurs in matrimonial disputes. I described it in detail in an earlier section, but since we are focusing on lawyers here, let me repeat its basic outlines. The lawyer puts his own best interest above his client's, first by encouraging the formal split rather than trying to help patch up the relationship. Second, the wife's lawyer, when dependent on the husband for the payment of his fee, makes major concessions on behalf of his client in return for the guarantee of his own fat fee. This scam recurs in other types of negotiations. Try, if you can, to find out whether and when your lawyer has established his fee. The earlier it is set, assuming the other party is in effect paying it by the agreement, the greater the likelihood your lawyer will be tempted to or has already in fact sold you out.

A related reason clients often lose confidence in their lawyers is a lack of aggressiveness. This has not been a personal problem with me. A lack of aggressiveness can indicate a sellout. For example, a negligence lawyer represents you in connection with a car accident. You know you were in the right and the other party was in the wrong, and you've suffered significantly. Yet your lawyer is pushing you to settle for what you feel is a low figure. Why, you ask? He's getting a percentage of the settlement; isn't it in his best interest to make the settlement as high as possible? Not always! He may have twenty cases a year against this insurance company and its lawyer. It may be the end of the fiscal year and the lawyer for the insurance company may have shown your lawyer a memo his company has circulated to keep settlements low that month. The other lawyer might promise your lawyer to more than make it up to him next year. But, of course, no one makes it up to you— you have been sold out. You become a statistic to your own lawyer.

The problem with judging a lawyer on the grounds of apparent underaggressiveness is that such an appearance is a matter of style with some of the best lawyers. They appear to be almost unconcerned with pushing their clients' interests, but when it comes time for negotiations, on a central point, in a quiet solid way they become immovable objects. These lawyers are to be treasured, not fired.

Not all terrible lawyers are thieves. Many would never knowingly sell out their clients. Yet they too are to be feared. Why? As the Chief Justice of the United States baldly proclaimed in January 1978, about half of America's practicing attorneys are simply "incompetent." He may have been too kind.

It is very difficult to protect yourself from your own lawyer's incompetence, except in gross situations. Let me give you an example.

A client came in to transfer a personal-injury case to an acquaintance of mine, Allan Zaroff—a highly competent negligence attorney. Months before, the client had opened the door to an elevator and had fallen down the shaft, suffering very serious injuries. He had concluded his lawyer wasn't pursuing the case vigorously enough. Zaroff called the previous attorney to get the file transferred over to him. The other lawyer said, "Yes, I'll send you the file, but first I want 50 percent of my fee." Zaroff asked what he'd done. Had he conducted an examination before trial? "No. But the case is prepared to go on the calendar." Zaroff next asked him whether he'd gotten an engineering report on the condition of the elevator at the time of accident. "No," the lawyer replied. "Are you aware that the building has since been demolished?" "Yes." "Then, you must be aware that by failing to get engineering reports and photographs, you have made the case much more difficult and worth much less money in settlement. You are potentially subject to a rather large malpractice action." The other lawyer changed his tune suddenly from "I want 50 percent of my fee up front before transferring the file" to "I'll send you the case folder; why don't you look it over, see what needs to be done, and I'm sure we can work out a fair arrangement on the fee after the case has been completed."

The lesson from the story, which is sadly typical, is that a lawyer may sell out a client by failing to take critical steps when they are necessary. Here the lawyer was being cheap. Working on a contingency fee with a comparatively poor client, he tried to save a couple of hundred dollars in costs by failing to hire an engineer and professional photographer, who not only would have made a record of the condition of the premises at the time of the accident, but would later be able to give expert testimony. Instead, he figured he'd save the money and look at it himself, which was stupid in two respects: His eyes were not trained to see the worst, and his expertise was not such as to qualify him to testify as an expert.

What was critically important in this case was some expert testimony as to why the safety latch on the elevator door, which should have prevented anyone from walking into an open shaft, had failed to work. Because of this serious oversight on the part of the lawyer, the client's lifelong debilitating injuries, including permanent paralysis, which took six pages to list and which might have been worth a couple of million dollars in compensation, are instead worth very little. As a matter of fact, if forced to trial, such a case might not ever reach the ears of a sympathetic jury, for the judge could throw it out for failure of proof.

AVAILABILITY

I have not had problems with claims of sellout, overcharge or negligence. But a complaint which has been leveled at me is that I am unavailable. Of course, a lawyer should be on tap—always—for actual emergencies. But a client's need to consult does not always fit neatly with a lawyer's calendar. I am writing this in Perth, Australia, which I guess is about as far from New York as one can be. Yet, when I arrived yesterday at 5:00 A.M., at the home of friends with whom I'm staying, the office was on the phone from New York.

I'm just plain busy and overworked. So is every lawyer with any appreciable degree of success. I've always liked the saying "The only way to get the impossible done is by giving it to someone who's already too busy to do it." I cannot spend hours listening to irrelevant tales about what happened thirty years ago. I cannot refuse overseas or emergency calls because I'm "in conference." Thus, if someone complains—which I can understand—that they don't seem to get my undivided attention for long, I explain that I can recommend dozens of lawyers who have hour after hour to spare, and whose phone hardly ever rings.

Our switchboard is open from 8:30 A.M. until 8:00 or 9:00 P.M., and often on weekends. Nothing is more important in my profession than availability. But does that mean I must accept interruptions in the middle of every meal or at 7:00 A.M. on Sunday because a client in a matrimonial case has a totally unimportant question, or a report as to some horrible thing her husband did, such as bringing the children home half an hour late? Some clients batter me with letters and messages on obvious moves which, if sensible, are already being made.

This urgency is typical of wives in matrimonial cases. Understandably they are under great pressure, often trying to shield children from the ugly hatred and destructive passions of clashing parents. But the lawyer ordinarily is not the client's best friend or parent or psychiatrist. It is human nature, when you are greatly troubled and paying someone to help you, to come to think of your own problem as the only one that matters; but almost every good lawyer I know wishes certain clients would exercise a little judgment in separating "emergencies" from current events, and in distinguishing what counts from what clogs up a day.

Now, at the opposite pole, many clients are totally considerate. They call only when business requires it, and keep conversations brief and to the point. I can single out three examples which are supportive of my experience that the more affluent a person is, the more considerate s/he is likely to be. The finest exemplars of total brevity who unmistakably convey the message and then terminate the conversation were the late S. I. Newhouse, founder of one of the world's largest media empires and a man of almost superhuman modesty and gentleness; Mrs. Charles Allen, Jr., the pretty and charming wife of the investment banker; and John S. Samuels III, who combines his success in the coal business with cultural leadership of New York City. Never a wasted word from them.

But the point is: It's not my time a client's wasting—it's his. A lawyer soon learns which clients cry wolf, and the lawyer quickly develops instinctive priorities to determine whose calls to return and how really important is "important." It's not egomania that compels these observations, nor is it a swelled head. I've met many a sweller head than mine (don't press me for examples). But, truth is, less than complete availability is not always the sign of a negligent lawyer. On the contrary, that s/he doesn't answer every phone call, or give you hours at a time of undivided attention, may be a sign that you're being a foolish client.

THE WRONG LAWYER FOR YOU

Because there are thousands of tiny ways a lawyer can foul up in handling your case about which you'll never know, it becomes difficult if not impossible effectively to monitor the quality of your own legal care. It's difficult to know until the result whether you've been well served. (And even then it may not be clear, as not every good move wins, nor does every mistake cost.) The critical decision, therefore, is selecting the right lawyer in the first place. A layman relies on his lawyer for day-to-day competence. He should choose his lawyer with extreme care.

To hire a lawyer because he's cheaper, because he advertises in the paper, is a foolish economy. If he's advertising the cheapest rates, he will have to cut corners. And as with the elevator-accident case, a typical instance, to save $200 may mean later to forfeit $2 million. Expertise and care are intangibles. Usually they are worth paying for. While there are many high-priced horrible attorneys, there are few dirt-cheap excellent ones. Don't cut your costs to spite your claim.

In choosing a lawyer, you must ultimately rely on other people's recommendations. And we all know that reputations of all sorts are often unmerited. Your friend may have been well served because her case involved the lawyer's strengths, whereas yours does not; because the attorney took a personal interest in her, although he will not in you; because her case came at a fallow time for the lawyer, whereas now he has personal problems at home. Suppose you conclude that you made a mistake in your initial selection of a lawyer?

SWITCHING LAWYERS. If you conclude that your lawyer is placing self-interest above or, worse, in opposition to your own best interests, or that s/he is negligent, incompetent or timid, you should seriously consider switching attorneys. Make a confidential visit to another lawyer who is respected and get a second opinion. Are you embarrassed? We've discussed that already. Don't be! We are too overawed by professionals. They speak a fancy language of their own; they seem comfortable in a world that is all so much mystery, to you.

But ours is an age in which the tyranny of the professional is finally being resisted. It's about time. In the '60s and early '70s the psychiatrists often ruled the courtroom, and juries and judges kow-towed to their moral judgments of a defendant's sanity or insanity couched in scientific jargon. Now we've come to realize that we, the people, are the best judges of ultimate criminal responsibility. For years, the surgeons told us it was time to cut up our body, and we, unthinking, unquestioning, yielded. Finally, we're starting to wake up to the idea of informed consent, and second opinions. Your life, your assets, your emotional and financial well-being are at stake. And as the beer commercial says, you only go around once. So if you feel your lawyer is giving you the go-around, if you feel mistakes are being made and each time you ask you're confused by technical terms carefully calculated not to let you understand, then seek a second opinion. It only makes sense; either you'll be convinced that your suspicions were mistaken, in which case you'll have more faith in your attorney and greater peace of mind, or you'll find out, and the sooner the better, that you're not really represented by counsel, in which case it's time to switch.

If you should decide a change is in order, make it quickly and decisively. Don't use it as a threat. In the vast majority of cases, a lawyer threatened will react very defensively and, if s/he desires to keep you as a client, will change appearances, seeming more concerned with your welfare while subconsciously resenting you. Remember again, it's your life. And don't worry about what the first lawyer knows that can hurt you. You are protected by a lawyer/client privilege. Nothing you've told the lawyer in confidence can ever be revealed unless you say so.

A lawyer ought, on request, to turn over your file to the new lawyer. We've seen that on occasion a lawyer will resist turning over the file until s/he's paid. This doesn't happen often. But take, for example, a personal-injury case in which your first lawyer agrees to settle with the insurance company for $6,200. Suppose you conclude that the proposed settlement is grossly too small and that your lawyer is pressuring you to accept it because his best interests, though not yours, dictate quickly concluding your suit. You say no and, having lost confidence in your lawyer, now look to switch. The first lawyer technically has a lien against you for his percentage of that $6,200 settlement. Theoretically, s/he can demand that you pay it up front before you obtain the case folder. The lawyer will almost never do this, however, because the client either will not have the ready cash to pay before winning the case or, in any event, will most likely refuse. Then things can get nasty for the first lawyer, who now has a second lawyer as well as a dissatisfied client as his adversary. What generally happens, especially in personal-injury situations, is that the first lawyer negotiates his fee with the new lawyer—either a percentage of the recovery or a flat fee guaranteed out of the proceeds of the suit.

If the lawyer refuses to turn over the file, in most instances a court will order it. If there has been no agreement on the first lawyer's share, the second lawyer's proper first remedy is a suit for fees. (If this happens, watch out. The bar association protects its own by permitting a lawyer to reveal a confidence when necessary to collect a fee.) Remember again, it's your life and it's your right to have it counseled well.

This is a lesson I learned the hard way. Just before the beginning of a criminal trial in which I was the defendant, I came to the conclusion that my lawyer—one of the most highly respected members of the bar who was so decent that he refused a fee—was wrong for my case. I believed him to be wrong in that the trial judge was totally hostile to me and this lawyer's style was to stay completely in the good graces of all judges. Ordinarily there is nothing wrong with this, and many a "fighting" attorney, while apparently "zealously" doing battle for a client is actually doing more harm than good. But I saw this as a rare case in which nothing we could do would get us fair treatment from this judge: The case would have to be addressed strictly to the jury, even to the extent of open battles with the judge in front of the jury. This is always a dangerous strategy, as jurors tend to like and respect trial judges.

I went to my partner Tom Bolan. We talked it out and agreed that we must change our lawyer. I was embarrassed and felt ungrateful, but it was *my* life at stake. We changed. (Another prominent person under similar circumstances knew he should change, but didn't want to hurt his lawyer's feelings, and didn't. To this day, I believe this mistake caused his conviction and imprisonment.)

If the lawyer you're bouncing is a nice fellow, there is a selection of mixed truths and white lies you can use—for example, "I can't afford the continuing expense of the litigation, and some friends have agreed to help me if I use their lawyer, who is on a retainer with them," or "My family insists I use their regular lawyer so they can keep an eye on the case through him," etc. If you are a compulsive truth teller even at the unnecessary expense of someone's feelings, just write and say you've decided to change. If you're a devout coward, as I was, you can dispatch a mutual friend. Another way of steering clear is to have your new lawyer handle the substitution by making a friendly call, in the course of which he will tell the lawyer he's replacing that, of course, he won't come into the case if the other lawyer is not agreeable. The lawyer getting the ax will ritualistically reply that he couldn't be more pleased, particularly considering who is replacing him. Make sure there are no loose ends left. By that, I mean make sure, preferably in writing, that the lawyer being replaced is to do no further work in the matter. That prevents last-minute bill-padding. If there is a balance due, before notifying him of the switch, very casually pin down the amount. This prevents him from sticking it to you later when he finds out you're changing.

Don't change every five minutes, and don't be a pain in the neck. Ask yourself: Is there any real basis for my dissatisfaction? Am I being petulant because I want to be treated like a child with everyone's attention only on my problems, or do I have the honest, supportable feeling that I am not being adequately represented? If there is a real, rather than fanciful, reason to do so, go ahead; fire your lawyer. Change.

PRESSING CLAIMS AGAINST YOUR LAWYER. Suppose, in spite of all your care and caution, you've fallen prey to your own lawyer. What can you do? Your first resort should be to the organized bar association—but only because your only remaining resort is a costly malpractice suit, in which, again, you will likely need the help of a lawyer.

The standard professional histories of the organized bar that are found even in some otherwise excellent judicial opinions claim, to take a typical example, that the bar "arose from a need to protect the public from unskilled persons practicing law." The cant continues today. The bar makes self-serving statements about protecting the public, when in fact it is protecting the livelihood of lawyers who are overcharging clients of modest means who would prefer, if they could, to do without them.

Few lawyers know, and those who do like to forget, the true origins of the organized bar. It did not, as is standardly claimed, arise in England in the twelfth century. It arose, not surprisingly, in ancient Greece. Here's why. The ancient Athenians struggled vainly against the rise of a professional class of lawyers. There was big money to be made in helping other people with their problems, and in instituting criminal prosecutions. The system of justice was a people's system; anyone could institute a prosecution. A professional class of prosecutors flourished. If a prosecutor was successful, he got a piece of the fine imposed. These clearly professional lawyers posed as public benefactors; they claimed they were prosecuting for the public good and that their own share was not of primary importance. But, of course, the opposite was true. The easiest way to make the most money was to successfully prosecute defendants who were totally innocent of any financial irregularities. Once a lawyer established his reputation for being able to convict anyone he wished, the next step was easy: to blackmail the rich by threatening to prosecute them unless they paid off. The hush money from this shakedown became the bread and butter of the large number of "sycophants," as they were called, who infested ancient Athens. Even the totally innocent were willing to pay in order to avoid the uncertainties and hardships of a trial. For, even then, it was already observed that "many things turn out contrary to expectation in a court. Luck, rather than justice, determines the issue. It is much wiser to pay a small sum and be free from trouble."

But, for this huge-scale organized blackmail scheme to succeed, a person who paid hush money to these professional accusers had to be guaranteed that his one-time payment of the agreed sum would protect him from further demands not only by one particular lawyer but by all. What good does it do to pay off once, only to be threatened with prosecution by someone else for the same thing? Without such a guarantee that he would be left alone for a while, an accused person would prefer to risk paying a fine or damages to a continual bleeding at the hands of these professional lawyer-extortionists. So there flourished organized clubs of professional sycophants who could enforce an agreement among themselves. There was, at the beginning, little distinction between the organized bar and organized crime. The bar began in order to protect the economic welfare of its members, and for no other reason.* Things have not changed all that much in the succeeding twenty-five centuries.

The way things have evolved, the bar associations regulate the right of an individual to practice law. They impose the terms and conditions. They are often supported in this role by the courts. Why? Because, as the associations tell us, it is all solely for the protection of the public. They want to ensure that when you go to a licensed lawyer you will be able to trust that your problem is being handled with skill and warm zeal to maximize your interests. By its own profession, therefore, the bar exists to serve the public in two complementary ways: to keep out of the legal profession the unqualified—by taking legal action to prevent "the unauthorized practice of law"—and to ensure that those licensed to practice law serve their clients competently, by disciplining and disbarring attorneys. Is the eagerness to keep people from practicing law matched by a zeal to keep the practitioners worthy of their calling? No.

How can you fight back against your corrupt or incompetent lawyer who has done you ill? Can you fight back? In 1977, 124 lawyers were disbarred. Let's look at some who were not.

---

* For a detailed account of this fascinating period, see Robert J. Bonner, *Lawyers and litigants in ancient Athens*, New York: Barnes & Noble, 1969

Mrs. Ragsdale was a fifty-year-old widow with a first-grade education. She had been employed as a maid in a San Francisco hotel for about seventeen years and had had to stop working because of illness. She first met Thomas J. Clancy, attorney at law, when someone recommended she consult him in connection with a personal-injury claim. Satisfied with her lawyer's performance on that occasion, she retained Mr. Clancy to handle the probate of her husband's estate, from which she received, on final distribution, the modest sum of $10,000. Clancy also helped her obtain a widow's pension from the Veterans Administration and drafted an agreement between her and a songwriter. He later drafted her will. A relationship of trust and dependence grew. This is common between a lawyer and a client. The lawyer handles matters of intimacy and importance and often comes to be regarded as an important and trusted friend. When it works and is not abused, this relationship is the most worthwhile part of a lawyer's professional life. Mrs. Ragsdale and Mr. Clancy talked about their families, and she "thought of him as a brother, and he seemed like the best friend I had here." And, after all, what are "best friends" for if not to share financial opportunities?

So one day lawyer Clancy phoned widow Ragsdale at home and said that, in going over her will, he had noticed she had a little money in the bank. He inquired whether she would like to make a good investment. He told her a long, complicated story about contingent interests in real estate which she didn't understand. She asked him whether she could lose her money and he apparently "guaranteed" that she couldn't. He omitted to inform her of one small detail. He was in personal financial straits. His wife had filed a divorce action against him, and he was awaiting the release of some other hoped-for funds and was not able to borrow any money. So Mrs. Ragsdale "invested" $1,000. He gave her what she thought was a "receipt" but turned out to be an unsecured interest-free promissory note.

A few weeks later the lawyer called her back, telling her he had "good news" for her. "You made $200 on the investment," he said. But first he had to "fix" certain "deeds and things" and then he would have a check for her, in a few weeks.

The uneducated poor widow heard nothing from her trusted investment counselor at law for several weeks. When she then telephoned his office, she received a recorded message that the telephone number was no longer in service. She went to his office, where she learned that Mr. Clancy had moved out. She couldn't locate him and didn't hear from him.

In the meantime, Clancy had used the funds for his personal expenses and to discharge some of his debts. He had given up his office and sold its furnishings to pay back rent. He was unemployed for a year afterward.

Mrs. Ragsdale *complained to the bar association*. She fought back. A hearing was held, and findings were made that, among other things, Clancy had "willfully failed to communicate with her and to make a fair disclosure of his inability to repay her; and that [Clancy] used his position as an attorney for Mrs. Ragsdale and his knowledge of her lack of understanding of financial matters and her trust and confidence in him to obtain money from her fraudulently for his personal use without full, fair, and truthful disclosure of the purpose for which the funds were to be used and of his then existing financial condition which if it had been disclosed, would have thwarted" his scheme.

After the initial findings against him, Clancy filed for bankruptcy and Mrs. Ragsdale was notified along with the other "creditors." The findings of the board were appealed, and the case wound up in the supreme court of California.

The court found that "in a little over five years after he was admitted to practice, Clancy had abused the trust and confidence placed in him by an elderly, uneducated woman of moderate means and in ill health to gain a monetary advantage for himself. His intentional breach of his fiduciary duty and his dishonest conduct in dealing with Mrs. Ragsdale constitute acts of moral turpitude."

What happens to a man like Clancy who, with a license, steals from a helpless client? He was *suspended* from the practice of law for *six months* and placed on probation for another two and a half years, provided that he pay back the promised $1,200, without any additional interest!

Unfair, you say? What worse could a lawyer do? Let's follow the exploits of Kenneth I. Persion, attorney at law.

Persion was hired to handle an estate. He too deceived his client, Viola Ives, the executrix, and ripped her off for $12,500. Only he went a step further than Clancy. Whereas Clancy had done it by half-truths and omissions calculated to deceive, Persion was not so indirect. He made false representations and induced Ives to deliver to him two checks signed by her in blank. (Stop! Do not give anyone blank checks, even your lawyer, *especially* your lawyer! There are better ways of proving you trust your lawyer.) Persion told Mrs. Ives he would destroy the two checks. He did destroy their blankness, by filling them in to his own order in the amounts of $2,000 and $3,000 and cashing them. (Stop! Don't accept a merchant's representation that he will later destroy a check, or refund the balance. Tell him your spouse or accountant or somebody demands that the check at all times accurately reflect the exact payment and wishes it returned.) Then, having fraudulently obtained blank checks and falsely promised to return them while, instead, cashing them, Persion took one additional step. Without Mrs. Ives' knowledge or consent, he forged her signature to a withdrawal slip for $7,500 on the estate's savings account at the Union Bank. He then had this deposited in the estate's commercial account, once again forged her signature to an estate account check for $7,500 payable to his trust account, deposited it, commingled it with his own funds and spent it.

Mrs. Ives complained. A bar committee held a hearing and recommended punishment. The lawyer appealed and once again the case came before the California supreme court.

Persion candidly admitted that his conduct, "regardless of any compelling circumstances, was indeed disgraceful, abhorrent and inexcusable." But there were mitigating circumstances, the California high court found. What were they? Get this. His excuse was that he had "financial difficulties." Perhaps his child needed an expensive medical operation they couldn't otherwise afford? No. He was having great difficulty "maintaining an extremely high standard of living." You see, his wife didn't want him to sell either of his two houses, and, what with orthodontics for the children, and the payments on the boats and automobiles . . . He trotted out an assistant professor of psychiatry at UCLA to testify that the risk of any future occurrence of misconduct was "quite minimum." What result here? He paid back the money, and was *suspended* for *one year* and placed on probation for two more years. Unbelievable but true.

MALPRACTICE SUITS. Only with great difficulty can you fight back against the lawyer who steals—by going through a bar association or court. And you can fight back for excessive fees by going through the bar association. But how about incompetence? Can you fight back against incompetence? Yes!

Malpractice suits can be brought against lawyers as well as doctors and other professionals. They're difficult to win because a lawyer is held only to a *reasonable* level of skill, and generally will not be held financially liable for strategic choices which backfire. But if your lawyer really screws up, demand not only that you not pay the fee, but also that you be made whole. His home-court advantage can be overcome.

Rosemary Smith found that out. Rosemary Smith married General Clarence D. Smith and lived with him for the next nineteen years, while the general's state and federal pensions mounted up. Rosemary hired attorney Jerome R. Lewis to represent her in a divorce proceeding. For some strange reason, the lawyer decided that General Smith's pension, accrued during the marriage but to be paid in the future, was not part of the Smiths' community property. He did not plead it and it was not considered by the trial court, which awarded Mrs. Smith $400 per month in alimony and child support. The lawyer later realized his mistake—pensions are usually included in community property—and filed to amend the decree, admitting under oath that because of his own mistake, inadvertence, and excusable neglect the retirement benefits had been omitted from the list of community assets owned by the parties. His motion was denied on the ground of untimeliness.

Mrs. Smith fought back. She retained other counsel and filed a malpractice action. A jury awarded her $100,000. The lawyer appealed. Guess how much the supreme court of California cut down the award on appeal? Not one bit. Mrs. Smith was awarded $100,000. I hope she didn't have to give too much of it away to her second lawyer.

A piece of advice in protecting yourself which has been given elsewhere is worth repeating here. Don't sign anything until you've read it. Be sure that if it's understandable, *you* understand it. If your lawyer draws up a document and his explanation doesn't seem to jibe with the plain meaning of the words, don't sign it! Dr. Berman learned the hard way. He and his wife were getting a divorce. Attorney Rubin negotiated the property settlement. The settlement agreement read: "At the present time, the Husband earns approximately [a stipulated amount]. To the extent that in any one year, the Husband shall earn in excess of this said sum, the amount of child support per child for that year and alimony for the wife for that year shall be increased by 15 percent of such increase."

The good doctor had three children and a wife. What percentage of additional income would he have to give to them? The doctor asked his attorney precisely this question and was told that only *a total* of 15 percent of the excess would go to his family. Dr. Berman made the mistake of believing his lawyer. He was wrong. He had to pay out 60 percent—15 percent to each child and 15 percent to his wife.

He had read the agreement and initialed each page. And, since it was in plain language, he was unsuccessful in suing Attorney Rubin for malpractice. The court held that, since the agreement was "not ambiguous, nor is it technical or laced with 'legal jargon,' " the doctor therefore would be held responsible. There's a certain irony here. Legalese, that mysterious language of lawyers which in the vast majority of cases hurts consumers, in this case would have protected the doctor from responsibility had it only been more mysterious.

Still, all things considered, responsibility is a price worth paying for ultimately understandable documents. Read them before you sign. Or to the adverse consequences of your neglect yourself resign.

Why do these unscrupulous and incompetent lawyers flourish? Largely because of the bar associations' inaction against their own fraternity. Are lawyers really necessary to all of the many phases of life which they have come to regulate and exploit? No. Why does the legal profession take such a bite out of the assets accumulated through the honest toil of others' sweat? Once again, the bar association is a cause, but this time not a passive cause.

PARAPROFESSIONALS

Rosemary Furman was an experienced secretary. She worked at a lawyer's office and handled many of the routine matters of divorces, adoptions and estates. Her boss collected the fees, while she, as a secretary, did much of the work and acquired a vast understanding of the practical realities of the operation of the court system. Ms. Furman became aware of a very cruel Catch-22. Middle-class wives were being battered by their husbands. The wives would want a divorce or a restraining order of some sort, but had no access to funds of their own in order to pay a lawyer. Legal-aid societies declined to represent them because *their husbands* earned too much money.

Furman stepped into the breach. She counseled these women on how to fill out the necessary forms, and on what to say in court in order to get the most for themselves and their children. She told them which judges to avoid, and to what kind of arguments each would be sympathetic. In short, Furman helped otherwise helpless people to help themselves to their legal rights and fight back.

Nor was she alone. All across the country there sprang up such services. And all across the country state bar associations sued. But some paraprofessionals are fighting back, and continuing to provide such services. Virginia Cramer, for example, in Michigan for about $100 prepared a complaint, summons and all other documents necessary for a divorce. For another $10 she had the documents served by a process server. By the time her business had come to the attention of the courts, Cramer was handling only *uncontested* divorces, which did not involve any questions relative to children, alimony or property division. Any client who desired alimony was told to get a lawyer. (She had referred over 600 cases to lawyers.)

No one complained, no one that is, except the bar association. The way Cramer saw it she was helping people avail themselves of their constitutional right to represent themselves. The way the bar association saw it, she was practicing law without a license. The judge, who was himself, of course, a lawyer, agreed and issued a permanent injuction prohibiting Cramer from continuing to help people through a maze of forms. Cramer respected judges' orders about as much as she respected lawyers' claimed monopoly on expertise. She ignored the injunction and kept on doing business, for this she went to jail three times.

While every state prohibits the unauthorized practice of law, none defines it. For instance, in reviewing the conviction of Virginia Cramer for "practicing law" without a license, the Michigan supreme court agreed that "in an ever changing business and social order" any attempt to define what constitutes practicing law was "doomed to failure." But, omitting all reference to the bar's seamy origins in ancient Greece, the majority nevertheless issued the well-known self-serving statement that the bar "arose from a need to protect the public from unskilled persons practicing law." Yes, there are many unskilled persons practicing law. Some of them don't have licenses.

In short, as the profession sees it, everybody has the right to represent himself and dispense with a lawyer. And for that purpose we will provide you forms, but if you can't fill them out, you can't get help except through us. And whether or not there are people who can effectively help you for very little money, it is in *your* best interests for us to ban them and force you to pay us more.

A little too tough to swallow? The fact is that Furman and Cramer are "only a symptom of the problem created by the failure of the legal profession to see that sufficient skilled legal services are reasonably available and within the means of all people. A vacuum has been allowed to exist. If Virginia Cramer had not sought to fill it, someone like her would have done so. So said Justice Williams in a dissenting opinion. "The very rich and the very poor have access to lawyers, but it is generally admitted that middle-income groups do not have adequate legal services."

The realism of the dissent lies in the fact that those who can afford to will always go to lawyers of their choice. The question is: Why should we make it difficult for those who otherwise can't afford competent help to get it?

In other words, one of the functions that Cramer and others have been performing is to exercise a judgment whether and when a person really needs the assistance of a lawyer. It seems a bit circular to require someone to pay a lawyer's fees to decide whether it is necessary to pay a lawyer's fee. How come only a lawyer, charging like a lawyer, can help a layperson decide whether s/he needs a lawyer in the first place? (I've always thought this unfair, which is why I make it a practice *not* to charge anybody for an initial consultation during which it is decided whether the individual needs a lawyer and whether I am to be the one.)

Under the welfare psychology which has prevailed these past few decades, the federal government has footed the legal bill for the poor, leaving the middle class to struggle and pay. But the 1980s are a time when the country is returning to Constitutional limits on federal involvement with local and state affairs. The effort to balance the federal budget includes justifiable cuts for many agencies including the already flawed Legal Services Corporation. When the funding is removed, this problem—inadequate access of all to their legal rights—will only increase. At the very least the responsibility of the organized bar is clear: as individuals, to *step forward* voluntarily and take more cases *pro bono*, free of charge. At the same time, as an organized interest group the bar must *step aside* to allow the people—poor and middle class—the necessary means to help themselves.

But even as I write, more cases are being brought against the Furmans and Cramers and against our right to have them. Nevertheless, if you are of moderate means in a no-fault state, and desire a divorce without children or alimony at issue, or need a will, or you're fighting a landlord, etc., think of doing it yourself with whatever expert paralegal assistance is available. Whatever your means, participate more in your own fate. For twenty five centuries we've striven for a rule of law. Instead, we've achieved a rule of lawyers.

III

WRONGS AND REMEDIES: LAST RESORTS

SO MANY of us when we were children were always getting scrapes and burns. They didn't seem our fault at the time. And it was so unfair that we'd get hit the way we did. But there was always the school nurse to put a Band-Aid on it and Mommy or Daddy to make it all right, or take us to the doctor. We get older and the burns and scrapes get deeper and the world remains unfair, but, happily and sadly, sooner or later we're on our own. We may hook up for life with a roommate. That's what the first section of this book is largely about. Together we take serious decisions like buying a house, and pleasant ones like taking a trip. That's in the second section, including foul-ups which force us to and from our lawyers.

Here, we end with the hits out of the blue from the most casual relationships, or none at all. You put on a pair of pants and get bitten by a black widow spider hiding within. Weird, but it happens, and to the person to whom it happens, getting a leg up on the situation may be very important. That spider bite or fly in the pie may ruin you. Other people unfairly injure you. They call you foul names in print; they con you out of your life savings or just take you to the cleaners, and while at the cleaners, you give them your favorite suit to press, which they lose. That's what life's about. That's what this last section's about, scrapes and bruises. Life . . . and afterlife, what it's going to be like immediately after you're gone: your funeral, and for a longer time afterward the world that you helped make and foresaw—your last will.

8.
TORTS

ASSUME FOR the moment that you have discovered a cockroach in the last swallow of a bottle of soda. Foreign objects found in soda bottles range from partially decomposed worms and hairless rats to unpacked prophylactics. Although not poisonous in themselves, these objects tend, when recognized as they are about to be consumed, to cause nausea, vomiting and, sometimes, lasting trauma. If proved in court, these unwelcome consequences can also cause a consumer who fights back to be thousands of dollars richer.

Traditionally the law did not allow plaintiffs to recover for "fright, terror, alarm, anxiety or distress or mind unaccompanied by some physical injury." The theory was that in tort—i.e., claims for wrongful injury—there would be too many phony, subjective claims for mental anguish unless there was also an objective check of a demonstrable accompanying physical injury, however slight. But most states have scrapped this rule and now allow a person to collect for emotional suffering as long as there are objectively manifested *symptoms*. Therefore, should anything like our hypothetical cockroach turn up in your food, the obvious rule is to make sure you allow your symptoms to manifest themselves. Don't hold them in. If your pain is real, get medical help, and carefully document your suffering.

A perfect example of the carefully prepared fight is that of Mr. Santine, who witnessed his wife convulse in pain a half hour after she drank a Coke. Santine discovered decayed wormlike sediment at the bottom of some other unopened bottles he had bought at a Safeway store.

He took the bottles to a local university, but the matter could not be identified there. He took them next to an independent testing laboratory, which determined they contained insect larvae and speculated at trial that they might also have contained insecticide. Mrs. Santine saw a doctor several times, who diagnosed her malady as "gastritis, an ulcer, or a digestive disturbance." At trial, Mrs. Santine testified she still experienced nausea, frequent cramps, and poor vision which came and went. She testified that as a result she had been forced to sell one of her two small beauty shops.

By the time this came to trial, the doctor hired by the defendant bottling plant conceded that he could not run meaningful tests on her because it was "a very cold trail by now." The president of the bottlers testified as to the cleaning process of Coca-Cola bottles, but once again the well-prepared Santines countered with the testimony of a former plant employee who swore he'd seen cigar and cigarette butts and even a toothbrush in unopened Coke bottles. As a result of her injuries, objectively manifested and carefully documented at the time, a jury awarded Mrs. Santine $50,000, which award in 1979 was upheld on appeal, demonstrating, perhaps, that on occasion "things go better with Coke."

Often the bottle itself and not its contents is the problem. In one year alone there were 32,000 injuries from bottles of carbonated drinks.* A common cause of injury is inadequate threading on twist-off caps. The process of manufacture involves dropping an aluminum cylinder onto the bottle and imprinting it with grooves. If the grooves are defective, the cap will be held in place only by a closure ring, and when the ring is broken the cap can be propelled with tremendous force. Many of these injuries were serious, and the legal damages collected on their account can be substantial. For example, in 1979 a thirty-one-year-old Kansas English teacher

---

* Consumer Products Safety Commission estimate for 1974.

who was struck in the eye by a twist-off cap that exploded settled for $25,000. A sixty-three-year-old retired postal worker who sustained a cataract when he was struck by a twist-off cap collected $57,500, and Seven Up Co. recently gave $75,000 to a twenty-one-year-old man who had been struck in the eye by a twist-off cap.*

Be careful when you open twist-off caps on carbonated drinks. Make a habit of covering the cap with the palm of your hand or turning your face away. Many people who have been injured suffer not only physically but financially. Don't be one of them. If you are injured, fight back. Manufacturers know that a certain percentage of their bottles are defectively produced. To them it's a planned risk; to you it's real pain and suffering. To them a settlement of a suit is a cost of doing business; to you it's your due, at least.

My favorite story in this area happened in Dayton, Ohio, in 1977 during a trial in which Pepsi-Cola Bottlers was defending itself against charges of having produced defective bottles. The plaintiff, James Massay, had charged that one such bottle had exploded and flying glass from it had cut his Achilles tendon. As Pepsi was to begin its high-priced and elaborate defense, two unopened Pepsi bottles which were exhibits at the trial suddenly exploded in the courtroom, showering the chambers with broken glass and soda. It would seem to a person of common sense that the things had spoken for themselves. Perhaps in an ideal world the judge would have stopped the case right there and then and allowed the jury to find for the plaintiff. In fact, the judge did step in and stop the case. But he found this well-timed object lesson too prejudicial to permit an impartial verdict from the jury. He declared a mistrial.

Now consider Robert Susser, who purchased a 1969 Chrysler Imperial in 1977 and spent about $450 improving it. Two months later, Susser legally parked his car on an Upper West Side Manhattan street. The next day his car was gone. He reported the theft to the police precinct at once and was told that an alarm describing

---

* ATLA Journal, October 1979.

it had been issued. The police cautioned him that in the unlikely event he located his car he was to call them immediately and not attempt to move it himself.

The next day, Susser prevailed on a friend to delay a trip to Massachusetts and scour the local streets to search for the car. Just as they were about to give up they discovered the car parked at the side of a street. As he had been instructed, Susser called the precinct. While he waited for the police to arrive he entertained visions of their dusting the car for fingerprints and lying in wait to catch the thief. The police didn't come. He dialed the police emergency number. Still no police. Again and again he called the emergency number. No police.

Exasperated, he sent his friend to the precinct house while he remained to guard his car. While his friend was gone, Susser flagged down a passing patrol car and told the officer his tale of woe. He opened the door of his Chrysler and the officer observed that the ignition switch had been punched out and replaced by a jack. The officer requested that Susser accompany him to the precinct to fill out some forms and "clear the alarm." Susser challenged the wisdom of this plan. Who would safeguard the car in their absence? he asked. The police officer removed the coil wire and assured Susser that the car had thereby become inoperable. Unconvinced, Susser stated his intention to stay with his car and suggested the officer "clear the alarm" on his squad-car radio. The cop refused, saying it had to be done at the stationhouse and that Susser could not take possession of his car until the alarm had been cleared and the proper forms filled out.

Reluctantly, Susser went to the precinct house with the cop. His friend, quite late for his trip, left for Massachusetts. At the precinct house Susser was kept waiting. After a while he asked why he had to wait so long and was told that it sometimes takes up to three hours to clear an alarm.

Susser had had enough. He bolted from the precinct, found a mechanic and returned to his car, only to find—you guessed it—it was gone!

He sued the city of New York. Before trial he produced proof of purchase of his car—$620—plus sales tax of about $50 plus repairs of about $450, plus $656.42 for rental cars. Nothwithstanding the list, he was willing to accept $800 in full satisfaction of his claim.

The city refused and forced him to trial. The Court found that Susser "advanced a valid, honest claim. . . . Had Mr. Susser resorted to self-help, he would have his car today. Instead, as a reasonable person acting in a responsible fashion, he asked the police for help. By so doing, he unwittingly unleashed upon himself the bureaucratic inefficiency of both the police department and Corporation Counsel whose behavior was at best comical and at worst cruel." Instead of the $800 he was willing to settle for before trial, in January 1979 the court awarded him $1,775.64.

The lesson, once again, is: If you suffer a wrongful injury, suffer outwardly, but stay calm inside.

Many cases in the tort field grow out of defective consumer goods. Let's step back a moment and notice some general rules of law. The Uniform Commercial Code (UCC) has been adopted countrywide and regulates the rights of buyers and sellers of all types. It guarantees consumers that, above and beyond any specific promises a manufacturer may make about a product, there is an implied promise that products are "merchantable," i.e., that they are "fit for the ordinary purposes for which such goods are used . . . and are adequately contained, packaged and labeled." If food, for instance, is inedible, it's unfit for its ordinary purpose—to be eaten. If its container explodes, it, too, is unfit.

We've seen how merchants try to weasel out of implied warranties by disclaiming all responsibility in microscopic print. But the UCC makes it very difficult for sellers of consumer goods to avoid their responsibility to provide basically consumable items. The statute requires a manufacturer to give you "special precautions" if it is opting out of a normal warranty of fitness. So if you want your money back or if you want to avoid paying for defective products, don't worry about fine-print disclaimers you never read. Indeed, most people who are injured by defective products want much more than their money back. There's pain and suffering, doctor's bills, lost time at work, etc. Traditionally courts have been hesitant to allow you to sue for "breach of contract" and collect more than your lost profits for another's unfulfilled promises.

But as we've seen, there is another area of law, called tort, which complements contract law and is even more favorable to the consumer. The most important rule here is that of "general strict liability." What that means in a nutshell is that anybody who sells any product "in a defective condition unreasonably dangerous to the user or consumer" is liable for all physical harm caused to the ultimate consumer *even if* "the seller has exercised all possible care" in the sale of his product. This is true as long as the person selling you the item is in the business of selling such products. With the UCC's "implied warranty of merchantability" coupled with tort law's "strict liability," you've got a lot going for you on paper to help you fight back. In practice, how far does this extend?

For example, suppose you order a glass of wine at a restaurant and while you are taking your first or second sip the wineglass breaks in your hand, causing permanent injury? This happened to Daniel Shaffer, who sued the restaurant under a combined theory of UCC-implied warranty of merchantability and strict liability in tort. The restaurant defended by pointing out that it was not *selling* the glass and was therefore not liable under the UCC. Furthermore, it denied responsibility in tort on the ground that it had not been negligent in failing to detect the glass's defect.

The trial court agreed and threw the case out, and the appellate court affirmed, holding that the restaurant was not a "merchant" in respect to the glass and therefore did not impliedly warrant its merchantability. The appellate court also rejected Shaffer's strict-liability tort claim:

> Were the wine glass in question held to be a mere facet of the sale of the "glass of wine" and thus a "product," the theory of strict liability would be greatly and unnecessarily expanded. . . . If a wine glass renders a restaurateur strictly liable because he could not sell wine without it, what of other tablewear, the waiters and the bus boys, the furnishings to

effect an attractive atmosphere, or the building housing the establishment?

It looked as if Shaffer had lost, as if in order to fight back successfully he had to prove negligence on the part of the restaurant, which he could not do. But the Washington State high court rejected the views of the lower courts, holding it "immaterial" that no property interests actually passed in the glass. "Plaintiff ordered a drink (a glass of wine) from defendant. Defendant sold and served the glass of wine to plaintiff to be consumed by plaintiff on the premises. The wine could not be served as a drink nor could it be consumed without an adequate container. The drink sold includes the wine and the container, both of which must be fit for the ordinary purpose for which used."

Significantly, the court also held that Shaffer could sue for his injuries under a strict liability in tort theory. Rejecting the lower appellate court's fear of an "uncontrollable extension" of the strict liability doctrine, the court said, "We do not agree with the gloomy view of the Court of Appeals of the consequences of allowing the plaintiff to proceed with this action. We hold the sale of a glass of wine is subject to the strict liability provisions . . . If their predictions as to future lawsuits come to pass, we will deal with the litigation at that time." This view has been spreading in recent years.

Speaking of glass, Mrs. Betty Deris chewed on some in her banana split. Perhaps the waitress misheard her and thought she'd asked for a banana shatter. There was no physical injury, but there was $500 worth of mental and emotional anxiety. In this case as with foreign objects in soda bottles, the negligence is obvious. But where, as we saw, it is often very difficult if not impossible to prove negligence, strict-liability-theory recovery is critical to the success of the injured consumer.

The implied warranty that any food served is "fit for human consumption," regardless of whether or not the food server was negligent, protects the customer who is served the unfit food. But this exchanges one problem for another. What does it mean to be "fit for human consumption"? What about a walnut shell in a Chock Full o' Nuts "nutted cheese" sandwich? When Marjorie Stark broke her tooth on one, could she recover? A difficult question. Is a walnut shell "foreign" matter? A New York appellate court adopted the so-called "reasonable expectation" doctrine, according to which a person can recover for a breach of the implied warranty of fitness if it is found that the natural substance was not to be reasonably anticipated in the food, as served. $575 for Marjorie.

Problems concerning "foreign" matter get even more subtle. Miriam Carpenter was injured by a pointy chicken bone embedded in, of all things, a chicken breast. Doesn't a consumer naturally expect chicken bones in a chicken breast? Not necessarily; this particularly sharp bone was found in the meaty part of the chicken which she had torn off and hastily consumed. Finding the chicken "was in a defective and unreasonably dangerous condition making it unfit for human consumption," the jury awarded her $1,500.

The appellate court reviewed the rule of strict liability. Once again, if they serve you food unfit for human consumption, they're liable regardless of whether they're negligent. Next the court noted other cases, including one in which an injured consumer was denied any recovery when he broke a tooth by biting on a cherry pit concealed in a cherry pie. Cases such as this distinguish between injuries caused by food containing a "foreign" substance on the one hand and injuries caused by a substance *natural* to the product sold on the other. Under this "foreign/natural" test, you can collect only for foreign substances and not for natural ones.

Other courts, as we saw with the nutshell in the sandwich, reject this test in favor of the "reasonable expectation" test. Following this latter approach, a Wisconsin court had allowed a restaurant patron to collect for an injury caused by a chicken bone in a chicken sandwich. There the court had stated, "There is a distinction between what a consumer expects to find in a fish stick and in a baked or fried fish, or in a chicken sandwich made from sliced white meat and in roast chicken. The test should be what is reasonably expected by the consumer in the food as served, not what might be natural to the ingredients of that food prior to preparation.''

In our case, with a pointy chicken bone embedded in the fleshy part of a chicken breast, it is not easy to apply the standard of the "reasonable expectations" of an average consumer. In effect, the appellate court conceded the difficulty—"reasonable minds could differ''—and since twelve jurors had agreed to give Miriam $1,500, the court let her keep it.

Where strict liability protects the consumer we've seen that negligence is irrelevant. Therefore, the fact that when the restaurant served you unwholesome food you were negligent in not discovering the monster roach staring right at you hopping up and down on your spoon is of no consequence. The fancy legal way of saying the same thing is that your "contributory negligence is not available as a defense when such negligence consists merely in the failure to discover the defect in the product.''

But there is one catch in the net of strict-liability protection. Whereas your "contributory negligence" is no problem, your "assumption of the risk" will cancel even strict liability.

For example, Ann Bronson was invited to dine at Club Comanche in the Virgin Islands. After eating some fish that was poisonous, she became violently ill that night. She was unable to eat or digest her food for a long time thereafter. As a result she lost considerable weight, and was very weakened, as well as disabled from performing her responsibilities at work or around the house. She was lucky, really. The diagnosis was ciguatera, a serious disease. Individual fish of certain species in the Caribbean and Pacific areas carry this toxin. The disease is characterized by "nausea, vomiting, diarrhea, cramps in the extremities, muscle weakness, sweating, chills and fever. The skin becomes flushed, there is a tingling and severe itching, metallic or peppery taste in the mouth, a generalized inability to coordinate, and a general complaint of hot objects being cold and cold objects being hot. In severe cases, loss of speech, respiratory and body paralysis, coma and death may result.'' Careful inspection does not reveal whether a particular fish contains ciguatera toxin, and cooking does not destroy the poison.

It was no one's fault. The only way to prevent the disease was to not eat the fish. But, as we know, "the implied warranty of a restaurant keeper is that the food he serves his customers is wholesome, contains no deleterious substances and is fit for human consumption. The implied warranty imposes a strict liability upon him making him liable to his customers even though in the exercise of all possible care in the purchase and preparation of the food he could not discover its unwholesome nature." So it would seem that Ann collects.

But here's the catch which made her lose. She'd been a resident of the Virgin Islands for twenty years and admitted on cross-examination that she had known of other cases of fish poisoning. In short, the court concluded that she had voluntarily "assumed the risk." "If the consumer is fully aware of the danger and nevertheless proceeds voluntarily to make use of the product and is injured by it he is barred from recovery." Ann collected nothing.

This "assumes-the-risk" exception could potentially swallow up the entire rule of protection. A court could find that because of a restaurant's poor reputation in the community, its patrons assumed all sorts of risks. Fortunately, the exception has not been applied often.

I've given a few examples of common troubles with food. But I've saved for last perhaps the most common: a confrontation between you and the restaurant which has served you food without foreign objects or poison, but which is nevertheless just plain bad. If you refuse to pay, which you have every right to do, things can get nasty.

Consider this true-life scenario. You've had a wonderful day's outing at Surf City, New Jersey. En route home to Philadelphia you, your husband, your son and your mother stop for dinner at the Dutchman's Restaurant. Mother and daughter order fish, and while waiting for it, eat the bread and salad. The potato is undercooked and the fish is inedible, and you complain to the waitress, who summons the hostess. She tells you that the fish is "fresh" and there can't be anything wrong with it. You tell her to taste it. She refuses, informing you she isn't hungry and has already had her dinner. She walks away.

You are indignant. You will not pay for food you find inedible; you don't want to order anything else. You demand the bill from the waitress, who charges you for all the food ordered. You offer instead an amount you calculate equals the food you actually consumed. The waitress begs you to leave her out of this squabble, and you offer the money to the hostess, who takes you to settle the dispute with the bartender. He makes some sarcastic comment about a full moon that night. The hostess overpolitely informs you that either you pay the bill in full or she will call the police.

You are furious; this is extortion and you know it. It happens thousands of times every day. At this point the disgruntled patron usually gives in, pays the bill and announces s/he will bad-mouth the restaurant throughout the neighborhood.

But Diane Lind and Helen Sprecher decided not to take it and to fight back. In effect they told their "hostess," "Do what you're going to do. We're not paying for inedible food." The local police soon thereafter burst in through the back door and arrested mother and daughter. Joan Schmid, the "hostess," signed a complaint charging them with "obtaining food with an intent to defraud." Bail was fixed at $200 each, and Mr. Sprecher, who hadn't ordered fish and wasn't involved in the protest, drove back to Philadelphia to get the money. The two women remained in jail from 8:30 P.M. until 3:30 A.M., when they were finally bailed out.

Six days later they were tried before a local magistrate, who found that the food was indeed bad, but that Lind and Sprecher were guilty because they should have paid for the food and sued the restaurant to get their money back, and because they had not ordered additional food. The case was retried by a county court solely on the transcript of the lower court's proceeding. This court reversed, holding that the women had refused to pay the balance of the bill because they truly believed the fish was inedible, and that they had the money to pay for the food and did not try to "sneak out" without paying. Because the state had not met its burden of proof that either woman was attempting to defraud the restaurant, the convictions were reversed.

This was far from a full vindication. The women had been

subjected to inedible food. Fighting back so far had cost them seven hours in jail and the time and expense of a trial and appeal. All this because of Joan Schmid. Lind and her mother were determined to fight back some more. So they sued Schmid for "malicious prosecution"—an intentional tort upon which the courts generally frown. This form of fighting back is disfavored because we want citizens to be able to call to the attention of the authorities apparent criminal violations without fear that they themselves will later be sued for doing so. Nevertheless an action for "malicious prosecution" does lie when, with *malice,* a person has *instituted a criminal action* against another *without probable cause* for doing so, *and* when the prosecution was *terminated favorably to* the accused.

Here, the women's convictions had been overturned—therefore they met the "terminated favorably" part of the requirement. The obvious key question was whether hostess Schmid had "probable cause" to believe that the patrons had committed a crime when she caused them to be arrested. At the time, the majority rule across the country and in New Jersey was that a conviction at the trial level necessarily amounted to probable cause. The logic was that if you've been convicted then I must have had at least some legitimate basis for pushing your prosecution in the first place and therefore you can't later sue me for malicious prosecution after your conviction has been reversed on appeal. With this rule controlling here, the lower courts threw out the women's suit.

"Unfair!" they argued. Schmid had been malicious in prosecuting them and the first court had been clearly erroneous in convicting them while at the same time finding the food served them had been inedible. The higher court had recognized the lower court's clear error and corrected it, so why should they be punished twice by it? It all made sense, except the prevailing rule was contrary. Their fledgling lawyer, M. Jefferson Davis, convinced the high court, which broke with tradition and allowed the malicious-prosecution suit.

If this story had a just and happy ending, perhaps Lind and Sprecher would have settled handsomely and been repaid for their indignities. But it didn't work out that way. The restaurant's insurance company, which stood to pay any adverse judgment, refused to settle. Instead, it submitted counsel and sent in an outstanding trial lawyer against the inexperienced but so far successful Davis. At trial the company's attorney skillfully stoked the smoldering temper of Sprecher and got her to flare up in anger. He also managed to make it appear that the women had gone to jail in order to make themselves martyrs. The local jury found for the local restaurant owner.

So, all told, Lind and Sprecher had been served bad food, spent seven hours in jail, and been through two trials and appeals for which they had spent thousands of dollars. All for what? They had changed the law, making it easier in the future for the public to fight back in situations where people maliciously prosecute us for our righteous refusal to pay for defective goods and services. Although their efforts resulted in no financial benefits to themselves, their place in the fight-backer's hall of fame is assured. Let us ensure that their efforts have not been in vain.

9.
BAILMENTS

WE ARE our bodies and our memories. People we love pass on, memories fade, and the records of our lives we treasure. Suppose, then, our life's record consists of thirty-two fifty-foot reels of movie film—first steps, family pets, weddings, birthdays, Little League games, etc. After carefully placing the thirty-two reels in order, we take this treasured collection to our local drugstore, where we bought the film, to have the segments spliced into four larger reels. The manager gives us a receipt with some fine print. We don't read it; after all, it's only a receipt. Instead, our parting words are: "Don't lose these. They are my life."

The store sends them out to a GAF lab for splicing. And what happens next? "The best guess is that the plaintiff's film went from GAF's lab to the garbage dumpster to a truck to a barge to an up-Sound landfill where it may yet repose."

This was the final journey of the Mieskes' film. They sued the drugstore and GAF. A jury awarded them $7,500. The defendants appealed, and the supreme court of Washington was faced with two questions: Should the fine print limit the liability to replacing thirty-two blank rolls of film, and, if not, can a person collect for the lost film's sentimental value?

Once again, the fair colors prevailed over the black and white. In April 1979 the Washington supreme court unanimously held that, whatever the usual practice in the film trade, the Mieskes weren't on notice as to the proposed limits on liability. The film didn't have a market value and it couldn't be replaced. Therefore, the value to the owner was the proper measure of damages. Sentiment which "indulg[ed] in feeling to an unwarranted extent" being "affectedly or mawkishly emotional" was not to be compensated. But simple sentimental value—"governed by feeling, sensibility or emotional idealism"—was the proper measure of the loss. The $7,500 award was affirmed.

In a variety of such situations we pay someone to care for our possessions. For example, before going on a trip, you store your furs, garage your car. Each time, you're given a claim check. In legal terms you, the owner, are the "bailor," they, the keeper, are the "bailee," and the contractual relationship is called a "bailment."

Perhaps even more than in the business of safekeeping, bailees are in the business of limiting their own liability with fine print. Sometimes it works; sometimes it doesn't. Let's look at different situations, and then try to draw general conclusions about fighting back.

Evelyn McKissick delivered to R. Connely Jewelers two rings valued at $4,000 to be made smaller. When she returned to pick them up, she found they had been made so much smaller they had disappeared. Unfortunately, as the jeweler informed her, there had been a break-in by burglars who had pried open a locked metal door between the jewelry store and an adjoining vacant building and had entered the vault by knocking off the dial to the combination lock and ripping open the door with a crowbar. The walk-in vault, eight feet tall and five feet wide, was built into the building and had steel and concrete walls and floor six to eight inches thick. All this was very impressive except that Evelyn's rings were gone.

It so happened that this jeweler didn't carry insurance. It appeared the poor jeweler would now have to pay Evelyn out of his own pocket. But the North Carolina courts didn't see it that way. The trial court held, and it was affirmed unanimously in May 1979, that because there was no contract requiring the jeweler to purchase insurance against loss by theft, and as long as he had used due care to safeguard Evelyn's property, and since the loss occurred without his fault, he didn't have to make her whole. Unfair, isn't it? Presumably it had never occurred to Evelyn McKissick to ask the jeweler whether he carried insurance; she had assumed it. Wouldn't you? No matter, said the court: "There was no contract requiring the defendant to purchase insurance. . . . The defendant was under no duty to inform [her] that there was no such insurance."

Had it cared to, the court could have awarded Evelyn her $4,000. Its opinion might have read: "One who entrusts valuables to a jeweler rightfully and reasonably assumes that implicit in a contract to repair is a guarantee that the valuable jewelry will be returned. And absent clear notice to the contrary, a person reasonably assumes that the jeweler is insured against loss by theft. If the bailee is so confident about the inviolability of his own safe as to not insure, he takes the risk of being wrong. Of course, it is open to a jeweler not to insure and pass on the savings to the bailor in the form of lower prices, and it is open to the bailor consciously to take the option to leave her rings at her own risk. But to hold that this occurred here is to ignore reality."

All this is so much wishful thinking. Evelyn was out $4,000 for doing absolutely nothing wrong. The lesson is to acquire a habit of not assuming the obvious and distrusting all bailment relationships. Suppose she'd asked the jeweler whether her rings were insured. If he falsely assured her they were, the court would have almost certainly found an implied contract and held him liable. If Evelyn had been smart, she would have gotten him to guarantee it in writing, but that's so embarrassing. What were the odds of losing the rings? Better than either of them imagined.

Suppose the jeweler had answered truthfully that he wasn't insured. Evelyn's next move would be to ask him why not. He might answer that this building had been a bank and that the safe had not been broken into in its twenty-six years of operation. "Since there is no risk," Evelyn might say sweetly, "you won't mind calming the irrational fears of this overcautious lady by guaranteeing in writing that in case the impossible happens, I get paid back.'' Most likely the jeweler would have been willing to do this. The same false confidence he felt in his safe which caused him to decline insurance in the first place might well impel him to act as insurer rather than lose the business.

One of the most common bailments involves cars. The standard sign at the parking lot reads, ''Not responsible for articles left in the car.'' Atlanta Parking Services, even if it were negligent in failing to protect R. J. White's car while parked in its reserved space, was not liable for the $2,000 of equipment stolen from its trunk. By *prominently* displaying the sign, the lot had limited the bailment to the car, excluding its contents, toward which it had no responsibility whatever. This is fair. Two people should be free knowingly to contract just about anything that doesn't injure society.

But *fine-print* ''contracts'' are another story. Carl Shroeder drove his car into the Allright Parking lot in downtown Houston. He handed over the car to an attendant and received a claim ticket:

ALLRIGHT, INC.
320 TRAVIS
WE CLOSE AT 6:00 P.M.

IMPORTANT ·· READ CAREFULLY

In consideration of low rates charged for parking, customer agrees that parking operator won't be responsible for loss by fire, misdelivery or theft, except with loss be occasioned by negligence of operator, and then only up to a maximum value of $100. Proportionately greater rates must be paid in advance if customer sets larger limits of liability.

Articles Left In Car At Own Risk

191

ALLRIGHT AUTO PARKS

Notice the words ''we close at 6:00 P.M.'' were printed on the ticket in heavy type. If you happen to have microscopic vision you might also notice that the garage limited its liability to $100, even in the case of its own negligence, after that hour. Signs were located throughout the parking lot which stated that the lot closed at 6:00, and that anyone returning after that time could pick up his keys at another parking lot (also operated by Allright). When Mr. Shroeder returned to the lot around midnight his car was missing. He inquired at the other lot, but no one knew anything about his car or its keys. It was later recovered, partially stripped, worth $1,000 less than it had been.

Mr. Shroeder sued. The parking lot claimed that Shroeder had impliedly agreed to the limitation of liability provision printed on the stub of the parking ticket. A jury, however, awarded him the $1,000. A Texas appeals court affirmed:

> Where parking lot owners attempt to limit liability by posting notices on the wall or by printing such a limitation on the claim check, the limitation must be called to the attention of the bailor before they may become part of the bailment contract. . . . The limitation provision printed on the claim check was not specifically called to the attention of the bailor at the time he left his automobile at the parking lot. . . . There is no evidence that the plaintiff read the material appearing on the claim check which was given him.

Now this is interesting, when you think about it. If Mr. Shroeder *had* read the claim check and later honestly admitted it, presumably he would have lost his case. But by not being so diligent, the fact that the limitation was in tiny print absolved him of the responsibility to read it. So it seems that sometimes, in bailments at least, not only does the red, white and blue prevail over the black and white, but ignorance is bliss. Your best strategy, therefore, may well be to forget this entire chapter so that if you're ever hurt by a bailee's lack of due care, you can honestly say it never occurred to you that you might be agreeing to its low liability in case of its negligence.

Car complaints traditionally head the bailment list. A few years ago there were 110 million automobiles and 134 million motorists in the United States. The figures are probably higher today. Nearly $50 billion is spent each year to repair and maintain cars. Although your car is in need of repairs, the screws are often put to you instead. The National Highway Traffic Safety Administration estimated in 1978 that $20 billion was wasted on poor, needless, or fraudulent auto repairs.* Before 1973 only three states gave con-

---

* "Consumer Problems with Auto Repair," published by the Office of Public and Consumer Affairs, U.S. Department of Transportation.

sumers any protection in their dealings with auto-repair shops. Now about half the states do; typically, the shop is required to give you a written estimate before doing any work and to inform you and get your permission to exceed the estimate by more than 10 percent. It is standard and good advice for you to demand the return of all replaced parts.

Getting a written estimate as to price and completion date is fine, except the price is often going to be higher and the delivery date later than promised. Furthermore, you think you are helpless because the shop has your car and won't release it without cash or a certified check. You are indeed a prisoner. This happens daily to thousands of people all over America. For example, it happened to William F. Buckley, Jr., although with a boat, not a car. His motor-sailer ran into trouble off the coast of Bermuda. He was to catch a plane to New York, arriving just in time to introduce the Vice President of the United States at a dinner. When he got the bill for the simple rescue, he nearly passed out. In fact, he is still writing fuming columns about it.

It happened to a dentist from Scranton, Pennsylvania, who left his car for repairs at a "reputable" New York repair shop. The work was to be completed in a week. Three months later, the car was ready at "triple" the estimated price; and then it was released for cash or certified check only—and still isn't functioning properly.

If it happens to you, you feel furious but defeated. You are stuck. Must you pay their excessive demands and go away licking your wounds? Not at all.

1. Here is something few people seem to know. You can give the shop a certified check and then stop payment on it just as you can stop payment on a regular check. You have your car or boat, and the shop has a check on which it can't collect without coming to you on non-blackmail terms. Or:

2. You can go to court and get an *order of release,* with a method for determining how much you actually owe. Or:

3. You can *pay now,* and *sue later* for damages and return of the overcharge.

Let me give you some actual examples of how this works. Our firm owned an old Mercedes limousine (God help whoever has it now). It broke down in Long Island. A Mercedes place nearby was glad to take it in for repairs. We were given an estimate of "under $1,000 and ready in a few days." The few days came and went. No car. Finally, weeks later, the repairs were complete and the tab was $4,500—cash or certified check. I swore to myself there was no way I was going to get taken. The owner, incidentally, professed great personal friendship and admiration for me—and referred to a wealthy and socially prominent family in Long Island as his customers, knowing they were clients and good friends of mine, commenting that "even they always pay cash in advance."

My first stratagem—unsuccessful—was to arrange for our driver to test-run the car (all the way into New York). The shop owner didn't fall for that. My next idea was to use our duplicate set of keys and just have the car driven away. He was too smart for that. When his mechanics finished work on a car, they promptly moved it to a secret location away from the body shop. I then devised the idea of a trial run, with our driver agreeing to be accompanied by a representative of the repair shop, who a few miles later would politely be told to get out of the car. I was dissuaded from this by some of my partners, on the theory that the representative of the repair shop might claim to have been kidnapped. If it were up to me, I would have done it that way—but I sometimes bow to wiser heads, or at least cooler ones. So that brought us to our last alternative—give the shop a certified check, get back the car, and then stop payment on the certified check. We did it. As soon as the phone-booth call came that the car was returned, a letter was hand-delivered to the bank, stopping payment. About two days later the body shop found out what had happened. They threatened the bank in every which way. They called the Superintendent of Banks—all to no avail. What certification of a check means is that there is and will continue to be enough money in the account of the issuer to make good the check —it does not turn the check into automatic cash like a bank check, or prevent the issuer from stopping payment on it.* A few days later, realizing that it had been outfoxed for once, the shop called to negotiate a settlement. I was in a charitable mood, and knocked off only about a third of the bill.

Earlier we looked at trips and luggage, now we've discussed jewels and cars. No chapter on bailments would be complete without furs.

In the spring of 1973, Florence Carter brought her fur coat to Reichlin Furs for cleaning and storage until the next winter season. She was given a printed form, on the front of which the furrier had written $100 as the valuation of the coat. There was no discussion at the time of its true value, nor did Carter realize that $100 had been written on the receipt, which she didn't read. If she had, she would have noticed on the other side of the contract fifteen conditions, one of which limited the liability of the storer to the actual value of the coat or its declared value, whichever was less.

Spring and summer passed and the autumn chill returned. It was time to take the fur out of storage. After Ms. Carter had paid the bill for storage and other services on the coat, the furrier informed her that the coat was lost and offered her $100. She sued. A trial court awarded her $450, the coat's true value, and an appeals court affirmed.

A similar case arose in Arizona. Hyman Brettschneider of Mr. Brett Furs and Fashions stored two furs belonging to Janet Lerner. Again, a $100 valuation was placed in the blank, the true value was not discussed, and the disclaimer limited liability. Six years later, when Janet was in the shop, she asked after her fur and about the failure to have been billed for storage fees. Claiming to be too busy to search for the mink in the vault, Mr. Brettschneider told her the storage fees would accrue until she decided to retrieve the mink,

---

* However, a bank may not be obligated to honor your stop payment request. And if it does, the bank still may require you to post a bond equal to double the amount on the face of the check to protect itself in the event the payee sues. A lot depends on your standing and relationship with the bank. Often, a threatening letter from a mean lawyer (try me) can block an account. If the bank gets uppity and wants a bond, do it—particularly if the amount is not large. The fact is that by successfully blocking the enemy from getting his/her money, you have the leverage, and chances of a settlement at a reasonable figure are excellent.

which he offered to buy. Five years later she attempted to retrieve her mink. Without searching his storage vault for it. Mr. Brettschneider stated he didn't have it any longer. Janet, he said, had left the fur in storage too long for him to be required to keep it. This excuse was rather flimsy, as he had never sent her any notice of inquiry, and had stored other furs for this length of time.

At trial he claimed that it was a well-settled principle of law that acceptance of storage receipt at the same time the goods are bailed constitutes an assent to the terms and conditions of the receipt, and therefore his liability would be limited to $100.

In May 1979, however, the appellate court unanimously "reject[ed] this inflexible approach." Instead, it offered seven factors to be considered in determining the reasonableness of the furrier's belief that the customer had knowingly entered into a contract with the stated limitation:

1. Whether bailee notified bailor of the limitation.
2. The conspicuousness of the limitation.
3. The intelligibility of the language of the limitation provision to a layperson.
4. Whether bailor signed the storage receipt.
5. Whether bailor assented to the $100 valuation.
6. The status of the bailor as business person or layperson.
7. The purpose of the limitation.

Using these factors in this case, the court noted that "bailee did not discuss the valuation with bailor, nor did he notify her of the limitation. He did not ask her to read or sign the receipt, and she did neither. The limitation is inconspicuously placed in the midst of a lengthy paragraph printed in small type. A lay person may not readily understand the import of the limitation provision which is couched in legalese. Bailor is a lay person, not a business person chargeable with general knowledge that bailment contracts often contain liability limitations. Bailee arbitrarily limited a known risk." Consequently, Janet Lerner's $4,000 judgment was affirmed.

Again the lessons of fine print. It can come back to haunt you. Bailments can be nasty things. If you've been burned, fight back!

When they offer you a paltry sum and wave the fine-print "contract" by which you've given up all your rights, you wave the flag. Although you've lost by the black and white, you may yet win under the red, white and blue. I say it over and over but it's true over and over, and if more people only believed it, fewer of us would be taken advantage of and more of us would take the advantages the law allows.

If you're absolutely committed in advance to leaving your property with a particular bailor, then you're probably better off not reading the fine print at all. But remember Evelyn McKissick —out $4,000 for her stolen rings. Learn from her mistake. Don't be embarrassed to ask questions and ensure your important possessions are protected. Don't be overtrusting. The world is not out to screw you, but it's not out to protect you either. The law, like the Lord, helps those who help themselves.

10.
FRAUD

PROBABLY LESS often than once in a lifetime a truly once-in-a-lifetime good deal is offered the public. Why do so many people get sucked into apparent opportunities only to end up with real disappointments? I'm not sure. Perhaps it's a tendency of human nature to assume that luck is on our side. People tend to make their hopes the foundation for their beliefs. How else explain the number of people who consistently lose money at gambling tables playing games by rules they know are stacked against them? Like the man who walked into a gambling casino saying: "I sure hope I break even—I need the money."

The vultures who run business-opportunity, merchandising and mail frauds often possess a refined skill in sizing up and seizing on a person's hopes and fears, and playing a cruel opportunistic tune on others' vulnerabilities. Frauds come in all forms and reach heights of sophistication, propelled by high-powered, white-collared Ph.D.'s in ripoff psychology. Some professional con artists hang out at Madison Avenue and work for the largest corporations, fleecing millions of people of billions of dollars of hard-earned money in return for goods and services, the desire for which they create. These pros at cons are called advertising executives. They present annual awards and have achieved the height of respectability. Others who zero in on more specific targets are more often labeled con artists, but sadly only after their targets are hit.

The possible patterns of fraud are infinite. They have one thing in common: They appeal to hope and fear to eliminate reason. There are some general rules devised by those experienced in prosecuting such frauds which are helpful in avoiding being victimized. I'll mention them in a while. First, it might be helpful to take a look at two of the millions of simple folk across this land who fell prey—and fought back!

Michael Joyner was born in Mexico in 1919. His formal education ended at sixth grade in a Mexican school. For twenty-two years he was employed as a factory worker, earning less than $5,000 a year. In June 1969, as a result of reading ads in the New York subway and seeing television commercials, Joyner decided to accept one of the many invitations which constantly assaulted him to enter a promising career at a good salary. This trusting fellow who barely spoke English visited the Albert Merrill School in order to discuss the possibility of becoming a computer programmer.

He was interviewed and told Merrill representatives that he was fifty years old with no more than the sixth-grade education. First he was given a so-called "aptitude" test. This is a common first step; you must be convinced that you are in some sense the elect, that your luck is not only absolute, it is good relative to that of others, who, unlike you, could not survive such an initial talent screening. Furthermore, having completed it, you have a stake in continuing. These "aptitude tests" are as various as the schemes of man. They may consist of an analysis of your finances which reveals that you are one of the few who will be allowed to invest in the get-rich-quick scheme, etc. Well, Michael Joyner had so much trouble with this "aptitude" test that he couldn't understand it or complete it within the time usually allotted. But the sympathetic tester gave him extra time.

What was Joyner's score? B+! This must be the ultimate in grade inflation, which puts to shame our colleges, known in the '70s for their grade gifts. Having given him the B+ on his aptitude test, the tester told Joyner he had a "good head, worth a $10,000 job." Joyner told the Merrill representative that his sole purpose in signing up for the computer programming training was to get a good job, and he was assured that the school would place him in such a job following his completion of the course.

Following this conversation, Joyner completed an "Application for Admission" to an IBM Data Processing/Computer Programming Course offered by Merrill. All he had to do was print his name, address and date of birth and then sign on the dotted line on the *front* of the document. He did not read his "application," but just signed it. He was given a photocopy of the front, but not the back. On the reverse side of this "application" were, among other things, the statements: "I understand that this application if accepted by the school, constitutes a binding contract," and "I understand that this application contains all the terms of the contract." (This insidious legal device called "merger" is used to allow the ripoff artist to deny any legal effect to any other oral promises which may have accompanied the written signed document. All collateral conditions are said to "merge" into the written document and if it's not on the piece of paper in black and white it's not enforceable.) There was one other statement on the reverse of this so-called "application" contract: "I understand that upon successful completion of the course, I will be eligible for the services of the school's placement department for free job counseling. I further understand that this is not a guarantee of a job or an offer of employment."

By signing the application, this semiliterate, $5,000-a-year factory worker had unknowingly enrolled himself in a $1,468.90 course consisting of "360 class hours in the theory and practical operation of IBM tabulation machines."

In July 1969, Joyner began the course. Twice thereafter Merrill representatives called him out of the evening classes he was attending and presented him with documents to sign. Without asking for or being given any explanation as to what they were, he signed them. It was not for lack of effort that Joyner failed to raise himself by his own bootstraps. He attended all 360 hours of class without any absence. During these classes he repeatedly informed his instructors that he couldn't understand the subject matter of the courses. He told them "he wanted to quit and didn't want to lose money." They talked him out of exercising his contractual right to quit and get a refund, advising him "not to panic; everybody here graduates." They waved the promised land before his longing eyes. Just make it through and a good job awaited him. And he in turn had unwittingly released them from their promises.

In April 1970 he completed the course, although he never understood the tests which he took in order to "graduate." The school outdid most of its collegiate counterparts. The students were given open-book tests, during which they were permitted to copy from other students. They gave Joyner a supplementary course. And he graduated. At graduation he was informed that the two additional papers he'd signed were New York State loans which he wouldn't have to pay off until he got his promised job in the computer field.

Joyner visited Merrill's placement office. Personnel there made out a phony résumé for him falsifying his date of birth, making him twelve years younger. They also put down that he had completed two years of high school and a bookkeeping course, and puffed the nature of his present factory job. Over the next five years, Joyner went on fifty to sixty job interviews. He failed every test given to him by prospective employers and received no job offers. Finally in the spring of 1975 the Merrill School burst the bubble and told Joyner he was unemployable.

To add insult to injury, Merrill entered a default judgment on his tuition loan, and $500, his life savings, were seized. Threatened with an attachment on his lowly salary, and fearing for the loss of his job, he made monthly payments to the sheriff of New York County.

You don't need a formal education to know when you've been had. Joyner hired a lawyer, who sued for breach of contract and fraud and for punitive damages. At trial Joyner needed an interpreter.

Unfortunately, the lawyer he went to wasn't from the school of fighting fully for the client. He requested only a return of the money plus $2,500 punitive damages. Punitive damages are the key. If someone rips you off, and you prove it, a jury or judge may award damages in excess of your particular loss as a punishment to the person who screwed you. But they are limited to the amount you request. Any good fighting lawyer will request a lot. It doesn't take much ink to add two zeros to the $2,500 prayer for punitive damages.

As the court said about Joyner's case, "Punitive damages are necessary here to prevent defendants in the future from defrauding those similarly seeking to improve their training and employment. As a consequence of defendants' defective practices, plaintiff wasted his valuable time and, to him, a considerable sum of money. Plaintiff seeks only $2,500 in punitive damages. The court is restricted to the demand and, accordingly, punitive damages are hereby assessed at $2,500. The court would, however, have been willing to assess a greater sum to serve as a more convincing deterrent to the defendants and to discourage them from engaging in the future in the deceptive sale of courses neither suited to an applicant's needs nor the job market."

Joyner got back about $4,000, modest by most standards, huge by his. Fighting back had paid off.

Another self-improvement ripoff which gives some insight into the techniques used by these vultures was perpetrated on Agnes Syester, a lonely and elderly widow, living alone, without family, working as a "coffee girl" at a restaurant.

She went to the Arthur Murray Dance Studio as a gift from a friend. On the first visit no attempt was made to sell her any lessons but she was invited to return a few days later. Over the course of the next few years, through flattery and false promises that she would become a professional dancer, and successive presentations of phony medals, Agnes was conned into purchasing 4,057 hours of dance lessons at a total cost of about $30,000. This included three lifetime memberships and a "gold star" course, which was "the type of dancing done by Ginger Rogers and Fred Astaire, only about twice as difficult." The instructor in fact had no idea of what he was doing but "faked it."

One of the more instructive aspects of the case was a twenty-two-page booklet the studio distributed to its sales personnel. Entitled "Eight Good Rules for Interviewing," it covered the following points:

1. Discourage a prospect from consulting his banker, lawyer, wife or friend.

2. Avoid permitting your prospect to think the matter over.

3. Tell the prospect that has never danced before that it is an advantage and tell the prospect that has danced before that it is an advantage.

4. Dance with prospects and then tell them that their rhythm is very good, their animation or self-confidence is good, and their natural ability is very good.

5. Summarize the prospect's ability to learn as follows: "Did you know that the three most important points on this Dancing Aptitude are: rhythm, natural ability and animation? You've been graded Excellent in all three."

6. In quoting the price for various courses, the instructor is supposed to say, "The trouble with most people is that they dance lifelessly, but as I told you on your analysis, you have animation —vitality in your dancing. No matter what course you decide on, you're going to be a really smooth dancer (men would rather be a smooth dancer—women would rather be a beautiful graceful dancer)."

7. Use "emotional selling." You have proved to him by now that he can learn to dance; now you must appeal to his emotions in such a way that he will want lessons regardless of the cost.

The jury awarded the widow $14,300 in actual damages and $40,000 punitive damages. The studio appealed. The appellate court began its opinion: "Since the beginning of recorded history men and women have persisted in selling their birthrights for a mess of pottage and courts cannot protect against the folly of bad judgment. We can, however, insist on honesty in selling. The old doctrine of *caveat emptor*—'let the buyer beware'—is no longer the pole star for business."

That's correct. The times they're a-changing. "The fact that she was so gullible as to be an easy victim does not justify taking over $29,000 of her money. She may have been willing and easily sold but nevertheless a victim."

Now you may rightfully feel that you are more sophisticated than these two unfortunates. Yes you are, but the self-improvement schemes and business opportunities presented to you will themselves be more sophisticated and subtle on a grander scale. The bigger you are, the harder you fall.

The National District Attorneys Association, composed of the people who prosecute these frauds, has written a couple of booklets titled "Business Opportunity Frauds" and "Merchandising Frauds." They contain some helpful advice, which I'd like to repeat.

Business-opportunity frauds take various forms, the most common of which are franchises, distributorships and work-at-home schemes. No matter what it's called, look for: large initial investment (they want your money); and "guaranteed" profits, market. Frequently the company promises (1) to buy back your product after you manufacture it, (2) an exclusive territory of operations, (3) a refund on request, and (4) complete training, marketing assistance and company advertising. The fraud occurs when some or all of these promises aren't kept.

According to the association, the most important ways to avoid fraudulent *business* opportunities are to *get all promises in writing* and *tape-record the presentation*. In addition, you should ask for written financial statements and references, names of company owners and officers, the names of all investors, and the exact locations of already-established product outlets. And *don't be rushed*. Check out the information, show the proposed contract to other people, preferably a lawyer, or a banker. Check with the Better Business Bureau, police, and DA's office.

The booklet gives some danger signals: there is a delay in receiving equipment or product; the company becomes uncooperative and your calls aren't returned; you get a runaround rather than a refund. Be wary of hastily called meetings in hotel rooms or temporary offices.

Two final cautions: Once they get your money it's very difficult to get it back. But if you are taken, complain to the district attorney's office. You owe it not only to yourselves but to the rest of us. Fight back. You may lose the battle, but together we will win the war. They're fighting back against the criminals in the subways of New York. Let's join together and fight against the con artists in offices with their phony titles and testimonials. I feel as if I'm campaigning, and in a sense I am. Join the party: Stand up and fight back; together we stand a shot.

Merchandising frauds are closely related to business-opportunity frauds. You are sold a bill of goods you don't really want. If you buy a product in your home for $25 or more and later change your mind, you should notify the seller's company in writing that you want to cancel the sale. Your letter should be postmarked no later than the third business day after the purchase.

Direct sales are those that occur when you are directly contacted by the company over the phone, at your door or through the mail. Remember, a direct salesperson must contact many people before a sale is made. This means the salesperson must make a large profit on each sale. As a result you often end up paying a high price for a product you didn't even want. You're at a disadvantage with direct-sales solicitations. If the sale is made in your home, you have no other merchandise to compare it to, as you would if you were in a store.

Beware: To get into your door, the salesperson may begin by asking you to fill out a questionnaire, or advise you that you've been selected to receive a free gift or sample.

The unordered-merchandise game is another fraud. Here's how it works from their perspective. You don't order it but they send it to you. Then they bill you for it. You may think you ordered it and therefore pay for it. Or with constant billing, you must pay for it to get them off your back. But the federal law is that anything sent to you which you didn't order is an unconditional *gift*. Keep it, use it, or throw it away, as you wish. But don't pay for it! If the sender claims you ordered it, make him prove it first.

You're protected in theory against most mail ripoffs. When it involves the U.S. Postal Service, it involves the feds. Here is the federal statute:

> Whoever, having devised . . . any scheme or artifice to defraud, or for obtaining money or property by means of false or fraudulent pretenses, representations, or promises . . . for the purpose of executing such scheme or artifice . . . places in any post office . . . any matter or thing whatever to be sent or delivered by the Postal Service . . . shall be fined not more than $1,000 or imprisoned not more than five years, or both.

The Federal Trade Commission, the agency which is supposed to keep track of frauds of all types, estimates that more than a quarter of all complaints involve a purchase through the mail. The commission has adopted a rule that you must receive merchandise when promised, or if there is no promise, then within thirty days. If you do not receive it shortly thereafter you can cancel your order and get your money back. If he can't meet the delivery date, the seller must notify you, give a new date and offer you the option to either cancel and receive a full refund or agree to the new shipping date. The seller must give you a free way to send back your answer, such as a stamped envelope. If you don't answer, it means you agree to the shipping delay. If you cancel a prepaid order, the seller must mail a refund within seven business days. There are some exceptions to this rule: photo finishing, magazine subscriptions, mail-order seeds and plants, and COD orders.

In its most informative "Shopping by Mail," the Federal Trade Commission wisely advises some precautions. A word of specification can be worth a thousand pictures. "Read the product description. Don't rely on pictures only." Make a record of the merchant's name, address, promised date, date payment sent. Hold onto your canceled checks.

If you do get ripped off in a mail fraud, complain to your local district attorney or state attorney general, Consumer Frauds Division, and send a copy of all correspondence to the FTC, Washington, D.C. 20580.

There is a mail-order industry group which polices the rotten apples in the group. It's important to the mail-order industry as a whole that people can trust to do business by the mail. Friends of mine who had failed to get action on a claim for several months received a full refund within days after contacting the Direct Mail

Marketing Association, Inc. (6 East 43rd Street, New York, NY 10017 or 1730 K Street, NW, Washington, DC 20006). Don't fall for it, but if you do, don't lie there steaming or crying. Get up and fight!

11.
LIBEL
AND
SLANDER

SHAKESPEARE SAID that the "edge" of slander "is sharper than the sword." Every day hundreds of thousands of people angrily proclaim, "I ought to sue that so-and-so for libel" or "for slander." Many are correct; they should sue. More are not and would make a big mistake. What is libel? What is slander?

Slander is defamation by spoken words, whereas libel is defamation by any other means—usually a written statement (or pictures or other signs). The difference between libel and slander is not always as clear as it might seem. For example, suppose a defamatory statement is spoken over TV or radio. It has been held to be libel if such spoken words are read from a script.

For most purposes, it doesn't matter much whether the offending words are considered libel or slander. What is significant, rather is that: (1) The words must be *published* by the offender, i.e., heard or seen by at least one other than the offended party. (2) The statements must be *of and concerning the plaintiff*. (3) They must be *defamatory*. (4) They must have *damaged* the plaintiff. This composite—a published defamatory damaging statement concerning the plaintiff—which constitutes libel or slander contains within it a number of important qualifiers. Let's look at it piece by piece.

The *published* requirement essentially means that the statement must have been made to a third person. In the case of a printed statement, especially with a mass readership, it is presumed that at least one person actually read the statement. With slander, the oral statement must have been made in the presence of another person—and have been understood by that person.

The statement must be of or concerning plaintiff. If I am a devotee of George Washington and some historian accuses Washington of corruption, I may be offended that my hero is defamed, but I may not sue the defamer for libel or slander. Suppose the statement is not about the father of my country but rather about my own father, who has died. Here "the general rule is that a libel upon the memory of a deceased person that does not directly cast any personal reflection upon his relatives does not give them any right of action, although they may have thereby suffered mental anguish or sustained an impairment of their social standing among a considerable class of respectable people of the community in which they live by the disclosure that they were related to the deceased."*

Although the statement must be "about me" it need not specifically identify me by name. "The son of the New York Appellate Judge Albert Cohn" is a description uniquely referring to me. So, too, "the lawyer for Tom Milbank in his divorce action against Loycex" uniquely refers to me. The point is this: A person may be identified in context in such a way that either the general public or some significant special subgroup knows to whom the statement refers. In order to defame, it is not necessary to name names. Descriptions which alert other people to the identity are adequate.

Let me give you two examples in which naming the plaintiff was not necessary for libel.

In April 1974, Donnie Cholmondelay, age twelve, and Jeff Girdler, age eleven, got into a fight. As Jeff raised himself off the ground, Donnie hit him on the head. This one blow caused Jeff to go into a coma and die a year later. Ten days after this tragic incident, there appeared an article in the *Kentucky Post* written by

---

* *Hughes* v. *New England Newspaper Pub. Co* 312 Mass. 178, 43 NE 2d 657 (1942)

Jim Blair which stated that Jeff had been hit *repeatedly* on the head. Five months later, Blair wrote another article in the *Post* which stated that Jeff's head had been pounded over and over again against the pavement, and that Jeff had been savagely beaten into insensibility. Donnie's name was never mentioned in either article. Nevertheless, the article was found libelous. The Kentucky court of appeals observed that "Donnie's friends and acquaintances who were familiar with the incident were certain to recognize Donnie as the unnamed perpetrator of the offense."

In the other example, *Hustler* magazine ran a feature article about William Loeb, the feisty and powerful publisher of the Manchester, New Hampshire, *Union Leader,* which described the protracted fight over his mother's million-dollar estate. Loeb's mother had disinherited her son in favor of his daughter, her granddaughter. One sentence in the article read: "Loeb . . . let high-priced New York lawyers eat up over $800,000 before withdrawing his complaint. . . ." Philip Handleman, one of three lawyers to be paid by the estate, having been appointed by the executors, had received about $90,000, the bulk of the legal fees actually paid. He sued *Hustler,* citing the sentence above (which never mentioned his name) as libel in that it suggested he charged excessive fees, thus damaging his professional reputation. In deciding that the libelous statement was published "of and concerning him," the federal court observed that "the libel designates the plaintiff in such a way as to let those who knew him understand that he was the person meant. It is not necessary that all the world should understand the libel; it is sufficient if those who knew the plaintiff can make out that he is the person meant."

(Incidentally, if someone slanders or libels a small group of persons, an individual member may recover if the group is so small that the matter can reasonably be understood to refer to the particular member, or if the circumstances reasonably give rise to the conclusion that there is a particular implicit reference to the member. Whether the offending statement is "about me" is for the jury to decide.)

What is *defamatory?* A statement which unjustly subjects another person to ridicule and diminished esteem and respect by others in the community is defamatory.

But, you may ask, aren't we a society that adheres to the ancient adage that "sticks and stones will break my bones, but names will never hurt me?" To a degree this is true. How many times each day does one person call another a "son of a bitch" or a "bastard" with others looking on. If each one of these outbursts gave rise to a slander suit, our courts would do nothing else. If these suits were successful, we would all feel chilled in our ability to express our daily irritations. Calling someone a "bastard" in most contexts would be understood as little more than "I don't like you." It is not actionable. We can imagine, however, a situation in which someone's parentage is in question and in which the false claim is made in the presence of others, in a cold, modulated voice: "You are a bastard." Here there may be an actionable defamation, because in the context the words mean something different and tend to injure the reputation of another.

Affirming a defendant's claim that "bastard" and "son of a bitch" are phrases which "amount to nothing more than vulgar name-calling and would not be understood by reasonable persons to amount to anything else, and therefore would not be defamatory," a South Carolina court reiterated standard law: "A certain amount of vulgar name calling is tolerated, on the theory that it will necessarily be understood to amount to nothing more." * Such "hasty, ill tempered abuse," "pointless arrows of mere vulgarity," if they do not convey a "degrading charge or imputation," are not defamatory and therefore not actionable.

It's interesting that in deciding the profanity was nondefamatory, the court utilized not the *defamation* measure but the *of and concerning* one: ". . . while the words may have indeed been spoken *to* the plaintiff, they were not spoken *of* him." This suggests that you may in some circumstances use an epithet to hurl *at* another person, while you may not employ that same epithet to characterize him. The law respects a common-sense distinction between cursing someone and slandering that person.

---

* *Smith* v. *Phoenix Furniture Co.* 339 F. Supp. 969.

Therefore, as a Virginia court observed, "mere words of abuse indicating that one party dislikes another or that he had a low opinion of him, without more, does not amount to defamation. A certain amount of vulgar name calling, indicating hostility or ill will, under certain circumstances is tolerated by the law." On the other hand, for words to be defamatory and actionable, it is not necessary that the words charge directly. They may defame by "inference, implication, innuendo, or insinuation."*

The law generally adheres to the "sticks and stones" philosophy. For example, a killing committed in the heat of passionate fury occasioned by words of abuse is generally not considered adequately provoked, i.e., "mere words," however abusive, will not mitigate a murder to manslaughter. On the other hand, it is not always strictly true that "names will never harm me." Not long ago while flying down to Mexico to meet with my client the Baron Enrico diPortanova, I was jotting down some notes for this book when the stewardess came by with the newspapers of the day.

The front page of one sent shivers of anger up my spine and the wheels of libel spinning in my head. Why? All it was was a virtually full-page photograph of the concrete shell of a magnificent house. The banner headline read: "The Secret Life of the Shah." To appreciate the seriousness of this, I must give you some background.

Ricky diPortanova earlier had decided that he wanted to build *the* house in Acapulco. He bought several acres on the bay which adjoined a modern house owned by Merle Oberon's former husband, Bruno Pagliai, and began construction on his magnificent residence—fifty-foot scalloped ceilings, rooms gently terraced down to the water, etc. In the meantime Pagliai sold his house to the shah's sister. So, here is the shah in exile looking for a home, perhaps in Mexico, with his sister owning a modern gracious house, next door to which, under construction, is a palace fit for an emperor. To the press, speculating on the future home of the shah, it was obvious: $1 + 1 = 1$. The shah was building himself a house next to his sister. Newspapers had run articles to that ef-

---

* *Jones* v. *Buell*, 152 S.E. 539.

fect. A television network had even sent a crew to the site. In ordinary circumstances such false statements would be expected to irk the true owner, who after all was spending millions for the house for his baroness and himself. But these were no ordinary circumstances: The Ayatollah Khomeini and his people were in control of Iran and were not known either for their rationality or their friendliness toward the shah. Following the publication of these news accounts, Ricky had received an official visit in London from an Islamic (Khomeini's) ambassador, who informed him that he was in danger of being marked for assassination for having given aid and comfort to the shah. Ricky vigorously protested that he was building the house for himself and was by no means a front for anyone. In fact, he had never even met the shah. We forced retractions. All was quiet, relatively.

Now, suddenly, here I was sitting in the airplane looking at a front-page photo of Ricky's house with the banner headline "Secret Life of the Shah." Names can sometimes harm you. We are presently suing for libel. At this writing, we are ahead in one case, and behind in the other. Perhaps the shah's death has convinced the ayatollah that what is destined to be a classic structure of this century is of, for, and by the diPortanovas.

The short of the matter is that whenever words in context interpreted in their ordinary and usual sense would unjustly tarnish a person's reputation, they are defamatory. This is obviously connected with the previously considered requirements, publication and reference. It is also intimately connected with the total question of damages.

Damage is the heart of the matter. The question of damages is the sticking point in most libel and slander suits. In order to decide whether and when to press a libel or slander suit, you must be aware of some rules and principles relating to damages.

There are two types of damages, *compensatory* and *punitive,* and in slander/libel suits the plaintiffs seek both. Compensatory damages, as their name suggests, are monies awarded to the person slandered or libeled to compensate for the injury suffered. Punitive damages are monies awarded not to make the injured person whole, but rather to punish the slanderer (or libeler) and to deter others from committing similar transgressions.

Within compensatory damages, there are two kinds: *special* damages and *general* damages. Special damages are the actual consequences of the injury complained of. These are not damages which in the usual course of events would necessarily follow, but which *in this case* actually did follow. They are damages (to reputation with respect to business, profession or occupation) which are computable in money. In contrast, general damages are those which from the common sense and experience of mankind might naturally be expected to result from the kind of representation made. The law presumes general damages, without regarding the peculiar circumstances of the particular case.

It is important to distinguish special and general damages because ordinarily if you want to collect for slander you must first plead and prove special damages. You must persuade a jury that in your particular circumstances, you actually suffered a measurable loss because of the defendant's slanderous statement. Once you do that, additional general damages are presumed to follow, as natural and probable consequences, for which you collect without having to prove.

It may often be very difficult actually to prove that you suffered some measurable loss. A person may have said all sorts of horrible things about you; the accusations may have been repeated and may persist in surrounding you in a cloud of suspicion or contempt. Yet you may not be able to prove a measurable financial loss. There is, however, an important exception to the rule which ordinarily requires you to prove special damages before you can collect general damages. Certain types of statements are considered defamatory *per se*. The four major *per se* exceptions to the requirement that you must prove actual damages are statements which (1) accuse you of *committing a crime,* (2) accuse you of possessing a characteristic which is a *derogation of* an important trait to your *profession or business,* (3) accuse you of suffering from a *loathsome disease,* (4) accuse you (if you are a woman, not a man) of being *unchaste.*

Let's consider now the distinction between compensatory and punitive damages.

For many years, Joe Skjonsby worked the family farm in North Dakota with his father. Eventually Joe did all the work and the arrangement was for him to get one-third of the crop. At some point he became aware that his elderly parents were transferring rights in the farm to his sister, Joyce. Claiming his father was not mentally competent to make decisions, Joe petitioned a court, asking that a guardian be appointed for his father. Claims and counterclaims flew, and when things sorted out, a settlement was effected whereby the father was adjudged incompetent, thus requiring a guardian.

But bad blood persisted between brother and sister. Joyce complained that Joe was a "thief," that he had "repeatedly stolen from his father's estate," "repeatedly stolen from his mother and all of the rest of the family." Joyce made these statements to Joe's son and at least two other people. It soon got back to Joe; as Mark Twain once said, "It takes your enemy and your friend working together to hurt you to the heart; the one to slander you, the other to get the news to you."

By accusing her brother of committing a crime, Joyce had committed slander *per se*. This self-evident slander removed Joe's responsibility to prove that he actually suffered damages. The law presumed he'd suffered. So, although all witnesses who testified to having heard Joyce call Joe a thief said that they personally didn't believe the allegation, nevertheless, the statement *per se* entitled Joe to compensatory general damages, which a jury found amounted to $5,000. But as is often the case, compensatory damages were the least of it. In addition to the $5,000 in compensatory damages, for the slander *per se,* the jury added another $20,000 in punitive damages.

These so-called "punitive" or exemplary damages are the jackpot of most libel and slander suits. Recall, the purpose of punitive damages is not to compensate the victim for a harm actually suffered; it is, rather, to punish the slanderer (or libeler) and to deter others. In general, punitive damages must bear a reasonable relationship to compensatory damages. But that is not sufficient. Above and beyond the injury remedied by compensatory damages, you must prove, in order to get punitive damages, that the issuer of the statement acted with *malice*.

A Kansas City fireman, Robert Sweaney, retired on a disability pension as the result of a leg injury. Thereafter Sweaney worked in an auto body shop. Nearby was a used-car lot operated by Jack Bagby from which a 1965 yellow Oldsmobile 442 with dealer plates was stolen. A few days later, Sweaney was directed to deliver a car to an out-of-town car company, and there to pick up a 1965 yellow Oldsmobile 442 and return it to the body shop for repair. Coincidentally, the yellow Olds which Sweaney picked up also had dealer plates. As he was en route back to the body shop, caught in heavy traffic, Sweaney's car was spotted by Jack Bagby, who, looking through the window of his office, spotted what he wrongly assumed was the very car stolen from his lot a few days before. Bagby raced out of the office and ran down the street until he caught up with Sweaney.

Sweaney heard a man yelling, "Stop that car—stop that car." As Bagby approached Sweaney, demanding that he stop the car, Sweaney became frightened, stopped the car, left the motor running, and moved over to the right-hand side, from which he jumped out. He tripped and fell to the pavement, injuring his leg, but picked himself up and ran into a store. Bagby and a fellow employee followed in hot pursuit. They cornered Sweaney and yelled for someone to call the police, repeatedly accusing Sweaney of being a thief. A policeman arrived and Bagby repeated the allegations, in the hearing of twenty-five bystanders. Sweaney made a couple of requests that someone call his boss to verify the fact that the car was not stolen, but the cop denied his requests.

Meanwhile, Bagby, his accuser, went out to the car to make certain its serial number matched that of his stolen car. Of course, it did not. Bagby returned in a few minutes and said in a low voice, "I'm sorry; it's all a mistake." For Bagby, it was a costly mistake. For having "ignored Sweaney's basic rights" and because he "took the law into his own hands" and called Sweaney a thief several times in the presence of many witnesses, a jury awarded Sweaney $3,000 compensatory damages and $18,000 punitive damages. An appellate court upheld the damages in spite of the fact that Bagby may have acted under a reasonable and honest mistaken belief that Sweaney was the thief. The jury found malice, and the appellate court affirmed. Bagby did not help himself by "frankly admitt[ing] that come another time and place, he would do the same thing over again!" This enabled the jury to conclude that Bagby hadn't learned his lesson, which may have encouraged them to add the extra $18,000 in punitive damages. There are times when silence is golden and speech is costly.

An important lesson is clear from these and similar cases: Do not call someone a thief with other people present unless you are absolutely certain of his guilt or are willing to suffer severe consequences. And from the other perspective, if someone humiliates you by falsely calling you a thief in the presence of others, or if he groundlessly disparages your reliability or competence, fight back! You are likely to collect compensatory damages, and, more significantly, punitive damages, as long as the statements are not *privileged*. What does that mean?

Let me begin with a fairly recent example.

Michael Bow had been employed under a work-study program at the University of Georgia Chemistry Department when Dr. Melton was the head of that department. More than a year after Bow left the university a problem arose: Some phony paychecks were issued to Bow and cashed under his signature. The university police conducted an investigation, and as a result a Chemistry Department employee who had caused checks to be issued in the names of ex-employees (including Bow's) was convicted of forgery. Bow had no connection whatever with the scheme.

Nevertheless, Melton made statements during and after the investigation to the effect that Bow was a thief, had stolen hotplates from the chemistry lab, was a liar and was in trouble with the IRS.

At trial, Melton's defense was privilege. The idea behind privileged statements is this: In certain circumstances, society has an interest in the free flow of honestly believed information. One such situation is a criminal investigation. A person who is questioned in the course of a criminal investigation should feel free to tell the police all s/he knows or believes without fear of a libel or slander suit. As long as s/he communicates in good faith—without malice —to those who are empowered to make the investigation, such statements should be protected, or privileged.

We'll consider other examples in just a moment. Here the claim failed; Melton had defamed Bow to others not involved in the investigation and persisted in doing so after being informed of the innocence of Bow and the guilt of an embezzler who worked in his own department. The jury found "actual malice" and required Dr. Melton to pay Bow $200,000. Yes, $200,000. This award was affirmed on appeal, by the Georgia supreme court.

So far I've emphasized a form of slander *per se,* the accusation that someone has committed a crime. And we've seen one form of privilege: the privilege to help law enforcement in criminal investigations. There is another common form of slander or libel *per se* and a related qualified privilege. Earlier I mentioned that disparaging someone in such a way as to injure him in his profession or business constitutes a *per se* defamatory statement. Yet here too society has an interest in the free flow of information and assessment honestly felt. It is very common for a former employer to be asked to write a recommendation or assessment of a former employee. How frank, how blunt, how informative can an employer be in that assessment? On the other hand, how is a falsely maligned employee able to fight back? Shakespeare said: "For slander lives upon succession, for ever housed where it gets possession." Perhaps that is nowhere truer than with employer evaluations and credit ratings. Let's look at one example of each and then consider generally the doctrine of privilege.

Mario Calero, a college-trained public accountant, who had worked for several other companies in Wisconsin, applied for a position with Del Chemical Company. Calero was interviewed and hired by Rogert C. Bagemihl, whose assistant he became. Over the next three years, Calero received eleven consecutive raises and became director of purchasing. He designed a new filing system to help him in negotiations with suppliers. One day he had a fight with the company's president, who verbally abused him. The next day Calero told Bagemihl that he had quit and was looking for other employment. Bagemihl accepted Calero's resignation but asked him to stay on to train his replacement, assuring Calero he would be paid for untaken vacation time and given severance pay. Calero agreed to do this, and continued to work for another full week. That Friday, he received a call from another Del accountant who had been recently transferred to Reno, Nevada, to set up purchasing procedures for an affiliated company. This other accountant requested copies of the purchasing records in the system that Calero had designed. Immediately, in full view of others in the office, Calero photocopied the cards.

Monday, when Calero reported to work, his secretary told him to go directly to Mr. Bagemihl's office, where Bagemihl ordered him to leave the premises, informing Calero he was being dismissed because Bagemihl had heard that Calero was starting a competing company, was attempting to hire away various key personnel of the corporation, and was "helping himself" to confidential records about suppliers. At Bagemihl's request, Calero surrendered his corporate car keys, credit card and office keys and took a cab home. He never returned to the office. Later Bagemihl was to admit that he had no direct knowledge of Calero's intentions to compete and steal employees, but that, at the time, it was well-known office rumor.

For the next several months, Calero worked without pay for a company he had helped form. Then he began work as a general accountant at about half the salary he'd earned at Del. Within a few months, Calero was on the rise again, being considered for promotion to comptroller. His desk was just outside the door of the office of his superior, and he heard this man call Bagemihl to ask about Calero's work history. About fifteen minutes later Calero was called into his superior's office and fired, effective immediately.

He was unemployed thereafter for about two months, and

then joined a company which soon went out of business. During this time he averaged five job applications a week. Next, he worked for a company at his previous high salary, honestly listing Del Chemical as a previous employer, only to be fired a month later when this new company reviewed his work history. He was unemployed thereafter for about eight months, during which time he made more than two hundred job applications. On all these he listed Del Chemical as a previous employer but never as a reference.

As a result of this frustrating fruitless job experience, Calero felt humiliated and demoralized and moved from Wisconsin to Arizona in order to search for a job. But he eventually fought back against an unwarranted employer reference which trailed him. What had Bagemihl written that had turned off successive employers? "I dismissed Mr. Calero when I learned he was starting a competing company, 'helping' himself to confidential corporate records about suppliers and formulations and attempting to hire away from us various key personnel."

On another form, Bagemihl stated that he would not consider rehiring Calero and, when asked to rate Calero's character on a table from "above average" to "unsatisfactory," wrote in: "Yes —he was something of a character." And there were other damaging reference letters.

Calero fought to clear his name. The trial court in Wisconsin correctly informed the jury that these communications to prospective employers were entitled to a "qualified or conditional privilege." That is, public policy recognizes the social utility of encouraging the free flow of information in these circumstances even at the risk of causing harm by defamation. As the court correctly instructed the jury, an employer is privileged to give a critical appraisal of a former employee "as long as such appraisal was made for the valid purpose of enabling a prospective employer to evaluate the employee's qualifications." But the privilege is "conditional"—it must be reasonably calculated to accomplish the privileged purpose and it must be made without malice. Malice was not to be presumed. Rather, first it was the defendant's (Bagemihl's) burden to prove the existence of the privilege, and once that was done, it became the burden of the plaintiff, Calero, to prove malice.

Because this was a case in which a ruling of privilege was not constitutionally required, the plaintiff could prove "express malice"—spite or ill will—by a mere preponderance of the evidence. If Bagemihl's statements, the court instructed, had been "honestly believed to be true, based upon some tangible information and made from an honest desire to promote public justice," then they would have been made without malice. However, the jury concluded that the charges against Calero were untrue and that Bagemihl had relied only on office gossip without any attempt to verify or investigate the charges. The jury awarded Calero $3,000 for injuries to his feelings, $7,000 for loss of income, and another $9,000 for punitive damages. Bagemihl and Del Chemical appealed, but the entire jury award was sustained.

"Privilege" definitions vary from state to state, but almost all states attach a qualified privilege to credit ratings. In such a situation, in order to collect any compensatory damages, malice must be proved. Once malice is proved, the privilege no longer attaches and not only compensatory but punitive damages may be awarded.

For example, Ladonna Brown gave a check to a supermarket to pay for her groceries. The market failed to endorse the check, and when it was returned, the market sent it through once again, again without endorsing it. It was returned again, but this time it was marked nonnegotiable. The store called Ladonna's husband, who agreed to replace the check. Concerned lest his name inadvertently be given to a central Oklahoma credit-rating service—CVA —the next day Brown visited the store and was assured his check would not be placed on a list of problem checks. Once again the store made a mistake and sent out a report showing that the Browns' check had been returned because of insufficient funds. Nor did the store notify CVA of its error. As a result, the Browns found themselves unable to pay by check at any of several stores. A month later their name was removed from the list.

The Browns fought back. They sued for libel. Because their

check was perfectly valid, the market, by falsely reporting it was backed by insufficient funds, had falsely implied their guilt of a criminal act. The jury awarded them $20,000 compensatory and $10,000 punitive damages. Upholding the award, a federal appeals court recognized a qualified privilege in such reports, but the court allowed for a finding of malice, *even in the absence of ill will.* As long as there was gross recklessness—mere negligence would be insufficient—then malice could be inferred.

In sum, states recognize these non-constitutionally based privileges at their option. In general, privileges attach to statements made in official proceedings. Statements made to a grand jury or district attorney concerning matters in pending investigations are absolutely privileged, as are statements under oath in civil proceedings. The remedy for false testimony is a criminal complaint of perjury, not a civil action for libel or slander. Another common absolute privilege is that granted to legislators to make any statement they wish while on the floor of the legislature.

Where the press is involved, another kind of privilege enters in: the First Amendment to the United States Constitution, which guarantees press freedom. Censorship comes in many forms, not the least of which is liberal liability for libel. If a speech or writing is *constitutionally privileged,* then several states are not free to treat it as they wish. The United States has an overriding interest in such problems, and not surprisingly, the Supreme Court has preempted the field with two major decisions: *New York Times* v. *Sullivan* in 1964, and *Gertz* v. *Robert Welch, Inc.* in 1974.

In the famous *Times* case, L. B. Sullivan, an elected commissioner of Montgomery, Alabama, sued the *Times* and four black clergymen for libel because a full-page ad which the *Times* carried and the clergymen signed accused the police and elected officials —though not Sullivan by name—of many violent and illegal acts in suppressing civil-rights activity. Some of the statements were false.

The trial judge instructed the jury that, under Alabama law, the statements in the ad were "libelous *per se*" and were not privileged, so that the *Times* and the clergymen might be held liable if the jury found that they had published the ad and that the statements were made "of and concerning" Sullivan. The jury was further instructed that, because the statements were libelous *per se*, "the law implies legal injury from the bare fact of publication itself," "malice was presumed," "general damages need not be alleged or proved but are presumed" and "punitive damages may be awarded even though the amount of actual damages is neither found nor shown."

Had this been an ordinary case, not involving the media or public officials, the jury's $500,000 award, affirmed by the Alabama supreme court, would have been final. But, for the U.S. Supreme Court, basic freedoms guaranteed to each citizen, in whatever state, by the United States Constitution were at stake. There was a national interest, constitutionally protected, in free speech and open debate. This interest, as guaranteed by the First Amendment and applied to the states through the Fourteenth Amendment, limited "a state's power to award damages for libel in actions brought by public officials against critics of their official conduct." In short, in this context, "actual malice"—the intent to publish a false statement with reckless disregard as to its truth—could not be presumed. It had to be proved with "convincing clarity" by the public official. Not only truth was a defense; an honest belief in the truth of the statements was sufficient. Otherwise the press would impose self-censorship to avoid costly libel judgments, and our constitutional republic would itself be damaged.

Seven years later the Court extended this test beyond public officials to public figures as well. In 1971, in a plurality opinion, the Court held that even though the suit against the news organization was by a private person who was not a public official or public figure, nevertheless the protection of the First Amendment applied because the issue was of public interest. Once again, the Court held that not only must the private person who has been falsely defamed prove actual malice—intent or gross recklessness—s/he must prove it with convincing clarity. It appeared for a while that newspapers were virtually immune in publishing false and defaming statements about private citizens.

In 1974, however, the Burger Court retrenched. A police officer was convicted of murder and the attorney who represented the victim's family in a civil suit against the cop was falsely identified by the *John Birch Society Magazine* as a "Leninist" and "Communist fronter." Although the Court, in reinstating the jury's libel award, did not deny that the matters discussed in the publication about Gertz were of general public interest, it declined to extend the *Times* rule in the way it had been willing to three years before. The Court noted that a private individual has less opportunity than a public figure for effective rebuttal of defamatory statements and is therefore more vulnerable to injury. A public figure has to some extent voluntarily exposed himself to attention, comment and criticism, but a private person has a right to greater protection. Therefore, the Court held in *Gertz*—which remains the law of the land —that whereas (under the *Times* rule) a public person may not collect for libel unless s/he proves "actual malice," a private person in a state which permits it may collect compensatory damages without proving actual malice, and may recover presumed general damages and punitive damages where s/he can show actual malice. In essence, for a private individual to recover punitive damages from the media, s/he must meet the same burden of proof as to actual malice that a public official must meet to recover compensatory damages. And, as the law is now, the media have an affirmative duty to check facts and avoid extreme negligence. And that's where we are as the '80s begin.

One final question: whether to sue or not may be a difficult decision. If you don't bring suit, for example, your failure to do so may encourage a general belief that the libel or slander is true. Actually this can be handled by an appropriate statement to the effect that "I wouldn't dignify anything that well-known liar says by suing him. That's just what he'd like me to do so he can get more attention for his lies," etc.

I would venture to say that there are thousands of pages of false and defamatory statements about me in print. Yet I have sued for libel only twice. A libel suit can be very messy; if they've got a shot at proving the case, you may get hurt, and in any event the suit will generate publicity. On the other hand, if you've been slandered without cause, fight back! You might well win big. But don't forget the old maxim: "Don't sue for libel; they're liable to prove it!"

IV

TAXES, FUNERALS AND WILLS

WE ALL have to pay our dues. Sooner and later. Each year the IRS takes some away from us, and in the end we ourselves are taken. Life sometimes feels like a losing battle. But it's a fight worth making. The idea of dying bothers people more or less. It haunts some so much as to disable them from enjoying life, thus ironically making life itself a living death. Others accept death as a part of life and shrug it off. Still others use their mortality as an engine, to drive them to accomplish great things, and the prospect of the death of friends and loved ones becomes a constant reminder to cherish others while they live.

For the foreseeable future, death seems about even with taxes. Medical science and politicians are running neck and neck to reduce the burden of each. We are all going to die. The odd thing is that often the people most possessed by their own deaths are the least likely to provide for what follows. For that's the joke: because of taxes and the attempt to flee from them, the game of our estate goes on after our own death. But we get to play it now when we make a will. So those of us who long for an afterlife, and those who understand that the world goes on after we die will make arrangements as best we can in order to continue to be a positive influence in the lives of those we care about, beyond our own brief earthly stay.

12.
TAXES

SUPPOSEDLY WE fought the American Revolution to establish the principle of "no taxation without representation." History books tell us the people of the United States won that war. April 15th makes us wonder. More so than any other institution in these free and United States, the IRS smacks of a police state with police state methods. It can be cruelest to small people. From the ominous personal visit to one's home at unlikely hours, leaving an official card to contact Agent Jones, to the personal interrogation at IRS headquarters and routine haggling, few find the experience pleasant or pleasantly handled.

All this procedure must be viewed within the context of where tax money goes. Much of it goes to welfare recipients, many of whom file false claims and have undeclared full or part-time jobs on the side. Some of the rest goes to unemployment compensation for those who don't want to work, as distinguished from those who really want jobs and need unemployment benefits until they land one. Taxpayers also pay for civil service employees, many of whom are bloated bureaucrats frozen into needless jobs with fat lifetime pensions around the corner. Our taxes go as well to unnecessary political hacks, and to foreign aid, whereby money is ritualistically poured into countries whose people hate our guts. Little of it is used for the needy, but goes instead to the honchos who do the allocation and distribution. All of this hardly provides an incentive to overpay taxes or to earn more taxable income than we need.

Now, let's understand something. Does this mean I advocate not paying taxes that are due and owing? Absolutely not. I advocate total compliance with tax laws as well as all other laws, whether I personally think them equitable or not. But that doesn't mean citizens can't fight to change tax laws, as Californians did with the passage of Proposition 13, or as specified in the Kemp-Roth bill. These are essential steps in preventing situations such as we have in New York, where the "workers" support the "shirkers."

Avoidance and minimization (as opposed to evasion) of taxes is permissible. Such concepts as depreciation, depletion, and investment credit substantially reduce or wipe out the tax liability of many of the rich—and an argument can be made that it results in willingness, on the part of the rich, to build and take risks in business and industry. This in turn reduces unemployment rolls by creating jobs for those unemployed who want to work, thus the burden on the average taxpayer is reduced.

This is where I should be specific about my own circumstances. From printed stories of my battles with the IRS, incorrect conclusions are often drawn. One is that I advocate non-payment of taxes due. That is not true, as I have stated. Another is that I do not pay taxes. That is also untrue. In the past few years, I've paid substantially more than some Presidents of the United States. There is a problem, though.

Like other taxpayers, I file an annual return. Those returns must be audited to completion within a given number of years. If the IRS has not completed it by then, it loses its right to demand adjustments or make disallowances. The time limit can be extended only by you, the taxpayer. But it's not that simple. If you are asked to sign a waiver of the time limit and don't—then the IRS can arbitrarily disallow all disputed deductions, etc., and swoop down on you with a "jeopardy assessment." This may result in the tying up of your assets by IRS liens. So if you have assets, you are virtually forced to give the time extension.

My problem is that for an unprecedented twenty-year period, the IRS never completed auditing my returns. Thus in 1975, say, my 1959 return was still wide open. During this twenty-year period, a lot of things happened in my life. It is well known that "enemies lists," either formal or informal, have been kept during certain administrations. And it is well known that the IRS is an effective tool with which to harass or destroy an enemy. I could write a thousand pages on my experiences with the IRS. Instead, I'll mention the main events in a paragraph:

I was chief counsel to Senator Joseph McCarthy's Senate Investigating Committee, engaged in what I've always thought and still do (though some people in good faith disagree) was a well-justified struggle against Stalinist infiltration directly and indirectly into our government, defense, and foreign policy fabric. My assistant counsel at the time was Bobby Kennedy. Between us, it was dislike at first sight. A decade later, when Bobby, by then a darling of the liberals, became his brother's and the country's Attorney General, he turned loose the power of government to "get" me, among others. Three times I was indicted, tried and unanimously acquitted by juries of my peers. In other words, thirty-six jurors voted for me, not one for the "Government." The experience was so searing that I wrote a book, *A Fool for a Client,* recounting it. With my last acquittal, and the publication of the book, the trauma was behind me, an unpleasant memory with a silver lining that remains: the proven loyalty and devotion of friends and clients who stood beside me. Another of Bobby's weapons was the IRS. Thus was begun this twenty-year struggle between us, which has survived his tragic death and taken on a life of its own.

During these three trials (which spanned the years 1963 to 1971), my records were constantly subpoenaed; many were never returned. It was next to impossible for me to substantiate deductions going as far back as twenty years. Also, the IRS set up a squad of ten Special Agents, known as the "Cohn Squad," and headed by Special Agent "Red" Corcoran. The squad's job was to "get" me. After trying for a couple of years—aided by such techniques as intercepting my mail and that of my attorney—they came up with five suggested charges. Each one of the five was kicked out by the IRS Regional Counsel's office as being completely baseless.

So, after all, the IRS decided maybe it ought to complete the twenty years of open audits. The agency is in the process of doing so by disallowing every substantial deduction, including one found to have been perfectly proper by its own Regional Counsel's office. The revenue agents have been very decent—but they just follow orders. Over the twenty years of my open returns, three of the agents assigned to me have retired, one died, and still another got amnesia and couldn't remember where many of my files had been placed. The whole matter is still in dispute, and I suppose if I keep up my determination to fight back and win, I ultimately shall.

In the interim, I decided to have no assets. I have no need for any. I have no immediate family, and my law firm is in excellent financial condition. The firm pays the expenses I incur in developing and seeing through law business. My arrangement leaves enough income for me to take care of personal living expenses and current taxes.

I lived in and still love New York, and will all my life. But on top of federal taxes, New York State imposes a 15 percent income tax as well as property and gross occupancy taxes. I got tired of supporting our welfare and food stamp programs, so some years ago I moved to nearby Greenwich, Connecticut, where there are no state or city income taxes.

Judge Learned Hand, one of our outstanding jurists, once said, "There is nothing sinister in so arranging one's affairs as to keep taxes as low as possible." He's absolutely correct. Only a fool pays more tax than is legally required. Some people think it's a sign of patriotism to pay more taxes than they owe. It seems to me, however, that if you love your country and want to contribute to its improvement, there are more direct ways than to throw your money into the IRS coffers. Make gifts, earmarking them for purposes which you support, but don't pay taxes you don't owe.

I'll assume that you are not one of those who think it's the highest form of patriotism to overtax yourself, and that you desire to pay as little as is legally possible. "Legally" is the key word. There is a very fine line between tax avoidance—perfectly proper —and tax evasion, which is a crime. Often the line is a matter of interpretation, judgment as to what constitutes a business expense or proper deduction. If a deduction is reasonably arguable, argue it. You may ultimately lose it. But it may never be challenged in the first place. The point is, as Judge Hand suggests, there is nothing sinister about arranging your affairs so as to keep taxes as low as possible. But do it out in the open. Openly deduct it and carefully characterize it. And keep detailed records. The time to prepare for an audit is before you hear from the IRS. Most people are unconcerned about an audit until they hear from the IRS. Often that's too late. Be in a position to substantiate.

Turn what you can't avoid anyway to your own advantage. Many people want to keep their "private, personal and social" lives entirely separate from their "business, public" life. I understand and respect that, but there's a price attached. You have to pay more taxes. I've integrated my personal and professional life. I have an extended family of client/friends. In fact, it's an inevitable concomitant of the personal contact and day and night supervision of problems that my clients require. This makes life much more meaningful and less strained. It also makes deductible expenses legitimate. The first of two rules, then, in fighting back against the IRS: (1) Make business pleasure, and pleasure profitable. Integrate your life and take a businesslike attitude toward your personal affairs. A rose by some names is a write-off. (2) Keep detailed records in order to substantiate. A receipt of prevention is worth a ream of argument.

Why are some people audited and others not? Luck? Not entirely. I have known some accountants and IRS agents in my time. They tell me the same thing. A few audits occur as a result of vendettas involving a limited number of well-known people. That is not to say that audits don't turn into vendettas as they proceed and the taxpayer refuses to submit. Some audits, but very few, are merely random, the luck of the draw. Sometimes the IRS makes a "drive" on an industry. When, for example, the upper echelons in the agency determine that a particular group—doctors, art dealers not long ago, gasoline stations, head waiters—do a largely cash business and can hide income, they may heavily audit people engaged in that kind of enterprise. There's no way to protect against that except to have good records.

The IRS publishes guidelines for percentages of total reported income within which deductions such as charity and medical expenses should fall. If a deduction is out of that range, a computer is likely to kick out the return for further examination. Here's an example. Suppose your portfolio includes tax-exempt bonds, which your broker holds. The broker is likely to send to the IRS the total interest paid you, without breaking it down into tax-exempt and taxable. You, on the other hand, report only your taxable interest and dividends. If the discrepancy is large enough, the computer may kick out your return for audit. Lesson? Don't let brokers hold your stocks and bonds. Keep them in a safety deposit box. The fewer the people reporting your income for you, the better.

Another mechanism that activates the IRS is squealers. Who are they? Commonly they are disaffected employees. Your bookkeeper asks you for a raise; you refuse it. Resentful, the bookkeeper fumes silently: "The boss is underreporting or mischaracterizing, and drives around in a fancy car, lives high and won't give me the $50. I'll fix him." And s/he does. One anonymous tip to the IRS will start things rolling, especially when the complainant can supply facts and figures. Squealing can be profitable. The IRS can award squealers up to 15 percent of the additional taxes and penalties. Squealers are not only discontented employees; some may be rejected lovers, sometimes spouses. Earlier I counseled spreading the wealth—but not the information on how it's made. I reiterate it here. A loudmouth boasts at a party, "I take off my child's tuition and claim it's a charitable contribution to the university; they'll never find it," or, "I buy paintings for the office worth $10,000 and I depreciate them over five years until their book value is zero and I move them into my house and buy more. . . ." No one likes a braggart, and a not uncommon way of reacting is to tip off the IRS.

When a squeal comes into the IRS, it is turned over to the intelligence unit. Unlike the examining agents, the intelligence unit works from one assumption: everybody is a thief. They look for fraud. When they examine a business or personal taxpayer, they are ready, willing and able to follow any tangent. Under pressure, the taxpayer may claim he paid *you* a large sum as a referral fee and therefore is legitimately deducting it. Did *you* report it as income? The intelligence unit also has people reading newspapers. A house is sold, say, for $250,000 cash. The seller deposits the check in the bank. The bank is required to report to the IRS any non-normal cash deposit over $10,000. Without collusion between seller and teller, the $250,000 check will automatically be reported. The intelligence unit questions the seller as to how s/he came to deposit $250,000. "Oh, Buyer gave me the money." At this point, buyer had better be able to substantiate his source. In short, unless you want to draw attention to yourself, you should avoid paying large sums of cash to anybody even if the money is *legitimately* accounted for.

If you are in a low bracket, and the audit presents no dangers except a dispute about a small deduction or two, and if you possess reasonable intelligence, handle it yourself. Go down and try to talk the revenue agent out of disallowing anything ("no change"). Next best, give your hard luck story and indicate you'll have to fight unless things work out with a minor adjustment.

If you are in a high income bracket, or a corporation, don't meet with the agent yourself. If you do, you can be directly questioned (i.e., without the insulation of a middleman), and might make damaging admissions. You can avoid this by giving a power of attorney to a lawyer or accountant to represent you. The best type to get is a former IRS agent or a specialist in audits, as either one knows the boys at IRS and will know the ropes.

Many experienced people prefer "field" audits (they come to you) rather than "office" audits (you go to them). The typical office auditor, especially in large cities, is a clerk, paid very low wages, often uneducated, and almost never street- or business-wise. S/he plays it strictly by the book. You can't prove your phone calls? Disallowed. The office auditor is judged—despite protestations to the contrary—by the amount of money collected and the number of audits completed. S/he will therefore tend to be stupid and stubborn, rigid and unfair. S/he will almost never order a "no change return," and will force you to prove every bit of minutiae.

The field examiner, on the other hand, earns more, is supervised less and, more importantly, tends to have business and common sense that s/he will exercise more readily. If you can prove 90 percent of your itemized deductions, the field auditor will usually assume the other 10 percent to be legitimate. If, for example, you've had a fire, flood, or robbery, and your records have been destroyed, the good field auditor will look at prior years which are not under review, to get a good indication of the types of expenses you were likely to have encountered in the year for which you have no proof. The field auditor will accept "reasonable explanations" and will be more willing to compromise claims. This is not to say that the field auditors themselves will issue many "no change" returns. Few will. So be prepared to yield a little:

AUDITOR: $1,500 seems rather large for a business expense of this type.

YOU: That's my best estimate.

AUDITOR: Since you can't prove it, I'll have to disallow 50 percent of it.

At this point, if you know it's a good break, yield! Unless the amounts are large, don't fight the auditor down to the line. For their own good they have to come up with something. I know accountants who routinely include reasonably questionable items on every return, items which, while not amounting to enough to kick off the computer's initiated audit, are always there to be instantly yielded to an auditor. Similarly, some accountants keep in reserve some deductions which were not claimed on the return, to offset disallowances.

So, again, if you receive a letter saying that you are being audited, get a representative and insist on a field audit. If it is a corporate return, the reason is simple: the books are too big to lug to the IRS office. If it is a personal return, think of another excuse: you have a number of checkbooks and slips; you work odd hours and it would be very inconvenient to travel down to the office, etc.

It is likely that your initial letter or an early communication will inform you that not only are you being charged for unpaid taxes plus interest, but also are being fined a fraud penalty, which can be 50 percent of the tax itself. The rule is that no penalty can be assessed unless you've hidden a least 25 percent of the total. So, for example, if you've reported $70,000 in income, and they assert you've underreported by $20,000, even if they win they can't hit you with a fraud penalty. But the oldest trick in the book is to assess a frightened taxpayer the fraud penalty initially, and then compromise it as a *quid pro quo* for all taxes claimed. A good tax representative is used to this threat and should immediately dismiss it, as nonsense, or, if necessary, a subject for litigation.

This happened to a friend of mine who had not paid taxes on a Harvard law and humanities fellowship. The grant had been designed by Harvard Law School professors to be tax-free and at the time he was so informed in writing. Yet, four years later, from out of the blue, came a letter from the IRS not only demanding back taxes "due" plus interest, but also slapping on a willful fraud penalty. My friend didn't scare, and through his father, who was his accountant, he successfully demanded the removal of the penalty *before* discussing the rest of the claim.

If you do find yourself in an office audit, and even if you find yourself with an unreasonable field examiner, appeal to a supervisor. The higher up you go, the more reasonable and business-wise the agents. Furthermore, at the upper levels, known as "appellate," your dispute seems smaller in relation to the others there.

Be sure to watch for every piece of mail from the IRS. The agents are notorious for mistakes, and if you don't catch them, you may be barred from correcting them by some 60- or 90-day limit on protests. For example, we represent the beneficiary of a nine-million-dollar estate. The executor changed lawyers. The new lawyer—fortunately alert—found buried in a file a notice from the IRS disallowing five million dollars in deductions on the estate tax return. The agent was all wet, but if a protest hadn't been filed within a stipulated period, the disallowance would have become final, and the estate would have been in big trouble. No protest had been filed, but the new lawyer fortunately discovered the oversight just in time.

Of course, sometimes agents' goofs work the other way. One evening, when I arrived at my place in Greenwich and went through the mail, I saw an envelope from the IRS. Assuming it must be another of their aggravating communications, I figured I'd get a good night's sleep before opening it. The next morning I opened it. Out fell a check made out to me in the amount of $894,000. I couldn't for the life of me understand it. My partner Tom Bolan finally figured it out. I am an executor of the large Milbank estate, and, as such, sign its estate tax returns. As an exercise of caution, the accountants had overpaid the estate tax by an amount that later turned out to be $894,000. Instead of sending the refund to the Milbank estate, or to me as executor, the IRS made it out to me personally and mailed it to my home address! No, I didn't split for the Grand Canary Islands, or write IRS a letter of thanks for their sudden and generous change of attitude. It was handed over to the estate to which it belonged in the first place.

Suppose you just can't settle: not with the examiner, not with the supervisor. You can always prepare to force the case to litigation . The taxpayer has a sometime advantage, which also operates if the government is threatening to indict for criminal income tax evasion. For the fact is that the government has neither the time nor the staff to litigate all worthy claims. It must limit its activities by adopting such rules of thumb as not prosecuting criminally if only one year is involved, or settling unless there is a probability the case can be won—as the IRS is not the most popular plaintiff before juries.

To sum up, then: keep detailed records; report all income you receive; mix business and pleasure if you legitimately can; keep deductions in line, your bookkeepers happy, your lovers blissfully ignorant. Keep your stocks and bonds in your own possession, your deposits small, your mouth shut. If you get hit with an audit, be well represented; make them come to you; yield the small stuff, and let them know that your case is not an easy win for them. They have the burden to prove that the income was illegal or excessive. Ultimately you have your peers to judge your facts.

Maybe we're finally in for some tax relief. But in the meantime lie low and fight back.

13.
FUNERALS

WHEN DEATH us do part, the corpse of the beloved often comes to represent the person we loved; before it is buried, in that interval when the soul has departed but the body remains, the bereft are most vulnerable to ripoffs by their brother's keepers, the funeral parlors and cemeteries.

Funeral-industry ripoffs compound death's tragedy. What can we do about it?* *Ask someone who is not emotionally upset by the death to help with the funeral plans.* The closest relative will ultimately make decisions, but it is very helpful for the bereaved to bring along a level-headed friend who knows the family finances and is not emotionally involved with the death. This person will not be hesitant to look at the decisions to be made in dollars-and-cents terms, and can meet the funeral director on his own ground. An enormous range of options is available in disposing of the body. There is burial, cremation and organ donations to science. Burial is the most common choice. But, again, there is an enormous range of options. Not surprisingly, funeral directors generally wish to provide the most expensive. They have many subtle ways to bring this about—by suggesting that "paying your respects to the departed" is somehow bound up in the design of the box buried in

---

* Many of the observations in this chapter are suggested by a brief but informative pamphlet issued by the Department of Consumer Affairs of the City of New York called "Some Ideas About Planning Funerals."

the earth, or by playing on your guilt—"He would have been proud; he deserves the best," and so forth. Feelings of guilt are enormous: It's bad enough the person has died; the least we can do for him now is to bury him well.

Many states have enacted statutes to protect the family of the deceased from the hidden costs of funerals. California, for example, requires that

> no funeral director shall enter into a contract for furnishing services or property in connection with the burial or other disposal of a dead human body until he has first submitted to the potential purchasers of such services or property a written or printed memorandum containing the total charge for the funeral director's services and the use of his facilities . . . an itemization of charges for the casket, an outside receptacle and clothing [and] an itemization of fees or charges and total amount of cash advances made by the funeral director for transportation, flowers, cemetery or crematory charges, newspaper notices, clergy honorarium. . . .

Notice that under this statute the funeral director is responsible to inform you of the cost *before* entering into an agreement. It is a good, rule. But not all state statutes are quite as explicitly protective. New York, for example, also requires an itemized list of services and costs, but "at the time funeral arrangements are made." And Florida requires a detailed cost disclosure only on request. Request it, demand it!

An expensive item in a funeral is the casket. Caskets vary greatly in price. Many funeral homes have more than one casket selection room; some offer caskets other than those on display, caskets available on short notice through catalogs. But most proprietors will want to sell you only the most expensive. Consequently you should make exhaustive inquiries. Often the price of the entire funeral is pegged to the price of the casket. Again, some states require the funeral director to provide a list of the entire range for all caskets offered for sale, and further require that prices be prominently displayed on the caskets themselves, and that casket prices be entirely separate from the type of service purchased. But most states do not go so far, and proposed federal regulations are far from enactment; they must overcome the lobbying efforts of the funeral industry. It is important, therefore, to determine your options. Here is where a person not emotionally involved is most helpful. After being presented the options by the funeral director, ask for some time alone to discuss your decision among yourselves.

You should remember a few things. A recent Federal Trade Commission staff report notes that, despite what many people believe, decomposition cannot be prevented by the use of a sealed casket or vault, and modern embalming techniques are designed to preserve the body only for the period of the funeral—not "for decades and centuries." Score one for the ancient Egyptians.

You might keep in mind also that the amount of money spent on a funeral is not a sure indication of people's feelings for the dead. Spending money is supposed only by some to be a way of showing respect. Like time in youth, money on the dead is often misspent.

To be sure, symbolism can be very important. People do want to honor the dead, and whether it is rational or not their desire must be respected. But there are better ways to honor the dead than to transfer money from distraught survivors to funeral directors. Time and thought spent on composing funeral speeches and selecting music, and contributions of time or money to a charity or cause important to the deceased, are often better ways of serving the living while honoring the dead. Indeed, expensive funerals often dishonor the dead in that they directly contradict their wishes. A 1975 poll taken in New York showed that more than half of respondents would want $1,000 or less spent on their funerals, and less than 2 percent more than $2,000. Yet at that time the average funeral in New York cost more than $2,500.

Keep in mind, too, that valuables intended to be buried with the dead have a way of disappearing shortly before or after the funeral. My advice would be to take the valuables home.

Don't be passive and don't be embarrassed. Those salubrious

people in gray and black who express their condolences while they take your money away are in business. They are no better or worse than other types of business people. But you are more vulnerable. Unfortunately all evidence suggests that standing up and fighting back are reserved exclusively for the living.

What happens after you contract with the funeral parlor and things go awry?

Funerals are an exception to the general rule against damages for emotional distress unaccompanied by physical injury as a consequence of a contract breach. A Montana federal court said as much when it awarded damages for the distress of a family which had ordered a second autopsy of a deceased member only to discover the body floating in water and covered with mold within its leaky "permaseal" casket. "Rare indeed are the contracts which could give rise to a cause of action for liability based on mental suffering alone, but in my opinion a contract for the sale of a casket is one of those rare contracts," said the court. Similarly, courts have awarded damages for the emotional distress occasioned by grossly offensive odors emanating from a negligently embalmed body. The rule in recent trend-setting cases is that the defendant must have been guilty of "outrageous conduct."

What is outrageous conduct? The Iowa supreme court gave one definition in a case resulting from a botched double funeral in 1970: " 'Outrageous conduct,' " said the court, "may broadly be defined as 'conduct exceeding all bounds usually tolerated by decent society.' " Andrew Jackson Higgins, special judge of a Kansas City, Missouri, court of appeals, offered a better definition in a memorable case: "Generally, the case of extreme and outrageous conduct causing severe emotional distress is one in which the recitation of the facts to an average member of the community would arouse his resentment against the actor and lead him to exclaim, 'Outrageous.' " Well, what's your reaction to the fate of Mrs. Parker's remains?

On November 5, 1971, Eva Jane Parker died. Her sister, Mrs. Martin, and the deceased's son made arrangements for burial by Jones Mortuary. They contracted and paid for a two-piece sectional concrete "vault box liner urn" in Lincoln Cemetery. But that's not what they got.

Funeral services were held at Jones Chapel and were followed by burial at the selected gravesite. The grave was covered by a carpet or artificial turf and a lowering device. (Somehow it would bother me that my body rots while the "grass" above it lives forever.) In any case, following the service the family members returned by car to the funeral chapel.

Three months later, the deceased's sister and son went to the gravesite to pay respects and to see if the headstone had been placed. What they found was an open hole and Mrs. Parker's body, particularly the left side of her face, partially exposed through the dirt. Subsequent investigation determined that the grave was, at its deepest, thirty-one inches. Heavy machinery driven over the grave had struck the top of the casket, thus exposing the body. There was no vault.

Mrs. Martin was upset by her discovery and called the police. She also called lawyers and the Channel 9 Action Reporter, who took still and moving pictures.

The following history is standard. Suit. Defendant's claim of mere negligence and no malice and of no physical injury to the plaintiff. The court didn't buy it. "The damages recoverable in such a case are not for the injury done to the dead body, but are for the wrong or trespass on the right to the undisturbed possession and control of the body, measured by the mental anguish and suffering of the plaintiff occasioned thereby."

Again, quoting favorably from other opinions, the court said it "could imagine no clearer or dearer right in the gamut of civil liberty and security than to bury our dead in peace and unobstructed; none more sacred to the individual, nor more important of preservation and protection from the point of view of public welfare and decency; certainly none where the law need less hesitate to impose upon a willful violator responsibility for the uttermost consequences of his act."

Before burying this topic once and for all, I should mention one last, revealing phenomenon. Cryogenics is a science that concerns itself with the very cold. There is a theory that if a body has its blood drained and is frozen to a temperature close to absolute zero—minus 274 degrees fahrenheit—all further damage will cease. No decay, etc. This process has two advantages and one drawback. The first advantage is to the living: The body may be kept in a storage vault and observed without threat of deterioration. The second, although dubious, advantage is to the dead. The theory is that someday medical technology will have advanced sufficiently that whatever "killed" the victim can be undone and the body and mind can be brought back to life. For the person who is dying and knows s/he will be frozen, death may for the while be inevitable, but there remains the hope, however slim, that s/he may someday be brought back to life and experience a new world. Woody Allen brought cryogenics into popular consciousness with his movie *Sleeper*.

These two advantages make freezing for many the afterdeath of choice. But there is one drawback. It's expensive. The initial undertaking costs more than $15,000 and the upkeep runs into thousands per year. Moreover, it's more than usually subject to human foible.

Not long ago I had occasion to speak to one of the few people actually doing the freezing. He was a rather cynical fellow. Even though some wealthy people had left provisions in their wills for freezing and maintaining their bodies, and even though their wishes had been initially respected, after a while, he said, their children had tired of paying good money. The net result: They stopped paying, and this fellow got fed up with footing the bill for other people's refrigeration. He pulled the plugs and quit the business.

So stand up and fight back, while you still can.

14.
WILLS

OF 226 million people in the United States (not counting many of those hiding out in New York), probably at least 60 million have wills. Along with marital problems and real estate transactions (with which they are sometimes linked), wills and, more particularly, drawing them are perhaps the most common legal problem that laypeople face. We can tell this by observing what the legal profession advertises.

MODES OF PROVISION

Broadly speaking, there are three ways to provide for the disposition of your property after your death: by formal will, by holographic will, and by no will at all. Each way may be the best way in certain circumstances.

FORMAL WILLS

A formal will in most jurisdictions must be witnessed by two people. A beneficiary should *not* be a witness. In many jurisdictions a beneficiary is disqualified by law from witnessing a will. (An executor or trustee named in the will is not so disqualified.) But, if possible, witnesses ought to know the person making the will, the testator, well enough so they will remember being witnesses and, if necessary, later can testify that the testator knew what he or she was doing. The witnesses should be young enough to be expected to survive the testator.

In drawing your will, you must observe a formality which is very important. There may later be a dispute regarding the will, and strictly observing the formality greatly increases the chances that your wishes as to the disposition of your property will be respected after your death. The actual ceremonial part, on which the legality of it all may depend, goes as follows:

After the will is drawn, and the lawyer has it typed up, and the testator (or testatrix) reads the will and is satisfied with it, the lawyer will say, in the presence of witnesses, "Now, Mrs. Jones, is this your last will and testament?" She will say, "Yes, it is." "Have you read it carefully, and have you placed your initials on each page?" "Yes." "Is it your wish that my secretary, Ms. Smith here, and my law associate in my office, Mr. Stivers, be witnesses to the execution of this, your last will and testament?" And she will say, "Yes, I have asked them to be witnesses." At that point, with the two witnesses looking on—you may have three rather than two to allow for a margin of forgetfulness, or death, or disappearance—Mrs. Jones will place her signature on the signature page (whereupon there is a valid will). The witnesses, not having read the will, but having witnessed her agree to and sign the will, themselves will sign the document, as subscribing witnesses. Wills are not notarized.

Execute only one copy of the will. If there is more than one original, all must be produced at time of probate. To protect against loss or theft, you may arrange to have kept in other places several "conformed copies," which, if there is proof of the loss or destruction of the original, will suffice.

HOLOGRAPHIC WILLS AND INTESTACY

But you really don't need a lawyer for a will, nor do you actually need witnesses and the rest of the formality. You can simply write out your will in longhand on a single sheet of paper, and date and sign it: "I, Mary Jones, being of sound mind, knowing what I am doing, hereby write this will to dispose of my assets. I leave everything to my son Reginald save for my sterling collection, which I bequeath to our local museum.''

I see no objection to holographic wills if the matters to be dealt with are simple. You can save yourself a couple of hundred dollars in lawyer's fees and do just as well. But, beware—use a holographic will only if your estate and its disposition are uncomplicated.

Likewise, if your estate is modest and your family life is peaceful, in the ordinary course of things it is no big deal if you don't have any will at all. Generally, one-third of the estate will go to the spouse and two-thirds to the children with the spouse as guardian until the children come of age, which is probably what most people want anyway. There is, however, one drawback in not having a will: Because of the marital deduction permitted by federal estate tax laws and in all states, half of your estate can go to your spouse tax-free if provided for in your will, whereas if you die intestate only one-third will go to your spouse, and the other two-thirds, all taxable, to your children. Taxes can be reduced somewhat and the total estate increased, therefore, if you have a will and leave your spouse half the estate. But if your spouse has predeceased you, unless there are complications in the family— some of which I'll discuss at the end of this section—it's not important that you have a will.

CODICILS

Codicils are amendments to wills. Their execution must be done in precisely the same fashion as the will itself. Successive codicils are denominated "first codicil" etc. A codicil can be one paragraph or many.

A codicil can be challenged independently from the body of the will, because you can be of sound mind at the time you execute the will but not at the time you execute the codicil. The same reasoning applies to later wills, as we will see in the section on contests.

EXECUTORS AND TRUSTEES

You may have quite definite ideas about how you want to provide in the future after you're gone, but the future is largely out of your control, if for no other reason than that you can't predict it. Very simply, you cannot foresee what will happen. A close friend of mine thought he was setting up his children in a moderately comfortable standard of living by giving them $25,000 a year from a trust. But now, fifteen years later, the $25,000 may be worth what $10,000 was then. You must ultimately trust someone living to translate your wishes appropriately to the changing circumstances in which your heirs will live. Somebody living must have some substantial discretion to effect the substance of your wishes, even if it means violating the letter of your provisions.

These people, in the case of your will, are your executors; and in the case of your trusts, your trustees. You will name in your will one or more executors. Executors are simply people in whom you repose the duty of administering your estate. They execute your wishes as set forth in your will. As a practical matter, that means they make the decision how to liquidate your estate. Ordinarily it is the job of the executor to liquidate everything and turn it into cash to distribute. Thus the proverbial "estate sale."

However, although the standard legal duty is for the executors to sell everything as quickly as possible, you may not wish that done in certain circumstances. In that case you should say so, plainly and simply, in your will. When does this happen? A common exception to quick liquidation concerns a family business which you may want to be continued by members of the family. Or you may have owned controlling stock in a public corporation, which control you wish to continue in the family. A typical provision will read: "I devise the family business to pass in kind, without being sold" to various designated members of the family.

If you provide that your executors or trustees not liquidate a business, ordinarily, then, they will not turn that business ownership into cash to distribute. But even a provision in a will to that effect has been held not to relieve executors and trustees from a duty to exercise their "proper business judgment," which might require diversification despite the explicit instructions of the testator. The law has pointed toward a duty to diversify, not to put all the eggs in one basket, especially when economic conditions might change, or the family business might start going bad, or be banned by some federal regulations. The executors are not required to let the asset go down the drain. There comes a time when, despite the provisions of the will, they must use their independent business judgment.

A good executor may use his business judgment to delay liquidating an estate when it is composed largely of stock which at the moment is artificially depressed in price. I was an executor of the estate of Denny Slater, whose principal asset was Fanny Farmer stock, which at the time of Denny's death was selling at an all-time low, about $5 a share. We, the executors, after a careful study of the company, were convinced that the stock was bound to rise, so although we were under a legal mandate to liquidate as soon as possible, we applied a rule of reason and held the stock for almost five years—plenty long enough to make us nervous. In that time the stock went up to $15 and we effectively tripled the value of the estate. This shows we were geniuses. Of course, the stock might have gone to $2, in which case we would have had serious problems.

Whom you choose as your executor is an important decision. There is no formula I can give on how to choose correctly. It's just a common-sense thing, like whom to marry. The only hard and fast rules are to avoid idiots, profligates and thieves. The executor has to be someone in whom you have confidence, a person who, when you're not there, will be most likely to carry out your wishes. And if you're a rich person, someone who has the requisite sound business judgment not to mess up your estate, someone who is savvy, is conservative and has some guts. If you are very close to your surviving spouse, and s/he has the mental capacity and a degree of business sense, you will name your spouse as the executor. You might want to do that anyway, even if the requisites are not filled, in which case you might want to name two executors. You can actually name three, four or as many as you want; they are joint. If there are two, mutual agreement is required for decisions. If there are three (and there are rarely more), then two must concur in a decision. It is not too often that executors disagree, but when they do it can happen dramatically.

You also should name alternate executors in case your first choice dies before you do, or is unable to perform the role. As in the case of witnesses, it is a good idea to designate a person who is younger than you, although an executor will serve only until the estate is distributed, which shouldn't be for more than four or five years as an outside limit, and should be less, but often isn't.

Many wealthy people name a bank as sole executor, or as co-executor along with a spouse. The rationale behind this is that a bank is a very careful institution and will not do anything dishonest. It hires vast staffs of knowledgeable economists, who are at its beck and call. Do I regard this as a wise policy, to name a bank as executor? Absolutely not.

As a matter of fact, I, as co-executor of an estate left by a good friend of mine, the heir to a great fortune, had the option under the will to designate a bank as co-executor. Had we done so the bank would have gotten an executor's commission of some $300,000, whereas as it was, we were able to work out a deal with the bank whereby it gave us investment advice and handled our bookkeeping for $75,000.

Secondly, a lot of banks are notorious for the low return they receive for an estate or for a trust. Consider the case of the late financier Jesse Livermore, who created a trust with a prominent bank. In 1917, Livermore's trust amounted to $400,000. Under the guidance of the bank, guess what the corpus of the trust was worth in 1975 (bearing in mind, of course, that we had been through a depression, but had also been through some of the greatest growth periods in the country's history). I would have guessed $400,000 in 1917 would be worth about $3.5 million in 1975. The answer: $200,000. Under the prudent guidance of the bank the trust managed to shrink only to 50% which, after all, is less than 1 percent a year.

Let's now consider the advisability of trusts themselves. Often people don't do their children any favor by leaving them large sums of money. If there is any indication that the children lack wisdom or perspicacity in running their lives, that they're stoned all the time, or run around with a bad crowd, or simply don't know how to handle money, the remedy is to leave your bequest in trust with some strict trustees, and provide that the children get their hands on the principal only in gradual stages— for example, one-third at age twenty-five, one-third at thirty, one-third at thirty-five. (I suppose if somebody by the age of forty or forty-five doesn't know what to do with money, then s/he will never know.) In short, you create a trust because you don't. You can even attempt to influence your heirs' life-styles by conditioning the receipt of income or principal on certain behavior, as long as it is not against public policy.

You may want to choose your trustees on a more personalized basis than you do your executor, because you will usually give your trustees discretion to invade the trust's strict requirements in cases of an illness or other unanticipated need of the beneficiary. You therefore want someone who is a little more familiar with and sensitive to the requirements of the beneficiaries. It is very common, nevertheless, to name the same persons in your will as executors and trustees.

Executors and trustees usually are required to post a bond bearing some reasonable relationship to the size of the estate or trust in order to guarantee their faithful performance. But if your executor or trustee is somebody you trust very much, such as your spouse, you may state in your will, "I hereby provide that it shall be unnecessary for my executors or trustees to post any bond or security to guarantee their faithful performance." That does not exclude going after them for fraud at a later date. And their honesty in administering an estate or trust is further assured in that they must account to a court; they must file statements accounting for what they have done.

CONTESTS

Will contests are the stuff of a thousand novels. They are also the stuff of life. How does a testator protect against his own conniving spouse or children so as to defeat future claims of undue influence or testamentary incapacity against a will that is truly his own? Not uncommonly in the case of the wealthy (and less frequently among the middle-income and poor), the testator will put in the will what is known as an *in terrorem* clause which simply provides: "If any beneficiary of my estate or any person attempts to attack my will on the grounds of undue influence, lack of testamentary capacity or any other ground, that person shall automatically lose her or his entire inheritance as contained in this will."

For example, a person dies, leaving $300,000 in his estate, of which he leaves his child only $20,000, with the rest to his second wife, and his will includes an *in terrorem* clause. If the child chooses to fight it, s/he takes a risk. Fight it and win, in which case the child will stand to gain much; or lose, in which case the child loses all, forfeiting under the *in terrorem* clause. Most often, *in terrorem* clauses have been held to be valid.

This brings us to the next question. Suppose a person successfully challenges the will on the grounds of undue influence or lack of testamentary capacity. Does the estate then pass by operation of law, as if there had been no will in the first place? No! If you knock out a will, the next question to be answered is: Was there a prior will? If so, that prior will has just had pants put back on it, and its terms become controlling unless it too is knocked out. So, before attempting to knock out a will, see what the prior will provides. Otherwise you might well find yourself worse off than if you have accepted less than what you felt was your due.

After you die, your will is taken down to court. It is the duty of the person having actual possession of the will—sometimes a lawyer's secretary—immediately to present the will to the executors to file with the court. The first procedure of the court is to send notices not only to the beneficiaries named in the will, but also to all "heirs at law." These are all the people who might have taken under intestacy if there had been no will. (There are always laws of intestacy to cover those people who die without a will.) If there are no relatives at all, the property "escheats" to the state.

The purpose of these notices is to inform all interested parties that the will has been offered for probate, so that anyone wanting to object to the will's being received and probated may come in and object. You are *not* at this time to attack the contents of the will, or get into any accountings or the like. You face only the threshold question: Was this the last will and testament of Mrs. Jones, and was it a valid one—that is, was she of sound mind and memory when she executed the will and did she write the will free from undue influence?

You needn't immediately charge undue influence or lack of testamentary capacity in probate. Rather, you can put in a preliminary challenge that will not invoke the *in terrorem* clause. You have the right to examine all the witnesses *before* you make up your mind whether you want to challenge the will. No will can be probated unless all the witnesses are examined, or unless everybody concerned waives an examination of the witnesses. So what you do, if you're thinking of challenging the will, is to demand an examination of the witnesses: "Where was she when she executed the will? Was she in bed, out of bed, under medical treatment . . .?" You will give the main heir notice of examination before probate. You can explore and see whether or not you really have what your lawyer is going to feel is enough to warrant a challenge on the basis of undue influence or lack of testamentary capacity.

There is an initial presumption of the validity of the will. Therefore a person who would challenge it bears the burden of persuasion on the issues of testamentary capacity and undue influence. But the burden is not great. And many a successful challenge has been waged.

From the testator's perspective, the *in terrorem* clause takes care of only part of the problem. The children can still hold up the will to a certain extent in their preliminary examinations. But sooner than without the clause, they must make a decision whether to mount a full challenge and risk forfeiting their shares under the will. So the strategy for a testator who would like to cut off his children or others but wants the will to sail smoothly through and the distribution to be made quickly is to insert an *in terrorem* clause and leave just enough to the disaffectioned to make them grumble and accept their small shares rather than risk losing it all.

On the other hand, a child who has been nearly cut out, although having but a remote chance of ultimately upsetting the will, can use the power to delay admission to probate plus a later jury trial on the issues of "undue influence" to throw a serious monkey wrench into the settlement of the estate. Especially when the estate consists of a family business with nobody to run it, the named beneficiaries are likely to pay off the disgruntled heir to free themselves to sell the business, even if they're confident they would prevail after a long and costly fight. In most cases, a second wife, in order to expedite the probate and distribution, will add to what's been left the children, especially if they received more in earlier wills. This situation can be reversed. Christina Onassis, for example, reputedly increased Aristotle's bequest to Jackie rather than undergo a drawn-out struggle.

Let's examine now the two principal bases for challenge. One involved the founder and head of a large book publishing company. His wife died and he had two sons. One was a prominent banker; the other was constantly beset by problems. After the publisher's wife died, and when he was in a questionable state of mind, he executed a new will leaving the lion's share of his estate to a new wife, younger than he by about twenty years. She was a very strong woman, and the lawyers drawing the will were afraid that his sons by his deceased first wife would attack the will. So the execution was videotaped, which did not, however, prevent an attack on the will, which was successful to the extent we were able to force a settlement.

Why the videotape? Recording a will's execution can forestall one of the principal attacks: that the testator didn't know what he was doing because, clearly, he couldn't know what he was doing.

It is essential, in order to execute a will, that the testator be of sound mind and memory. If he's senile or *non compos mentis,* he does not have the mental capacity to execute a will, what is known as *testamentary capacity*—i.e., sound mind and memory. The videotape can powerfully convey to the court a person of sound mind, making a conscious decision, knowing and understanding the implications of what he is doing. But the tape does not parry another major attack. It cannot demonstrate that the testator, however conscious at that moment of his present act, was not subject to *undue influence*. That is the second great hurdle.

"Undue influence" is a very slippery phrase which caps a basic philosophy of human nature. To allow for undue influence as a ground for voiding a will is to recognize that in some situations a person may take an unfair advantage of another's weakness of mind, or take a grossly oppressive and unfair advantage of another's distress. In certain circumstances we recognize that a person may so control or affect the mind of another by persuasion or pressure as to substitute his or her own free will for the will of the testator.

We are a society that fundamentally believes in the possibility of free will. That is why we punish criminals and consider them as wicked, because they have chosen their act freely. So, too, we respect the free will of a person of property freely to choose to dispose of that property according to his own lights. But, as it is recognized in criminal law that in certain circumstances duress may overwhelm a person's free will, stripping him of the capacity to choose freely, and relieving him of the consequences of his act by converting him into a mere instrument of another, so, too, in this context (also with contracts) we recognize that sometimes a person may be subject to such intense pressure as to cease to be the responsible author of his own apparent choice. We excuse the criminal; we void the will.

Not uncommonly, a second wife will scheme to alienate her new spouse from his children, to cut them off and have him name her and hers as his sole heirs. Undue influence becomes a common objection of the children who seek to void the will. If the second wife has had enough time to do the dirty work, she will often bring about the alienation between the husband and the children. With a great disparity of ages, this is almost the rule. If the second wife is smart, however, and acts under the legal guidance of a scheming and skilled adviser, she can generate sufficient evidence to rebut in court a charge of undue influence. She will create supporting evidence like the fact of the children's long absence, coupled with letters from the father to the effect that "I never want to see my sons again because they've treated me so badly." A letter or comment to a friend that "I don't want them at my birthday party because they've been disloyal" will often aid greatly in establishing the very proposition that it really rebuts.

If a child sees this setting up, s/he can fight back from being cut off and establish undue influence, but only with great difficulty. Discuss the relationship with the parent. Do this early before the springs of affection are irrevocably poisoned. Of course this should not be done by phone, but in person. You should be direct but tactful. Acknowledge that the second spouse is devoted to your parent, but at the same time point out that she has every incentive to wish him to hate his children and cut them off. State your affection and establish some channel of communication independent from her.

To be sure, undue influence can work the other way. Children can make sure that the second wife of seventeen years gets a raw deal too. They can turn the father against her, telling him constantly, "She just married you for your money and can't wait for you to die. She's already telling her friends how she can't wait to be the rich widow on the Riviera."

If you are the testator, try to keep perspective and your wits about you. Human nature is such that your children and new wife will be jealous of each other. Discuss your will with each of them. Show them, if necessary, your will as it reads, the will locked in the safe of your lawyer. Then confide to your wife that you've drawn a codicil, leaving her more, and show that to her. And, finally, draw a will that no one knows about, leaving everything precisely as you wish. The key is: Always put in the last one, the will you want to count, "I hereby revoke all prior wills and codicils and declare this and only this to be my last will and testament." This way you'll have your cake and leave it: peace at home while you live, each one content with his share. And you'll have provided exactly as you truly saw fit. Embarrassed? Don't be: It's your afterlife.

DOWER

A common question asked me by someone contemplating drawing up a will is, "What's the least I have to leave my spouse and children?" Let's begin with the children. The answer in most places in the United States is: nothing. Not one cent must you leave your children. You can cut them off entirely with a single stroke of a pen. It is very different in many European countries, where—in France, for example—it's much easier to cut off your wife than to cut off your children. But in the United States generally you can totally disinherit your offspring.

The same is not true of your spouse—unless you have signed an ante-nuptial agreement which specifically provides otherwise. The reason is that most states have codified what are called dower rights. The principle of dower is that, no matter the testator's wishes, husbands and wives cannot totally deny each other participation in the other's estate. So, even if the husband's will leaves nothing to his wife, the wife has the option to "elect" against the will and take her "dower" share. This varies from state to state. In New York, for example, if there are children born to the testator of any marriage, the surviving spouse who's been cut off and elects against the will gets one-third of the entire estate. If there are no children, the one-third share increases to one-half.

Suppose you are married and have no premarital agreement —remember, such an ante-nuptial agreement annuls the elective right—and have come to hate your spouse and want your spouse to get the least possible share. The best way to leave the least— the closest you can come to cutting off your spouse—is to leave *in your will* the legal minimum which precludes an election against the will. The minimum is *not* the same as the share the wife or husband would receive if s/he chose to elect. It is less and it removes the right to elect. In New York, for example, you can defeat a right to election against an estate by a spouse if you leave that spouse *the income for life* from one-third of your estate. Follow the distinction. If, by will, you leave your spouse the *income* from one-third of your estate, that fulfills *all* your legal obligations. If you fail to do that and leave your spouse nothing, and your spouse then goes to court and exercises the right to elect against your estate (assuming there are children and the one-third is the entitlement), one-third of the estate is received outright rather than the income from one-third. That one-third is passed on forever by your spouse's will, whereas the income from one-third ceases at the survivor's death, and the corpus gets passed on as you dispose. So, half a loaf is less than none. Otherwise, by leaving less than you may you actually leave more than you might.

TAX CONSIDERATIONS

The estate tax is murder. Many legislators and others think it should be abolished on the ground that you pay taxes when the income is earned, and it is unfair to impose a second tax when you die and leave your property to your family or heirs. President Reagan has made out an excellent case against this double taxation. But as things are constituted, the federal estate taxes are enormous. The top of the range as this is written is 85 percent.

That used to be avoided by making gifts during your lifetime. The gift tax was much less confiscatory then, the theory being to encourage you to spread the wealth to others who would use it more actively. But recently the gift tax has been substantially increased, so now there is very little difference between it and the inheritance tax.

When it comes to gifts, however, each individual is allowed to give to as many people as s/he wishes $3,000 a year without paying a gift tax. A married couple can give $6,000 per year to each child without the transfer being taxed. If you do not exercise that option, the money becomes deductible from your estate for estate tax purposes.

Another major qualification is the *marital deduction*. You may leave your spouse up to 50 percent of your estate tax-free. There is no inheritance tax at all on 50 percent of your estate provided it is left to your spouse. (The same applies to a charity. You may leave 100 percent of your estate to a charity and there is no tax whatever.) But if you leave to anybody other than your spouse, and this includes children, your estate is subject to normal tax rates. Most lawyers, accountants and banks have copies of the tax schedule.

There is a legal way to avoid estate taxes on a major asset of an estate. If there are substantial monies involved, to avoid the life insurance going through the estate, have the *beneficiary* own the policy himself. Whether it be a person or a corporate firm, have the beneficiary pay the premium—you can give it to him to pay— and then when you die, the money will go directly to the beneficiary, who owns the policy, without being taxable as part of the estate.

SAFE-DEPOSIT BOXES

The middle-income and the rich sometimes store cash and other valuables—legally part of their estate—in a safe-deposit box. By law the contents of these boxes are to be included in the estate of the decedent for the purposes of computing inheritance taxes. Frequently, in fact, they are not.

As soon as someone dies, an obituary notice is posted. Usually the bank will seal the safe-deposit box, after which time it can be opened only in the presence of a representative of a state tax commission. In the olden days it was common practice to circumvent the law by giving the tax representative a $50 bill. Whereupon he would turn around and go to the corner of the room wherein the box had been placed, keeping his eyes glued to a pad making notes with his back to the executor, who cleaned out what he desired from the box. This procedure—greasing the palms of state tax officials while the executor filled his pockets—was so rampant that a friend of mine who was president of a major corporation used to refer to it as "executor's prerogative."

There has grown a second method which I also counsel against because it is illegal. What a lot of people do is to have a safe-deposit box not in their own name. They form a corporation whose name is disconnected from the person who has active control over the box. The corporation, by resolution filed with the bank, will provide signatories of those who have access to the box. The signatories will include the one who takes out the box, plus perhaps the spouse, lawyer, accountant, children, et al. Not being held in the name of the signatory, and it being impossible to keep a record of all possible signatories on a corporate deposit box because of the millions of them throughout the country, when the owner of the contents dies the corporate box is not blocked off because nobody knows that its contents belong to the deceased. Then, immediately following the death, the relatives of the deceased, or whoever is on the signature card, empties the box, and that's that. No one is the wiser, and the beneficiaries of the testator are the richer.

I repeat, I am not counseling this. It is illegal and therefore wrong. But it is widely done by the rich. I think that the estate tax is wrong; I believe that you should be able to pass your estate on to whomever you want without the government charging you for the privilege. My liberal friends violently disagree. In any event what both they and I concur in is that it is wrong to have two standards, one for the rich and another for the middle class.

But while you cannot legally avoid estate taxes through the use of a safe-deposit box, neither should you pay more than you legally must. There is no conclusive presumption that the contents of the box belong to the decedent. The spouse or child can claim and establish that s/he and the decedent shared the box and stored "her" jewelry over the years, which shouldn't be included in the estate. Therefore it is a good idea to allocate the contents of the box by leaving a note demarcating whose is whose. This too is subject to abuse in obvious ways.

THE CONTENTS OF YOUR WILL

We've spent this section in a look at procedures—how to execute, probate and challenge a will, how to translate your desires into reality after you're gone. I don't want to close the section without some comments on the problem of what to leave and to whom. You may have two children. One of them is sickly, averagely intelligent, struggling and poor. The other is clever, a successful surgeon, and married into a very wealthy family. Do you divide your estate equally between them? In principle you may say yes to yourself. But does "equality" mean that the same amount of money, or opportunity, or life-style, should be assured to each child? Does equality dictate giving to each according to his needs? This is a very difficult question, which is compounded by the fact that the relative circumstances of your children may change over the years. Your wealthy surgeon may get into a serious accident and be disabled while your poor inventor may suddenly score with a patent. I suppose you could include a clause in your will: "It is understood that should the disparity in my children's financial conditions reverse, because I love them equally, it is my hope and intention that Ann will give to Harry such funds as are necessary to essentially equalize their positions. It is on that assumption that I leave Ann the bulk of my estate." How much good this will do is sheer speculation.

Even if you solve the problem of a disparity between children, there is the additional problem of grandchildren. Suppose Ann has one child and Harry has three. If you divide your estate equally between Ann and Harry, bequeathing *per stirpes,* then you are greatly favoring Ann's child over Harry's children, in which case years later, all other things being equal, one of your grandchildren will be much wealthier than the others. On the other hand, if you leave equally to each grandchild, you've favored one child's family line over the other's. What if the succeeding generation is imbalanced in the other direction? The best you can hope to do is to leave lump sums to each child and establish equal trusts for the grandchildren, but this is not a perfect solution. In the end there may be no way not to be unfair to someone.

These difficult problems—illustrating how life's moral complexity often outstrips our capacity to plan—suggest no easy solutions here, save to do nothing and die intestate. But to do nothing is to trail your property behind you in just the manner prescribed by the state after it takes its heavy toll. No. Fight back against your impulse to sit back and "let things take their course." It's your course; run it your way, but run it. Where there's a will, there's a way.

About
the
Author

ROY COHN has been addicted to law since early childhood. As his
father climbed the judicial ladder in New York, young Roy spent
vacations in courtrooms instead of on handball courts or at movie
shows. At fifteen, he became a teenager in a hurry. He made a
$10,000 commission as broker in the sale of a radio station. He
invested part (in New York Giants baseball stock) and used the
balance to pay for his education. He took private lessons over the
summer of his junior year in high school, and was graduated in the
fall, skipping his senior year. On to Columbia—where he obtained
both college and law-school degrees in a record three and a half
years. In his spare time, he learned Gregg shorthand and touch-
typing—and helped manage some local political campaigns. Too
young to take the bar examination, he joined the United States
District Attorney's Office as a photostat operator, and then a law
clerk. On turning twenty-one, he was appointed an Assistant
United States Attorney. He prosecuted over two hundred defendants in narcotics and counterfeiting cases. By age twenty-three,
he was the confidential assistant to the federal prosecutor, and that
same year began his rise to national prominence as prosecutor in
the Julius and Ethel Rosenberg atom-spy trial. At twenty-five, he
went to Washington as special assistant for internal security to the
Democratic Attorney General of the United States. The next year
he became chief counsel to the United States Senate Permanent

Subcommittee on Investigations under the chairmanship of Senator Joseph McCarthy. Robert F. Kennedy was simultaneously named assistant counsel. They never hit it off. In 1954, Cohn was at the center of the nationally televised Army-McCarthy hearings, and attained international recognition, which he has never lost in the years since then. An expert at picking powerful enemies, he left Washington top on the enemies list of young Kennedy and his appointed United States Attorney in New York. Cohn was indicted and tried on criminal charges on three occasions between 1963 and 1971. On each occasion, he was acquitted on all charges by a 12–0 vote of the jury. Cohn's "big trial" became sensational when his lawyer suffered a heart attack, and Cohn delivered his own successful two-day summation to the jury.

Now a leading partner in the eighty-seven-year-old New York firm of Saxe, Bacon & Bolan, his clients have ranged from Benson Ford and Warren Avis (as in Rent-A-Car) to Carmine Galante, from Bianca Jagger to the Cullen oil heir and international philanthropist and statesman Baron Enrico diPortanova, from builder Donald Trump (New York's Convention Center, Grand Hyatt Hotel, Tiffany, etc.) to the Catholic Church in New York; from "21" Club to Studio 54.

In his spare time, he works for the Humane Society of New York as director of special projects; is board chairman of an organization called P.A.C.E., which supplies art and music materials to prisoners to foster their rehabilitation; is involved in building a nonsectarian athletic field in Jerusalem; has spent twenty years as a regent of St. Francis College; teaches ethics at New York Law School; and for recreation, water-skis and travels, almost invariably accompanied by a Cavalier King Charles spaniel named Charlie Brown.

In this book—his favorite of the three he has written because it embraces his philosophy on how to fight back—he has drawn on his experience as a prosecutor, investigative counsel, successful defense attorney, law professor, witness and, several times, defendant.